G. D. H. COLE:
SELECTED WORKS

# ECONOMIC TRACTS FOR THE TIMES

# ECONOMIC TRACTS FOR THE TIMES

G. D. H. COLE

Volume 7

LONDON AND NEW YORK

First published 1932 by Routledge

2 Park Square, Milton Park, Abingdon, Oxfordshire OX14 4RN
711 Third Avenue, New York, NY 10017

*Routledge is an imprint of the Taylor & Francis Group, an informa business*

First issued in paperback 2017

Copyright © 1932 H A Cole

All rights reserved. No part of this book may be reprinted or reproduced or utilised in any form or by any electronic, mechanical, or other means, now known or hereafter invented, including photocopying and recording, or in any information storage or retrieval system, without permission in writing from the publishers.

Notice:
Product or corporate names may be trademarks or registered trademarks, and are used only for identification and explanation without intent to infringe.

*British Library Cataloguing in Publication Data*
A catalogue record for this book is available from the British Library

ISBN 13: 978-0-415-56651-3 (Set)
ISBN 13: 978-0-415-59838-5 (Volume 7) (hbk)
ISBN 13: 978-1-138-56250-9 (Volume 7) (hbk)

**Publisher's Note**
The publisher has gone to great lengths to ensure the quality of this reprint but points out that some imperfections in the original copies may be apparent.

**Disclaimer**
The publisher has made every effort to trace copyright holders and would welcome correspondence from those they have been unable to trace.

# ECONOMIC TRACTS
# FOR THE TIMES

BY

G. D. H. COLE

MACMILLAN & CO., LIMITED
ST. MARTIN'S STREET, LONDON
1932

COPYRIGHT

PRINTED IN GREAT BRITAIN

# CONTENTS

## PART I
### THE ECONOMIC CRISIS

| CHAPTER | PAGE |
|---|---|
| I. A Short Tract for the Times | 3 |
| II. The Crisis | 11 |
| III. Free Trade, Tariffs, and the Alternative | 66 |
| IV. Public Opinion and Monetary Policy | 89 |
| V. Why and How we must Socialise the Banks | 106 |
| VI. The World Economic Outlook from the Standpoint of Labour | 121 |
| VII. Wages and Employment | 151 |

## PART II
### ECONOMICS IN THEORY AND PRACTICE

| | |
|---|---|
| VIII. Towards a New Economic Theory | 183 |
| IX. The Use and Abuse of Economic Terms | 212 |
| X. The Nature of Profits | 231 |
| XI. The Abolition of the Wage System | 258 |

## PART III
### SOCIALISATION

| | |
|---|---|
| XII. Public and Semi-public Concerns | 269 |
| XIII. The Essentials of Socialisation | 285 |
| XIV. The Method of Social Legislation | 307 |
| XV. Why I am a Socialist | 321 |

# NOTE

OF the papers contained in this volume, numbers 3, 4, 5, 8, 9, 10, and 12 have not been printed before. Number 1 appeared in the first number of *Plan* in December 1931. Number 2 (*The Crisis*), which I wrote in collaboration with Mr. Ernest Bevin, was published as a pamphlet by the *New Statesman and Nation* in October 1931. Number 6 was written and printed as a paper for the International Transport Workers' Conference in September 1930, but not published. Number 7 was written for the International Labour Organisation in January 1931, and published in the I.L.O. Report on *Unemployment Problems in 1931*. Number 11 appeared in French and Italian in *Scientia* in November 1922, but has not been previously published in English. Number 13 appeared in part in the *Political Quarterly* for July 1931, and has been issued as a pamphlet by the New Fabian Research Bureau. Number 14 was written as a paper for the Institute of Public Administration, and published in *Public Administration* in January 1931. Number 15 appeared in the *Aryan Path* of February 1930. I have to thank the various bodies concerned for their permission to make use of the papers here reissued.

G. D. H. C.

*January*, 1932.

# PART I
## THE ECONOMIC CRISIS

# I

# A SHORT TRACT FOR THE TIMES

## I.—Wheat

THERE is a world glut of wheat. Accumulated stocks are the largest ever known, and are being held deliberately off the market.

Wheat prices have fallen to a point which threatens the growers all over the world with ruin; and the holding of stocks does not avail to check the fall.

Yet in China, where there has been a great famine owing to flood, millions of people are on the verge of starvation. But they cannot afford to buy the world's surplus wheat: nor will the owners of it give it to them for nothing.

Germany, compelled to find huge sums for Reparations and interest on borrowed capital, has to restrict imports in order to build up an export surplus. The Germans have to take to rye bread in order to reduce their imports of wheat.

If half the wheat in the world were destroyed, the remaining half would be worth far more money than the whole supply is now.

The wheat-growers, getting less for their wheat, have to buy less manufactured goods, whose prices have fallen less. This creates unemployment in the industrial countries.

We have grown so used to statements such as these that most of us read them without turning a hair, or realising that the world is mad.

## II.—Employment

Broadly speaking, employers can afford to employ labour only if they can make a profit by doing so. If the selling prices of goods fall, or the costs of producing them rise, or fall less than selling prices, the result is that less workers are employed.

By disemploying workers the employer saves the cost of their keep, except to the extent to which he contributes to it through taxation. But someone has to keep the unemployed, on however low a standard of life. In this country they are kept mainly at the State's expense.

It costs the State less, directly, to keep a man in idleness than to set him to work, because (*a*) he can be kept idle on a lower standard of living, and (*b*) employing him involves other costs, such as buying the materials on which he is to work.

States, therefore, usually keep most of the unemployed in idleness, though they may be driven by criticism to set a few of them to work.

This calculation of costs leaves out of account the value of what the unemployed man would produce if he were set to work. States defend this on the ground that most of the work to which the unemployed can readily be set may produce social values, but is not directly reproductive in a money sense. For to set the unemployed to reproductive work would involve competing with Capitalism. This would decrease capitalist profits, and cause yet more unemployment, until the State was left as the only employer, with no rich capitalists to tax in order to meet the cost.

The same would apply if the unemployed were set to make things for their own use; for this, too, would limit the market for capitalist products, and cause more unemployment.

Most people draw the conclusion that it is no use setting the unemployed to work, and that the only course is to keep them in idleness on the lowest standard of living they can be brought to endure.

This is called 'economy'.

### III.—Scarcity

Things are valuable, in terms of money, in proportion as they are scarce.

The object of Capitalism is not to make as many things as possible, but as much value as possible.

Therefore Capitalism aims at scarcity.

There are apparent exceptions to this, as when Henry Ford brings down the price of motor-cars by mass production, in order to enlarge the circle of consumers' demand.

But even Henry Ford will only reduce prices to the extent to which he thinks his net profits will be increased by reducing them.

If so many cars are being produced that this is no longer the case, he will restrict production, and sack workers or put them on short time. Even he cannot escape from the conditions which make plenty a curse and scarcity a good.

A million motor-cars may be worth less than half a million in money; but they cannot really be worth less. For they still include the first half-million, even if the second half-million be worth nothing.

So with wheat. An increased supply cannot reduce the real value, though it may reduce the total selling price.

### IV.—Economists

Most economists nowadays tell us to stop thinking about value, and to think only about price.

Or at least they say Economics must concern itself only with prices, and not with real values.

The effect of this is to shut up Economics in the coffin of Capitalism, and forbid it to make any contribution to the devising of an alternative system.

The true economist must know how the price system works; but he must also get outside it, in order to criticise its working.

For this criticism he needs a standard; and his standard must be that of real value as distinct from price.

Real value consists in the power of a thing to satisfy human needs and desires, irrespective of the power of those who have the needs or desires to pay for it.

It is true that, in certain cases, the more a man has of a thing the less satisfaction each unit of it affords; but it is not true that, in any branch of production, the world has reached the point at which additional units will afford no satisfaction at all.

Nor is it true that, even if the total price offered for the supply of a thing falls as the supply increases, this indicates a fall in the total satisfaction afforded; both because incomes are grossly unequal, and because men's satisfactions are not really proportionate to the prices they are prepared to pay. For prices are, under normal conditions, largely conventional; and what people are prepared to pay bears a close relation to what they have been used to paying.

The classical economists were nearer the truth than their successors, because they had at least a hazy conception of value as distinct from price, and were less completely dominated by the idea of a monetary economy.

Marx was nearest of all, though he muddled up his theory of value by accepting too many of his opponents' assumptions, and trying to score off them by this means. Exchange value is a hybrid concept, concealing a confusion of thought.

It was a bad day for Economics when 'value in use' was discarded as useless. We have to bring back use-value into our economic thinking, and use it as our standard in criticising the Economics of Prices.

## V.—Socialism

The objects of Socialism are summed up in the phrase— 'From each according to his capacities: to each according to his needs.'

The first of these is the Socialist law of production: the second is the Socialist law of distribution.

'From each according to his capacities' implies the aim of securing maximum production, limited only by the demand for leisure.

'To each according to his needs' implies that the distribution of income ought to be a function, not of the productive system, but of the community itself.

That is why Socialists are as much against wages as they are against profits. Every man's income ought to be a share in the national dividend, not a cost of production.

The system that makes wages, interest and rent (and even,

some say, normal profits) into costs is the chief cause of unemployment; for it makes it not pay to allow production unless the product can be sold at a price which will cover all the costs.

It would always pay a Socialist community to employ everybody, except those few whose net product, excluding wages, was less than zero.

For a Socialist community would not be able to 'save' by starving its unemployed.

## VI.—Russia

There are many complaints about Russian dumping.

Russia, it is said, sells her exports under cost price.

Yet the Russians do not go bankrupt, or have to stop producing. Why is this?

Russia's foreign trade is a public monopoly.

This makes it virtually barter. The Russians sell their exports for what they can get for them in foreign money, irrespective of their costs of production in Russian money. They then buy with the foreign money as much as they can afford to buy of the things they need to import, and price these imports in Russia high enough to earn the costs of the exports for which they have been exchanged.

This shocks the capitalist world. But it is sound sense all the same. It is how most countries will have to conduct their foreign trade before long.

It is not Socialism; but it is a big step towards Socialism.

## VII.—The Crisis

Some say the crisis is due to over-production. But even the orthodox boggle at the idea of general over-production. It is too obviously silly.

Some say it is due to relative over-production of certain goods. But which goods are being under-produced, in relation to market demand?

Some say it is due to under-consumption; and so it is, in a sense. But why does under-consumption occur?

Some say it is due to the failure of the United States market. But why did that market fail?

Some say it is due to over-speculation in America. But did not American speculation go wrong chiefly because the demand for goods failed to keep pace with production?

Some say it is due to monetary causes, making the world price-level fall. They blame the shortage, or the mal-distribution, of gold. But there is not yet a real shortage, though there is mal-distribution. Why does this mal-distribution arise?

Some say it is due to excessive wages. But surely a reduction in the standard of life is an odd way of increasing the world's consuming power.

The real trouble is that wages are too low over the world as a whole, and rising less fast than productive power. This was especially true of the United States before the slump.

But one country, except when it is self-contained, cannot raise wages unless others do the same. Indeed, if one country reduces wages, others are driven to reduce them too, though this makes the world situation worse.

That is why there is no sign of an end to the crisis.

### VIII.—'RENTIERS'

A *rentier* is a person who gets something for nothing. He is a burden on the community.

He may be a necessary burden, if he is not capable of work. Some *rentiers* would have to be kept anyway. But that is no reason why the community should carry a *rentier* class that is capable of work.

An inherent tendency of the economic system is to pile up debts until they reach such a point that they have to be wiped off, and a fresh start made.

The Greeks called this Seisachtheia (a shaking off of burdens). The modern world provides for it by legalising bankruptcy.

There are *rentier* nations as well as individuals. Great Britain has long been a *rentier* nation. So, nowadays, are the United States and France.

Most people in Great Britain now think the United States

ought to let us and the rest of Europe off our debts, as far as they arise out of the war, and that German Reparations ought to be cancelled.

But most people have not yet begun to ask how long Great Britain can expect to go on receiving interest and dividends on a huge mass of overseas investments.

Even those who speak of repudiating the National Debt usually do not think we ought to refuse interest on our investments. Mr. Lang was not popular.

It would upset our national economy very badly if we did have to forego this interest; for we use it to buy imports in excess of the value of our exports. But we had better prepare ourselves for foregoing it; for the world will hardly go on paying indefinitely. Even now there are many threats of default.

Lending is all right in moderation; but it wants watching. It has gone much too far in the world today. In addition, of course, the burden of debt has been swollen by the fall in the price-level.

The world needs to wipe the slate clean; and it will probably do so, however inconvenient that may be for any particular country.

### IX.—The Future

The world is in a horrible mess.

Most people, instead of trying hard to put it right, have got rattled.

When people are frightened, they do not think straight.

Each man gives up the problem as a whole, and tries only to keep his own vested interest intact.

Vested interests are strangling the world.

It is of no use now to think even nationally; for no country can save itself by itself. Least of all Great Britain.

Think then internationally. But do not be sentimental about it. Too many internationalists are inclined to be sloppy.

If you want to put the world to rights, you have to find a force capable of doing the job. It will not be done merely by pointing out how silly things—and people—are.

The only available force is the working-class movement.

'Workers of the world, unite.' That does not mean that only the horny-handed need apply. It means that all of us have to make the working-class movement our rallying-point.

And it cannot be a pleasant job, cleaning up the mess we have got into. But it has to be done, and the sooner we take off our coats to it the better.

## II

## THE CRISIS[1]

### BY WAY OF PREFACE

WE are living, we think, on the very eve of one of those great world upheavals which are the turning-points of history. For a long while up to now the civilised world has been ordering its affairs on the basis of a system which is commonly called Capitalism. This system is open to many objections, and has aroused growing criticism, especially from the working-classes, on whose exploitation it is mainly based. But it has at least worked hitherto after a fashion, and provided those who live under it with the common necessities of life. Through its centuries of growth it has become increasingly complicated, with the development of international trade in necessaries as well as luxuries, the specialisation of this or that area in certain branches of manufacture or production, and the evolution of a complex system of banking and credit for the financing of the huge volume of transactions involved in the exchange of goods and services both within each country and between one country and another.

From time to time, in the history of the capitalist system, things have gone seriously wrong, and there have been great commercial crises which have caused widespread unemployment and distress. But hitherto world Capitalism has always recovered from these crises, and been able to advance from them to fresh economic conquests. When the present world crisis began, most people were inclined to say that it was only another of these periodic depressions of world trade, and that before

[1] This tract, written in collaboration with Mr. Ernest Bevin, and published in October 1931, is here reprinted with the permission of my co-author and of the *New Statesman and Nation*, the original publishers.

long there would come a revival leading to greater prosperity than the world has yet enjoyed.

There seemed, indeed, to be good warrant for this view. For it was plain enough that, thanks to the progress of science, the world's power to produce all the material necessities of life was advancing faster than ever before. In industry and agriculture alike, productivity was increasing at a wondrous rate; and there seemed to be every reason why the growing ease with which goods could be produced should result for the whole world in a higher standard of life. For the poverty of the many has always been attributed to the toil and trouble of production; and if men can produce more than before, that seems to assure that there will be more for them to consume.

This should obviously follow as a matter of course; but of late years it has not followed in fact. The result of increased productive power has been instead a great mass of unemployment in the manufacturing countries, and a fall in the prices of foodstuffs and raw materials which has more and more impoverished the producers of these classes of goods. These impoverished producers cannot afford to buy as many manufactures as before, with the consequence that many businesses have gone bankrupt and many millions of industrial workers been thrown out of work.

Still for a long time most people went on saying that the depression, serious as it was, would pass away speedily, and prosperity return. But latterly a great many who were optimists a year ago have become more doubtful of the outcome; for they have to confess that there is no sign at all of the depression passing, and every indication that it is deepening into a crisis which threatens the very structure of the capitalist world. They are coming to see that the causes of the present trouble go far deeper than any temporary loss of equilibrium in the world economic system, and that the system itself is rotten at the core.

The signs of this inward rotting away of Capitalism are many. They appear most plainly on the surface in the working of the world financial system, and in the relations between debtor and creditor nations. To these two questions accordingly this booklet is mainly devoted. It is an attempt to explain in simple terms the immediate causes and the essential character of the present crisis, in relation both to Great Britain and to the world as a whole, and to propose *minimum* remedies. It may well prove that these proposals, drastic as they will seem to many readers, are less than the situation requires; for it is hardly possible to exaggerate its gravity. But it has been written on the assumption that an attempt should be made to avert collapse, and that it is still possible, if we use our wits, to make a transition to a better system without an intervening period of sheer chaos and disaster. This view may be too optimistic; for events are rushing forward at an appalling pace. But there is no doubt that the attempt should be made, or that the first step towards making it is to diffuse as widely as possible an understanding of what is wrong and needs putting right in the world's affairs. Hence this booklet—inadequate and sketchy at many points—but at any rate an honest attempt to state simply the essentials of a desperately tangled situation.

### I.—The Crisis

The plain man may be forgiven if he finds himself bewildered by the events of the past few months. Even before the present crisis began, the situation was absurd enough. The whole world was involved in a trade depression, by far the worst in living memory, the cause of which no one seemed to know—or at least no two persons to agree upon. We were all being urged to economise and to consume less; and yet at the same time the world's chief trouble seemed to be over-production. How diminished consumption could possibly be a remedy for over-production no one was able to explain. But in all the industrial countries the cry was going up that wages must come down, and less be spent on 'doles' and social services as the one way of restoring prosperity. Manufacturers were turning off hands and reducing output; and there were wild plans for destroying the surplus stocks of wheat and cotton and other agricultural products, in the hope of raising their prices. The world, in the opinion of business men, seemed to be cursed with abundance; and scarcity was being made a god.

All this was mad enough; but there was even worse to come. In the early summer Germany, under the double pressure of the demand for impossible Reparations and for interest on capital borrowed from abroad, threatened to default and came very near to total financial collapse. A German collapse would have involved disastrous consequences for the financiers of New York and London; and both the United States and Great Britain hastened to the rescue. Mr. Hoover put forward his plan for a moratorium on War Debts and Reparations, in order to afford a breathing-space; and the British and other bankers made or extended special loans to the Germans in order to help them to tide over the emergency. By these means, German default and probably German revolution as well, were prevented for the moment. But nothing was done to cure the trouble, or to stop its recurrence as soon as the effect of the emergency measures had worn off.

Moreover, the British bankers, in their lending to Germany, had long been making use of money that was not their own. The sums they lent to the Germans were in effect borrowed from French and American financiers, on terms which allowed these financiers to recall them whenever they chose. On the other hand, Germany was in no position to repay at short notice, or indeed at all, without a satisfactory settlement of the entire Reparations problem. Our bankers, therefore, had taken the heavy risk of lending for a long period money which they had only borrowed on short period terms. This meant that the French or Americans could at any time, by asking for their money back, put the British financiers into a very difficult situation.

At the same time, in consequence of the world slump, Great Britain had serious troubles of her own. Her exports had fallen heavily in quantity, and were still falling; and increased unemployment and reduced profits were both diminishing the revenue from taxation and increasing the national expenditure. The British Budget thus ceased to balance; and money had to be borrowed by the State to meet its current spendings.

The fall in the export trade would have had far more serious immediate consequences had it not been for the very sharp fall in the prices of the goods imported into this country. But, in fact, the prices of wheat and other imported foodstuffs and raw materials fell so much that, although we were importing no less than a year before, we were able to pay for our imports with far less of our own goods, because their prices had fallen a good deal less. What is called the 'visible adverse balance of trade'—that is, the difference between what we receive for our exports and what we have to pay for our imports—was no larger in 1931 than it had been in previous years. On the 'balance of trade' we were, despite the fall in exports, no worse off than before. Manifestly, then, the fall in our export trade is *not* the cause of the present crisis.

Always, however, Great Britain imports far more goods than she can pay for with the goods she exports. She is able to do this because she has other resources with which to pay for the extra imports. She has large masses of capital invested overseas, on which the borrowers pay her annual interest or dividends. She is a great carrying nation, and the profits of her shipping go to pay for a further part of her imports. And she does a large part of the world's financial business in trade bills, insurances and the like, and uses the profits made in these transactions to pay for yet more of her imports. Indeed, in normal years, when the total balance is struck, it is found that, despite the excess of imports over exports, Great Britain, after paying for all she imports, has still a large sum due to her from the rest of the world. A small part of this sum she may receive in gold; but most of it she does not receive, but reinvests overseas as capital which will earn more dividends in the future, and thus swell the total sum due to British capitalists from foreigners all over the world, or from citizens of other Empire countries.

Now, these large annual payments from overseas on which Great Britain so largely relies are broadly of two kinds. Some of them are fixed payments in money, such as interest on Government loans or foreign railway bonds, while others are a variable share in the profits of enterprises carried on overseas, such as dividends on rubber, tea, or oil shares, or on the ordinary stocks of railways or manufacturing concerns. When world trade is bad, obviously the latter will fall off, because the businesses in which the money is invested will only pay lower dividends, or none at all. Thus, in the past year most rubber companies have made heavy losses. There will accordingly be less income available from this source to pay for British imports or to reinvest overseas.

The same applies to the earnings of British shipping, which will obviously tend to fall off in times of trade depression, when many ships are laid up, and freight rates reduced in order to get traffic.

The same does *not* apply to those overseas investments on which interest is payable at a fixed rate. Indeed, to some extent the truth about them is quite the opposite. Our debtors are under contract to pay us the fixed interest on these loans whether they are making profits or not, and whatever happens to prices. In a depression, as prices fall, the fixed money payments mean that they have to pay their debts with a greatly increased quantity of the goods they produce, so that the burden upon the debtors becomes much heavier. So far, nearly all of them (except Chile and to a small extent Brazil) have gone on paying. But they have paid with ever-increasing difficulty, as in the well-known case of Australia; and there is no reason to suppose that most of them will, or can, go on paying much longer. If the present world depression lasts, there is danger of widespread defaults by the debtor countries; and this would mean, from the standpoint of Great Britain, the loss of income on which we rely in order to pay for our imports. The outlook in India, China, Australia, and many other countries makes defaults inevitable in the near future unless there is a recovery of trade and prices.

Meanwhile, although defaults have not yet taken place on a large scale, there has been a big reduction in our national income both from shipping and from overseas investments carrying a variable dividend; and the effect of these decreases has been to turn us for the time being into a country with an adverse balance. There is, moreover, every reason to believe that our receipts in dividends from overseas and our shipping earnings will fall still more in the near future, thus increasing the adverse balance against us, unless we either reduce our imports or increase our exports, or both.

This does not mean in the least that we are a bankrupt country. Foreigners owe us more—many times more—than we owe them; for we have the huge mass of our existing foreign investments to fall back on in case of need. We can, in the last resort, sell some of these investments to overseas buyers to balance the account.

The present time, however, is a very bad one for trying to sell our investments; for, on account of the world slump, the prices of most of them have fallen heavily. We can sell in the last resort, but only at a serious loss.

There is, then, at present a cause in the state of our international balance of payments for some uneasiness. But there is nothing in the amount of our adverse balance that could not, under normal conditions, be met with perfect ease by selling some of our securities abroad, or that, even under the present abnormal conditions, suffices by itself to explain the crisis. Our adverse balance of international payments is a factor in the situation; but it is only a factor of secondary importance. For the real causes of the present crisis it is necessary to look elsewhere.

Where, then, are we to look? In order to explain the real trouble we must go back to what was said earlier about the position of Germany. The Germans, by the terms of the Versailles Treaty, were put in an impossible economic position. They lost a large slice of their territory and population, and of their resources in coal and iron, as well as the whole of their mercantile marine. Their productive system had been thrown right out of gear during the war, and needed complete reconstruction at heavy capital cost. They needed to import foodstuffs to feed their people, and raw materials for their industries. And at the same time they were sentenced to pay huge sums in Reparations to the victorious Allies.

How could they pay? Only by exporting more goods than they imported, for they had no stock of gold and no foreign investments to pay with. But it was not easy for a country which needed to import large quantities of foodstuffs and raw materials to create a surplus of exports over imports, even if other countries had been willing to buy their goods. And, in fact, many other countries built up high tariff walls which helped to exclude German manufactures.

The Germans soon saw that there was only one conceivable way of carrying out the obligations thrust upon them—a complete reconstruction of their industries which would enable them to produce so cheaply as to be able to force their manufactures into foreign markets even over high tariff walls, coupled with a low standard of life for the German worker in order to reduce imports and keep down the costs of production. But they had no capital resources of their own with which to carry out this gigantic reconstruction of industry.

Nevertheless, they set to work. The long-term capital for rebuilding their industries they borrowed from America, and the short-term credit for financing their trade chiefly from America and Great Britain. With the aid of this borrowed money, and of a low standard of living, they achieved wonders in reorganising their industries and forcing their goods upon the world market, incidentally keeping down by their intense competition the standard of living of the workers in other countries. But, of course, they had to pay interest—and high interest, too, because of their precarious position—on all the capital they borrowed from abroad; and the burden of this interest was added to the already top-heavy burden of Reparations due to the Allies.

All the same, someone will say, Reparations have been paid. Yes, but they have never been paid out of any real surplus available to pay them. The Germans have borrowed from abroad a great deal more than they have paid in Reparations. In sober truth, the Americans, and to a less extent the British, have lent the Germans the money with which to pay the Reparations, which are then paid back to the Americans as interest on Europe's debts to them. The whole affair is a vicious circle—it would be mere farce if it were not tragedy as well.

This absurd state of affairs went on, without absolute breakdown, as long as the Americans went on pouring capital into Germany. But in 1928 came the American speculative boom, and in 1929 the world slump. During the boom, Americans found it more profitable to use their money in speculating at home than to lend it to the Germans, even at high interest; and the volume of American loans to Germany rapidly fell off. This upset the equilibrium of the German economic system; and when the world slump came, the Americans were not at all disposed to go on lending to a Germany that seemed on the brink of financial collapse, and perhaps revolution.

To a substantial degree, the British financiers stepped into the breach. They were not in a position to lend on anything like the scale on which the Americans had been lending before; but British policy was directed to preventing the collapse of Germany in order to avert European revolution and check the growth of French supremacy in Europe. There was, accordingly, a strong political motive behind the British loans.

But there was an economic motive as well, especially during the world slump; for our bankers found themselves with large sums left on their hands, which on account of the slump in trade capitalists left in the banks in preference to locking them up in long-term investments in Great Britain. The Germans, in their need, were prepared to pay high interest even for short-term loans that would help them to tide over their troubles; and the British financiers plunged heavily, in order to earn this high interest on the money in their hands.

But, despite these loans, the position in Germany grew more and more desperate as the world depression deepened. Indeed, each fresh loan only intensified the difficulties for the future, and in postponing the evil day, made it more evil still. But for the Hoover moratorium and the granting and extension of emergency credits to the Germans by the great Central Banks, total collapse would have been unavoidable some months ago; and even now Germany is barely tiding over, and collapse is still certain unless far more fundamental remedies are applied during the next few months. Germany's whole financial structure is utterly insecure; and, if she falls, she will bring down a good deal more with her, and quite possibly plunge a large part of Europe into revolution.

In order to prevent this, and to safeguard the large sums they had already in Germany, our financiers went on renewing their loans to the Germans. As we saw, they did this to a great extent, not with British money, but with money belonging to French and American financiers which its owners had deposited in London because they found they could earn better interest on it, or keep it safer, there than in Paris or New York. It suited the British financier to have this borrowed money, if he could use it to earn in Berlin higher interest than he paid for it—as long as Berlin went on paying. But he ran two risks—the risk of a German default, and the risk that the French or the Americans might recall their money at short notice, whereas it would be impossible for him to get back quickly what he had lent to the Germans.

Clearly, the more we lent to the Germans, the more our fortunes became involved with theirs. And the more desperate the position of Germany became, the more likely were those who had money on deposit or in short-term holdings in London to doubt its security, and to ask for it back. Our heavy plunge in lending money to the Germans was one, though by no means the only, cause of the loss of confidence in the security of money in London. A no less powerful cause was the Americans' loss of confidence in themselves, which made them take alarm at Germany's growing troubles, and scramble to recall and realise loans and investments which they had made in Europe.

For the United States were themselves passing through an economic crisis a good deal worse in its immediate effects than our own. In particular, the American banks, which had invested huge sums in American securities during the boom, found their resources disappearing as stock prices fell and fell in consequence of the depression. Many of them became virtually insolvent; and there followed a scramble to realise their liquid resources. This involved a hasty calling in of sums which they had to their credit in British and German banks, or had been using in the London money market. In other words, the British financiers were called upon suddenly to repay their American creditors, at a time when it was out of the question for them to collect the sums owing to them by their German, Australian, South American, and other debtors.

## II. THE CRISIS

In these circumstances, there were only two ways in which the repayment could be made—by shipping gold to America or by selling British-owned securities to the American capitalists. The second course, in view of the panic stock prices ruling on the American stock exchanges, would have meant heavy losses, even apart from the fact that it could not have been done without compelling the British owners of the securities in question to hand them over to the Government or the Bank of England for sale. This was not done; and large quantities of gold began to flow to the United States, until it became plain that, unless the flow was stopped, before long the entire British gold reserve was likely to disappear.

It was at this point that the political crisis was added to the economic. Faced with the threatened loss of gold, the late British Government, in conjunction with the Bank of England, set out to borrow large sums of money from France and America in order to offset the withdrawals. At first, such borrowings were successfully arranged. But the flood of American withdrawals continued, and the credits secured were soon exhausted, and the outflow of gold resumed. The British Government set out to borrow yet more, this time from America, which was now the chief cause of the trouble, though Holland, which was heavily involved in Germany, was a secondary cause, and was also draining gold from London on a considerable scale.

The renewed request for a loan from America led directly to the political crisis and the fall of the Labour Government. For the Government was told that it could have the loans it wanted only on certain conditions. One of these was that the Budget should be balanced, so as to remove the need for further Government borrowing to meet current expenditure. The other was that the method of balancing the Budget should include a drastic cut in the amount of unemployment benefit, and a drastic revision of the conditions on which the benefit was granted. The majority of the Labour Cabinet, while they were prepared to agree to balance the Budget in their own way, refused to accept this financial dictation on a political issue, or to agree to a reduction in the amount of benefit. Upon their refusal, the Prime Minister handed in the resignation of the

Government, and proceeded himself to organise a Coalition with the Tories and Liberals, into which he carried only a tiny handful of 'Labour' supporters. The Labour Party, under Mr. Henderson's leadership, resumed its place as the official Opposition.

It should be observed in passing that, while it is clear the Labour Government fell as a result of financial dictation, it is still far from clear whence the dictation really came. It has been denied by the American bankers that they imposed any condition other than the balancing of the Budget, or insisted that unemployment benefits should be cut down. But it is certain that most of the members of the Labour Cabinet understood from those of their number who met the representatives of the Bank of England—which acted as intermediary in the negotiations—that both conditions had been imposed. Here is a matter that badly needs clearing up. *Did the financial dictation that caused the fall of the Labour Government come from the American, or did it really come from the British financiers?* Did British finance use the Americans as an instrument to bring down the Labour Government? And what part did the Bank of England play in the affair?

The 'National' Government was formed with the clear and explicit object of yielding to the demands of the financiers, by balancing the Budget and economising on the unemployed, and of borrowing enough money from America to save the position of London as a financial centre and keep the gold standard intact. Yet within a week, although it had borrowed £80,000,000 from America on most onerous terms, confidence in London was at a lower ebb than ever. There was a still greater rush to withdraw funds from Great Britain; and it became clear that the new credits would soon be exhausted. Within a few weeks of its formation, the 'National' Government, created with the one great object of keeping Great Britain on the gold standard, itself abrogated that standard by prohibiting the export of gold.

The means proposed by the 'National' Government to keep us on the gold standard were, indeed, in the event a factor in causing its suspension. The proposed cuts in the salaries of teachers and the wages of Civil Servants and others produced widespread discontent. The reductions in unemployment benefit and the threat to deprive hundreds of thousands of the workless of the means of life created an ugly temper of resentment throughout the industrial districts. The attacks on the pay of the fighting services aroused such feeling that trouble burst out openly at Invergordon and elsewhere; and the continental press was filled with rumours of impending riot and revolt that caused a further stampede away from the pound. Moreover, the enforcement of certain of these cuts—against the teachers, for example—in flat breach of solemn contracts into which the State had entered seemed so clearly the act of a Government reduced to panic and despair that other countries naturally took our situation to be very much worse than it actually was. The newspapers did their level best to swell the panic, and thus undermined confidence still more. Indeed, the loss of confidence in British credit was far more the result of the insane behaviour of our newspapers and politicians than of anything really wrong with Great Britain's economic position. The newspapers and the National Government—those ardent defenders of the gold standard—were the chief agents in compelling its abandonment. But, before we go on to study further this Gilbertian situation, we must say something about what the gold standard is, and what our departure from it involves.

## II.—THE GOLD STANDARD

The gold standard, though many intelligent people seem to be afraid of trying to understand it, is in essence quite simple. It is above all a device for keeping the national currencies of different countries at a fixed relative value. If a unit of each currency—a pound, or a franc, or a dollar—can be at any time exchanged for a fixed quantity of gold, it is evident that the relative values of these currency units cannot vary much, though of course their purchasing power may vary a great deal, in accordance with changes in the world level of prices. The gold standard is a means of keeping stable, not the price-level, but the relative values of the moneys of different nations.

This relative stability is obviously, in normal times, a great advantage from the standpoint of international trade. For it means that traders of different countries can make bargains in terms of one another's currencies with full knowledge of the amounts they will get or pay in their own money. As most trade is done on a credit basis this is highly important; and where the relative values of national currencies are liable to vary a new and dangerous uncertainty is added to the normal risks of trade.

For this reason the countries which were forced off the gold standard during the war made a great effort to return to it when the war was over; and most of them had succeeded in re-establishing it before the present world crisis began. But somehow, in the years since the war, the gold standard has not been working as it used to do. Where it has been in operation, it has kept the relative value of money almost stable; for it is bound to do that by its very nature. But the struggles in which the countries have been involved in order to keep on it at all have brought most inconvenient and even disastrous consequences in their train. High bank rates, restriction of credits to industry, and a rapidly falling price-level—these have been the results of the gold standard in recent years.

Countries which are on the gold standard in any full sense have to keep in their banks a supply of actual gold. This gold serves two purposes. In the first place, if their currencies are exchangeable for gold at a fixed rate, they must be prepared to sell gold at that rate to those who ask for it in exchange for currency. As the gold is of no use to the buyer within the country, this usually means that he wants to export it, in order to pay a bill which he owes in some other country, or in order to change it into the money of some other country. If, for example, the same sum of money will buy more goods or earn higher profits in America than in Great Britain, a number of persons will want to change British money into American money in order to get the benefit of the difference. There may thus arise a demand for gold to be exported to America; and Great Britain, as long as she was on the gold standard, had to be prepared to supply gold for this purpose to those who demanded it. Moreover, a country like the United States, which exports more than it imports, has somehow to be paid by other countries for this excess; and, unless Americans are prepared to leave this excess on loan in the debtor countries, the payment can only be made in gold. That, incidentally, is why America has sucked up so large a part of the world's total gold supply since the war.

The second purpose for which gold standard countries use gold is to keep a reserve, usually fixed by law, as a backing for their issues of paper money. The precise arrangements vary from country to country: in Great Britain the Bank of England is allowed to print a fixed amount of paper money without gold backing, but must have a pound for pound backing in gold against all notes issued beyond that amount. A great many people think that this is quite unnecessary; and that all the gold a country needs in order to work the gold standard is enough to meet demands for export. But at present the keeping of a gold reserve against notes is almost everywhere enforced by law; and legislation would be needed to remove the obligation. It has actually at the present time been temporarily modified in Great Britain.

The real object of compelling the banks to keep reserves of gold against their notes is simply to limit the amount of currency they are able to issue, so as to prevent any undue rise in prices. For if the banks went on printing paper money irrespective of any increase in the supply of things to be bought and sold, prices would be bound to rise, as they did in Germany and in other countries during the period of inflation. Inflation is, indeed, simply an increase in the supply of money without a corresponding increase in the quantity of things for sale.

A country that is on the gold standard cannot inflate. For if it did, its price-level would rise. It would therefore pay financiers better to change its currency into gold, and export the gold to a country where prices were lower. The country with the inflated currency would soon find itself losing all its gold. It would be compelled before long to refuse to give gold in exchange for its currency, at all events at the old fixed rate. In other words, it would be driven off the gold standard.

In this indirect way, the gold standard does regulate a

country's price-level, as well as the relative value of its currency and those of other countries. But it does not keep prices stable Speaking very broadly, it causes them to fluctuate in accordance with the movements of prices in the world as a whole, or rather in other gold standard countries.

As we have seen, after the war most countries came back to the gold standard. Some, indeed, such as the United States, remained on it throughout the war; but all the belligerent nations in Europe were temporarily driven off gold as a basis for their currencies. When they came back to it, they did not all do this in the same way. There were two alternative courses open to them—deflation and devaluation. Great Britain deflated; France, Italy, Germany and Belgium all in various ways devaluated.

Deflation is the opposite of inflation. It means a reduction in the quantity of money without a corresponding reduction in the volume of things to be bought and sold. This reduction brings down the price-level, and so makes each unit of the currency worth more in terms of goods, and therefore of gold as well—for gold has a value like other commodities. The effect of deflation is therefore to increase the value of the deflated currency in terms of gold and of currencies based on gold. In the case of Great Britain after the war, deflation was pushed to the point at which it became just possible to restore the gold standard at pre-war parity—that is, to offer to give for a pound sterling the same quantity of gold as before the war. This brought the pound back to pre-war parity with the American dollar, which was also exchangeable for the same quantity of gold as in 1914.

The French and the Germans, equally with ourselves, came back to the gold standard. But their method was not deflation, but devaluation. The French did not attempt to make a franc worth as much gold as it had been in 1914, but only to fix for it a new and greatly reduced gold value (roughly one-fifth of its pre-war value) and then keep it stable at the new value. This was fully as effective and complete a restoration of the gold standard as ours; but it had quite different effects. The Germans went further than the French, by wiping out their old inflated paper currency altogether, and starting a new one, with a fixed value in gold.

Our policy of deflation had apparent advantages to us as a great creditor country. It compelled our debtors, who mostly owed us debts reckoned in our own currency, to pay us more in real things as the value of the pound went up. But it had far more serious disadvantages. In order to carry it through, the bankers kept bank rates of interest high and restricted the amount of credit, thus hampering industry and increasing unemployment. Moreover, as the value of the pound rose, the burden of the National Debt, and of all fixed interest charges, rose with it, putting a tremendous strain on our system of taxation, and burdening productive industry with higher real charges on all sorts of mortgages and debentures as well as in bank interest. A huge addition was made by these means to the unearned incomes of the *rentier* classes, and the seed sown has sprouted into the unbalanced Budget of today.

Moreover, even though deflation compelled the countries which owed us money to pay us more in goods or gold, it is more than doubtful whether we got any advantage from laying this extra burden upon them. The increase in their indebtedness helped in the long run to destroy their power to purchase our exports. This in turn caused severe unemployment in our export trades; and we had to maintain those who were thrown out of work. This meant that we had to take back in taxes to maintain the unemployed quite as much as we had exacted from the debtor countries. And, in addition, by pressing these countries too hard, we caused them to threaten to default in their payments; so that we ran the risk of losing what they owed us altogether and still being left with the unemployed to maintain. The gain from scaling up the debts due to us from other countries by means of deflation was therefore illusory. So far from gaining by it, we were heavy losers in the long run.

Devaluation, the alternative open to us when we decided to restore the gold standard, would have meant some loss on our foreign investments which bore a fixed rate of interest in pounds sterling. But it would have avoided the necessity of high bank rates and credit restriction, and it would not have made the huge unnecessary present which deflation made to the *rentier* class. It would have kept down the burden of the National Debt, and released the proceeds of taxation for more useful purposes, such as a policy of national development and the extension of the social services. Undoubtedly, devaluation was the right policy, and deflation hopelessly wrong.

Nor is this the whole of the case against deflation. When, in 1925, Mr. Churchill and the Bank of England restored the gold standard on a basis of pre-war parity, deflation had not really been carried far enough to enable the value of the pound to be easily maintained at the new fixed level. British prices and costs of production had not really been forced down far enough to make the pound sterling worth as much as we insisted on valuing it at, in terms of gold and dollars. Consequently, there has been ever since persistent pressure to bring down wages still further, in order to reduce costs, and the policy of restricting the supply of credit has had to be maintained. We have lost export trade because we have been charging more than the world prices for our exports in terms of gold and of our overvalued currency.

In order to retrieve these losses of trade, we have been driven ever since 1925 to a series of unsound and dangerous expedients. The first was the coal subsidy. Then came the Conservative Derating Act—a deliberate attempt to lower costs of production by transferring burdens from rates direct upon industry, which increase costs, in part to the national tax-payers and in part to the local householders. This meant in effect an indirect reduction in wages all round, as well as a bonus to profits in a number of flourishing trades which needed no help. The point here is that this measure arose directly out of our folly in restoring the gold standard. In doing so, we unnecessarily raised the prices of our exports; and we were then driven to one bad expedient after another in our attempts to get costs down again to a competitive level.

These expedients have failed. We have been left with a large persistent mass of unemployment; and the maintenance of the unemployed has combined with derating and the excessive interest on the National Debt to make our taxation the highest in the world. High taxation in itself need not be bad—that depends on how the proceeds are used. High taxation devoted mainly to keeping people in idleness is certainly very bad indeed. Yet this was the necessary result of deflation. It caused widespread unemployment; and it grossly increased the incomes of the *rentier* class—the latter being of course by far the heavier burden on the Exchequer.

Ever since 1925, Great Britain has been struggling vainly against the disastrous consequences of this colossal blunder. Our troubles arose, and arise, mainly not from the fact that we went back to the gold standard, but from our folly in doing this by deflation instead of devaluation. The mistake lay in forcing the pound back to pre-war parity, and so putting on it a value which exceeded its real worth.

We have now, in the midst of the world slump, been driven off the gold standard, in an attempt to reverse the consequences of our folly. By prohibiting the export of gold, or rather refusing to give gold in exchange for our currency, we have removed the pin which fixed the relative value of sterling and other currencies, and for the moment we are letting the gold value of the pound fluctuate. But we are told by those in authority that this is meant to be a purely temporary measure and that, as soon as the present emergency is over, we are to go back to the gold standard.

What does this mean? It may mean either of two things—either that we are to aim at bringing the pound back yet again to its old parity with gold and with other gold standard currencies, or that we now mean to devaluate, and, as soon as the emergency is over, to fix a new and lower gold value for the pound, as France has done for the franc and Italy for the lira. On this point, those in authority give us no clear information; but the hints which they drop sound as if they were still hankering after a return of the pound to the old parity.

This would be a disastrous policy. It would again force up the real burden of the National Debt, and of all fixed interest payments. It could be brought about only by a drastic reduction of wages and salaries, designed to force down costs of production, and by a continuance of high bank rates and credit restriction. It could be put into operation only over the prostrate body of the working-class movement. And, above all, it is entirely unnecessary.

The effect of allowing the pound to become worth less in terms of other currencies is, of course, to increase the cost in pounds of our imports, and to cheapen the prices of our exports to foreign purchasers. This is on the assumption that other countries do not follow our example, and devaluate their currencies as well. If they do, and devaluate to the same extent as ourselves, the position is as you were—we buy their goods, and they buy ours, on the same terms as before. Probably a substantial number of countries, in addition to those which had gone off the gold standard before we did, will, in fact, follow our example—as Denmark and Sweden, for instance, have done already. But at least France and America, with their huge stocks of gold, can hardly embark on a policy of devaluation. The effect of our going off gold is therefore likely to be a stimulus to our export trade at the expense of French and American exports, and of those of any other countries which remain on the gold standard.

A second effect will be some restriction of imports into Great Britain, at least from countries which still keep to gold as a basis. For, as we shall have to pay more in pounds for their goods, we shall tend to buy less from them, and either to make the goods at home, or to buy them from countries which are not on the gold standard. The tendency of our departure from the gold standard will thus be to reduce the British adverse balance of trade, and to hit seriously the export trade of those countries which, for one reason or another, do not follow our example.

To some extent, these effects will be temporary. If costs and prices in Great Britain were to rise to the full extent of the fall in the gold value of the pound, they would disappear altogether; for our manufacturers would then be charging so many more pounds for their exports as to make them no cheaper to foreign buyers than the exports of France and America, and imports from gold standard countries would again be able to compete at the higher prices with our own products or those of other countries with depreciated currencies. There is, however, no reason to suppose that, for some time at least, the internal price-level will rise to the same extent as the external value of the pound falls. The prices of many imported goods will doubtless rise, and this will cause the cost of living to increase to the extent to which we live on goods imported from gold standard countries. But there is no reason why the prices of goods and services produced at home should rise, or at any rate why they should rise to anything like the same extent. For some time at least the devaluation of sterling is likely to give a considerable stimulus to our export trade—the more powerful the further the depreciation goes.

If we attempted to restore the pound to its pre-war gold parity, we should totally throw away this most necessary advantage, and plunge our export trades back into the difficulties from which the suspension of the gold standard gives them a chance of emerging at last. For this as well as for the other reasons given above, it would be the worst sort of folly to attempt to go back to the old gold parity.

There remains the second policy, of returning to the gold standard at a new and lower gold parity—that is, of permanent devaluation of the pound in terms of gold. After allowing the pound to fluctuate for a time in terms of other currencies, so as to let it find its natural level, we can, if we will, stabilise it at a new gold value, based on its new actual ratio of exchange with the currencies of countries still on the gold standard.

This would be a far better policy than to attempt to restore the pound to its old parity. It would retain, at least for a long time, the advantage to our export trade; and it would reduce permanently the real burden of the War Debt and of other fixed interest obligations. Of course, it would mean some rise in prices, which would have to be met in due course by increasing wages and salaries; but, as we have seen, there is no reason why prices should rise to nearly the same extent as the gold value of the pound falls.

This policy of permanent devaluation has therefore much to recommend it. The chief argument used against it is its effect in reducing the sums owing to this country as interest on our investments abroad. But we shall find it far more to our advantage to reduce this interest than to provoke defaults all over the world by pressing for payment on the old terms. Countries like Australia and India, Chile and Brazil, the prices of whose products and the value of whose currencies have already suffered a severe fall, cannot possibly afford much longer to go on paying interest on their borrowings in pounds measured at the old rate. Unless their burdens are made lighter, they will default altogether. Devaluation, which does lighten their burdens, is from this standpoint a positive advantage.

But, although stabilisation of the pound at a new and lower gold parity is a possible policy with a good deal to recommend it, can we be at all certain at this stage that we shall wish to go back to the gold standard at all? For that standard, while it has the advantage of being international, has shown itself to possess very serious disadvantages. May it not be better to replace it by a new international standard, worked out in common among the countries which the crisis has driven off gold; or even, in default of this, to leave the pound to fluctuate in terms of other currencies, and concentrate on an attempt to stabilise our own internal prices? To the case for and against the gold standard itself—as distinct from the question of pre-war parity of the pound with gold and other currencies—we must next turn our attention.

### III.—The Gold Standard Breaks Down

The gold standard demands for its successful working that the available gold supply of the world shall be distributed among the leading nations roughly in proportion to their needs. This does not mean that each country in the world needs to have a supply of gold corresponding to the volume of its currency and the quantity of goods it needs to buy and sell. For many of the smaller countries can manage with a quite tiny amount of gold, by keeping always available large credits in the banks of the leading countries. Thus, as long as London was a free market for gold—*i.e.*, as long as gold for export could be got at a fixed rate in exchange for British currency—a credit on London was practically as good as gold; and many of the smaller nations, under what is known as the gold exchange standard, held claims on London instead of gold as a basis for a large part of their currency and credit operations. But the gold exchange standard has always been held to imply the existence of countries on the gold standard proper; and it is essential, if the gold standard is to work, that the available supply of gold should be distributed among these major financial centres roughly in accordance with their needs.

In the years since the war, this condition has never been fully satisfied; and there has been constant and serious danger of it not being satisfied at all. There has been a steady and persistent drift of the world's gold to the United States, and latterly to France, until these two countries have accumulated gold reserves far in excess of any rational estimate of their needs, while the rest of the world has been forced to go short. If the United States and France had followed the old course of banking orthodoxy by issuing currency and credit to the full extent apparently authorised by their stocks of gold, the inevitable effect would have been to raise their prices well above the level of prices in the rest of the world. This would have destroyed their export trade, and caused an increase of imports into their markets unless they had raised their tariffs to absolutely prohibitive heights. The result would have been that the gold accumulated by them would have flowed out and been redistributed over the world in payment for these increased imports.

But in fact neither France nor America has increased its issue of currency and credit in proportion to the growth of its stock of gold. Both countries, in order to prevent their prices from rising far beyond the world-level, have sterilised a large part of their gold by keeping it in the vaults of their banks without making any use of it at all. Of course, gold so sterilised is a dead loss. It earns no interest, and it performs no manner of service. But to keep it idle has seemed preferable to allowing the rise in prices which would have followed its use as a basis for a larger issue of currency and credit.

Moreover, in the case of the United States at least, the tariff, while it is not prohibitive, has been raised very high against most classes of manufactures, and does have a big effect in excluding imports. The gold stocks of France and the United States have therefore not been automatically redistributed to the rest of the world by that change in relative prices which, according to orthodox economics, is the natural means of correcting a mal-distribution of gold.

There remains, however, another way in which this redistribution can be brought about. If France and the United States, or rather their investing classes, are prepared to make large loans of capital to other countries, these loans can be made out of the surplus gold lying in the French and American banks. In the case of the United States, it is only because such loans have been made in past years on a very large scale that far more even of the world's total gold supply has not been locked up idle in the American banks.

But if at any time this flow of investment abroad ceases, or is seriously diminished, at once the flow of gold to the United States is resumed, and the rest of the world, finding itself short of the basis on which its currencies rely, proceeds to restrict credit at the cost of causing disastrous contraction of trade. Other countries raise their bank rates of interest, in the hope of attracting gold or at least preventing a further outflow. This raises their costs of production, hampers their trade, and adds to the burdens of taxation for the maintenance of the unemployed. As long as the present tendency of the world's gold to drift to France and the United States remains in being, the prosperity of other countries depends on the willingness of French and American investors to keep up a large and constant stream of foreign loans of capital.

But why, it will be asked, does this tendency for the world's gold to drift to France and America exist at all? The answer, though it is not quite the same in the two cases, is as easy as the tendency is hard to remove. Take the case of America first.

Before the war the United States was a debtor country. Its capitalists had borrowed large sums of money from the investors of Great Britain and other European countries for the purpose of developing the vast natural resources of the American continent. On these borrowings they owed and paid interest, chiefly in the form of exported foodstuffs and raw materials.

## II. THE CRISIS

The United States was, moreover, still borrowing capital from abroad, though at a diminishing rate.

During the war, all this was altered. The Americans bought back a large part of the stocks and bonds of American enterprises held by foreign investors; and they also lent huge sums to Europe, in order to enable the European nations to pay them for the foodstuffs and munitions which they supplied, at a time when the European export trades had been thrown out of gear by the war, and Europe had no means of paying with her exports for her inflated imports.

The United States therefore emerged from the war, no longer a debtor, but a great creditor country, to which European nations, and especially Great Britain, owed large sums in annual interest. How were these sums to be paid? The natural means of payment would have been for Europe to export to the United States far more goods than she imported from them. But this was impossible, both because Europe imperatively needed a huge volume of American goods, and because the United States maintained a high protective tariff in order to exclude just those manufactures in which alone Europe had the means to pay. Europe therefore owed America each year not only the interest on her debts, but also a further balance on account of the excess of European imports from America.

This unbalanced situation sufficiently accounts for the persistent tendency of gold to drift to the United States. Between 1920 and 1924 the gold holdings of the U.S.A. rose by over 1,600 million dollars; and in 1924 the U.S.A. had nearly as much gold as all the rest of the world put together, excluding only France. Thereafter, a further increase of the American gold stock was prevented, and even a small diminution secured, by heavy lending of American capital overseas. But when, in the American boom of 1929, the American investor saw more chance of making high profits by using his capital at home than by lending it abroad, the flow of gold to the United States was at once resumed; and a crisis at once arose in the financial affairs of other countries, which had to raise their bank rates and restrict credit on account of the loss of the gold. Not that America wanted the gold; far from it. She had far too much already, and could make no use of it at all. But that did not check the flow; for Europe had to pay its debts, and in face of the high American tariff there was no other means of payment.

Nor was the situation bettered when the American boom ended in the crisis which ushered in the world slump. For the American investor was now unwilling to lend because the world-wide slump made him distrustful of the profitableness, and even of the security, of foreign investment. American gold holdings grew rapidly in 1930; for, slump or no slump, the rest of the world was due to pay its debts, and these debts were mostly fixed in terms of gold dollars.

We have, then, in the case of the United States a supremely ludicrous situation. The Americans, on account of their great natural resources, have a tendency to export more goods than they import. They exaggerate this tendency by maintaining a high protective tariff against manufactured imports. They have large sums invested abroad, and large claims on foreign Governments, on which annual interest and dividends are due to be paid. Not all the world's gold would suffice for long to balance this account. It can be balanced only if American investors regularly lend enough abroad to balance it—in other words, if America forgoes present payment, with the result of adding the annual interest for ever to the sum due. In plain terms, America can never be paid. The logical end to her attempts to exact payment would be that she should gradually buy up the whole world on condition of receiving nothing from it.

The French situation is somewhat different, though France has, during the past few years, been drawing in gold quite as sensationally as the United States. France, too, is a creditor country, though not on the same colossal scale as the United States. The French situation, indeed, arises largely out of the history of the French financial system since the war.

France, as we have seen, returned to the gold standard on a basis, not of pre-war parity, but of drastic devaluation of the franc, roughly to one-fifth of its pre-war gold value. Stabilisation at this lower figure was preceded by a period of inflation, during which the value of the franc fell sharply over a long period. While the fall was in progress, there was a 'flight from the franc'—in other words, French capitalists changed their money into other more stable currencies in order to avoid the consequences of a further fall. Above all, they changed francs into pounds sterling, and kept large balances in London. London, in turn, used these balances to re-lend at interest to borrowers at home and abroad, and found them very useful as a protection for the British gold reserve against the drain of gold to America.

But in due course the franc was stabilised at its new value; and gradually the French capitalists began to take their money home again, thus causing a drain of gold from London to Paris. Between 1926 and 1929 French gold holdings much more than doubled; and again and again a serious strain was put on the British financial system. For it was impossible for British finance at once to recall the loans which it had made on the strength of the French balances, as any attempt to do this would have at once provoked a world financial crisis, and, above all, a collapse of German credit.

Now, France is to a considerable extent a self-contained country, depending less on imports and exports than either Great Britain or Germany, or even the United States. Her imports and exports are nearly balanced; and there is certainly no tendency for gold to flow out from Paris in payment for imports. Accordingly, the only way in which the surplus gold uselessly accumulating in France could be redistributed would be for the French capitalists to make foreign loans on a sufficient scale to cause an outflow of gold.

The French investor, however, especially since he has been badly bitten in the past, is very fearful of foreign investments; and the French have been in fact lending abroad less than the amount of their annual balance, thus accentuating the flow of gold to Paris. Moreover, what they have lent they have often preferred merely to deposit in foreign banks or to lend at short term, rather than invest in long-term securities. They are therefore in a position at any moment to upset the financial equilibrium of the rest of the world by a sudden recall of their loans; and such a recall may always be prompted by political as well as by economic motives. The large mass of French short-term credits still outstanding in London thus gives the French financiers a strong economic pull; and this is the more dangerous because Great Britain, holding French money on short-term conditions, has lent largely to Germany, against which French political animosity is especially directed.

The fundamental trouble, however, in relation to both the United States and France lies in their being creditor countries which are at present unwilling to invest enough capital abroad to offset the tendency of gold to drift into their banks in payment of the world's debts to them. This drift of gold accordingly results in locking up uselessly a large part of the world's gold supply, and in keeping the rest of the world short of gold. This shortage, in its turn, tends to force down the world price-level, by restricting the amounts of currency and credit which the world is able to create, in accordance with its existing laws and conceptions of financial rectitude. Thus restriction of currency and credit is added to the other factors, such as the collapse of the American market, making for a fall in world prices; and the fall in prices, thus accentuated, results everywhere in trade depression and in frantic efforts to restrict production in order to prevent prices from falling yet more.

The gold standard, under post-war conditions, thus produces highly unfortunate results for most of the world. It has indeed been evident for some time past that, failing a removal of existing tendencies, it could not possibly long continue in operation. For the debtor countries of the world had been, even before the recent crisis drove Great Britain off the gold standard, losing gold at such a rate as to make the total exhaustion of their supplies only a matter of two or three years at most. Several of these countries had been driven off the gold standard before Great Britain; and others are already following Great Britain's example.

In these circumstances, a return to the gold standard by Great Britain and the other countries which have abandoned it for the time would be likely to lead only to a resumption of the drain of gold to France and the United States, unless it were accompanied by far-reaching measures for the revision of existing international obligations and probably by a lowering of the

United States tariff wall. For, as long as Europe owes huge sums to America, she can pay only in goods or in gold; and even if the American tariff were greatly reduced, she could not hope to pay in goods and gold together nearly all she owes, even if all her gold were drained away. But the resumption of American lending, even on a scale sufficient temporarily to reduce the balance, can afford no lasting remedy; for its result is to swell each year the sum of European indebtedness, and the amount payable in interest upon it. There can be no remedy without a thoroughgoing revision of existing international debts, including Reparations payments. Given such a revision, the form and extent of which we must next proceed to consider, a return to the gold standard, at a new and lower gold parity of the pound, *may* prove to be desirable. Without such revision, emphatically it is not.

## IV.—Debtors and Creditors

The basis of world trade is mutual exchange of products. Some countries are best suited to produce certain types of goods, and other countries to produce other goods. In general, the prosperity of each country, as well as the total wealth of the world, will be greatest if each economic area specialises in producing the goods which it is best fitted to produce, and exchanges its surplus for the different surpluses of other areas. The basis of international trade is international barter, based on the different productive qualities, national and acquired, of the various countries and their inhabitants.

To this simple exchange of commodities, however, the modern world has added a new and growingly important kind of international trade based, not on the exchange of goods for goods, but on the lending by the richer and more developed countries of capital resources for the development of the less advanced. This form of trade involves, in the first instance, exports from the former countries to the latter without any equivalent return in goods; but it also creates on the part of the borrowers an obligation to pay interest—that is, to export in future years to the creditor countries goods for which no equivalent in their goods will be due. In the beginning, then, the lending countries have a surplus of exports over imports; but, when the lending has gone on for some time, the interest due on the capital already exported comes to exceed the amount of new capital annually lent abroad, and these countries accordingly show an excess of imports—commonly called an adverse balance of trade. This has long been the position of Great Britain, which has been for generations past the leading creditor country in the world.

This extensive lending of capital to the less developed countries is justified economically, and made attractive to investors in the older countries, by the fact that the exploitation of the unused resources of the less advanced areas often affords prospects of higher profits than can easily be made at home. In other words, the capital is more productive when used in this way than it would be if it were applied to the further development of home resources.

So far, so good. If the capital lent to the less advanced countries is so applied as rapidly to increase their riches and productive power, they can, out of their increased wealth, afford to pay interest on it to the creditor nations, and still retain a margin of profit for themselves. But if the loans so made are wasted in unproductive expenditure, or squandered on wars and armaments, the burden of interest on the debtor country may easily become unbearable; and there have been in the past many defaults due to this cause. Moreover, even if the loans are put to the best productive use, but the value of money changes, or there is a heavy fall in the prices of the goods chiefly produced by the debtor countries, or a serious and prolonged world depression of trade, it may become impossible for the debtors, through no fault of their own, to pay the interest due. For they can pay this only in goods; and if their exports fall off seriously in either quantity or price, they have no other resources out of which to pay, unless indeed they are able to resort to further borrowing—and that will only aggravate the problem in future years.

In face of the catastrophic fall of prices in recent years, the position of the countries which have borrowed large masses of foreign capital has become increasingly difficult, especially where their borrowings have been in terms of a gold standard currency. For the interest, in view of the lower prices, has come to represent a greatly increased debt in terms of commodities. Hence the recent defaults of Chile and Brazil, the threatened default of Australia, the extreme hardships involved for India and China in the meeting of their international obligations. In the case of India and China, the situation is further aggravated by the fall in the price of silver, which has depressed the purchasing power of the Far East even more than the fall in commodity prices.

It is not too much to say that, failing considerable modifications in the claims of creditor countries, widespread default is inevitable in the near future. As far as Great Britain is concerned, the position of debtors has been greatly eased by her departure from the gold standard; for the debtor countries will now be called upon to pay their interest only in sterling at a lower gold and commodity value. But the United States is still claiming to be paid in gold dollars, and so are other countries which remain on the gold standard. The danger of defaults has therefore not been averted, though in the case of Australia, which owes most of its debts to Great Britain, the position has been materially improved by our departure from gold.

In Europe, the great debtor nation is Germany. The Germans owe large sums in interest on the capital which they have borrowed for economic reconstruction since the war; and the greater part of this debt is owing to American creditors in gold dollars. The falling price-level has therefore added greatly to the dead weight of Germany's annual interest obligations.

But Germany is under obligation to pay not only interest on her commercial borrowings, but also large sums in Reparations and other Government debts. Under the Young Plan, the sums due for Reparations are fixed in gold, without any allowance for changes in the price-level. Accordingly, as prices have fallen, the real burden on Germany has proportionately increased, until it has become at the present time altogether impossible for her to meet the charges involved. As we saw, she has made of late years a tremendous effort to build up an export surplus, both by increasing the volume of her exports and by decreasing imports. By these means she succeeded in turning a large adverse trade balance in 1928 into a substantial favourable balance in 1930, at the expense of a very low standard of life for her own people. But, even so, the balance available is wholly inadequate to enable her to meet her international debts and to pay Reparations on anything like the scale laid down in the Young Plan. The moratorium declared in 1931 on the initiative of the Americans was the only possible alternative to a German default, followed by the collapse of the entire Young Plan and probably by most serious political complications as well.

By means of various moratoria, a temporary respite has been barely secured. But no sensible person supposes that Germany will be in a position to resume payment in 1932. Indeed, despite the Hoover moratorium, it has been touch and go with German finance all through the summer of 1931. The precarious condition of Germany has throughout added greatly to the difficulties of London; for it has been out of the question for London financiers to attempt to withdraw from Berlin the large loans which they have made. If they did attempt to do so, Germany would at once collapse, and her creditors would lose their money. London therefore has been called upon to meet the claims of American creditors at a time when she has been unable to draw in the sums due to her from her German debtors. This is partly the fault of the London financiers for locking up in loans which cannot be quickly recalled money borrowed on short term from America and France. But unless someone had lent Germany the money there would have been a complete German collapse long ere now.

The immediately critical time ahead is early in 1932, when the existing temporary loans to Germany through the Bank for International Settlements are due to expire. But it is abundantly evident that no mere moratorium can be of avail in dealing with the situation. It is futile merely to extend another short-term credit to Germany, or merely to extend for a further short period the moratorium on War Debt payments and Reparations. For it is plain to any rational person that Germany and other debtor countries are burdened with international obligations which they can never possibly meet, and that as long as these inflated claims are maintained in being they are bound to plunge the world into recurrent financial crises, unless indeed a point is swiftly reached at which crisis passes into revolution, and the entire structure of world finance, and perhaps Capitalism itself, goes up in smoke.

The only sound basis for world trade is mutual exchange of goods and services. This need not exclude capital loans from the more developed to the less developed countries, provided that these loans are kept within reasonable limits, that the proceeds are put to good productive use, and that the door is kept always open for revision of interest claims in the event of a serious change in the level of prices. But when interest claims are fixed in gold money in face of falling prices, when borrowing is allowed to pass the limits of sound productive expansion in the debtor country, when the proceeds of international loans are applied to non-productive uses, and, above all, when huge non-commercial claims to interest on War Debts or to Reparations payments are added to the burdens of ordinary borrowing, the entire equilibrium of the world financial system is bound to be upset, and a condition of economic crisis is bound to ensue.

The situation will be worst of all if to these other madnesses is added the raising of tariff walls to a height which seriously obstructs the buying and selling of goods across national frontiers, especially when such tariff walls are erected by creditor countries, which thus refuse to allow their debtors to pay in goods, attract to themselves an undue share of the world's gold, and cause the maintenance of equilibrium to depend on their will to make continuously huge investments of capital abroad, on a scale which can only add to the magnitude of the problem, by increasing constantly the payments due from the debtor nations.

Surely we have gone on long enough with this farce of War Debts and Reparations. What is needed here and now is a complete cancellation of all such claims. Great Britain would neither lose nor gain much directly if this were done; for she is on balance, in these respects, neither a large creditor nor a debtor.

The United States would give up a great deal—on paper; for she is a huge creditor. But what is the use of being a creditor if the condition of continuing to be one is that you go on lending the debtor the money to pay you with? Even the United States would lose nothing in reality by complete cancellation. Germany would obviously gain; for she is the worst sufferer by the present situation. But does even France really wish to keep the whole world in permanent and disastrous crisis in order to get her own back on the Germans? And, if she does, will a suffering world allow her?

France, indeed, stands to lose, for the simple reason that she has been receiving payments from Germany, while she has successfully evaded the payment of most of her debts to others. France, like Belgium, had doubtless special claims immediately after the war for the restoration of her devastated areas; and if she can substantiate even now reasonably small claims to special consideration, they can be considered by way of exception—a payment towards her high cost of war pensions, for example. But, if any such exception is to be made in France's favour, it must be only in return for a really large measure of disarmament. France cannot be allowed to wreck a world settlement by standing out for her pound of flesh, or to plead poverty as a reason for exceptional treatment while she continues to spend heavily on arming for the next war. But perhaps before long even the French will realise that it is not to their interest to pull the whole world economic system down in ruins for the sake of accumulating more and more useless gold in the cellars of the Banque de France.

Complete cancellation of War Debts and Reparations is the first obvious step towards the recovery of world equilibrium. But with this must go either monetary measures which will ensure a very considerable and lasting rise in the level of world wholesale prices, or a drastic scaling-down of all debts, international as well as internal, that are fixed in terms of gold. We have done this for our own debtors by going off the gold standard, and for as long as we remain off it, or at any rate allow the gold value of sterling to be greatly below the old parity. But corresponding concessions will have to be made by countries which remain on the gold standard to their debtors if a great sequence of national defaults is to be avoided.

For these and other purposes there ought to be, in the near future, a World Economic and Financial Conference, fully representative of the Governments of the nations involved—debtors as well as creditors. This Conference ought to have terms of reference wide enough to allow it to consider all the causes of the financial and economic crisis, and to accept remedies of the most far-reaching character and extent. It ought to deal at least with the following matters:—

(1) Complete cancellation of War Debts and Reparations.

(2) Scaling down of the interest obligations of debtor countries.

(3) The permanent raising and stabilisation of the world-level of wholesale prices.

(4) The reduction of tariffs.

(5) The regulation of the volume and direction of overseas lending.

These five points are not put forward as at all a complete summary of what the Conference would have to do, but merely in order to focus attention upon the immediate and outstanding issues.

This Conference certainly ought to be a real World Conference, representing all nations. But, if any nation refuses to attend, the Conference will have to be held without it; and it would be better to have a nation or two absent than to allow the agenda to be emasculated in order to secure their presence. For it is evident by now that only fundamental remedies are of any use in dealing with a world in imminent danger of total economic collapse. For years past we have been patching up an impossible situation. Now at last the time has come to end it once and for all.

Great Britain's part in the proposed Conference is clear enough. Her abandonment of the gold standard has given her back the initiative in the world's financial affairs; for she is no longer harried and helpless with the fear of losing her gold, and all the world is watching attentively to find out what her new policy will be. Moreover, as she stands neither to lose nor to gain much directly by cancellation of War Debts and Reparations, she is admirably placed for putting forward sane and far-reaching proposals. Given a strong and imaginative Government, concerned above all to get the economic life of the nations once more on a firm basis, Great Britain today could lead the world. Instead, she is hovering between her desire to get back to pre-war parity and her fears of losing her position as a creditor country, and letting her great opportunity go by. It will not long remain hers. For within a few months either some other country will have wrested the initiative from her, or the world financial system will have dissolved into chaos and, maybe, revolution. The time to act is now; and the action needed is plain enough for even politicians to see it.

### V.—What should we Do?

What should British policy be, both at such a Conference and in our other national and international measures to deal with the present crisis? We have seen that it would be disastrous for Great Britain to attempt, now or later, to bring the pound back to its old gold value; for this would involve a drastic downward revision of British incomes, an intolerable retrenchment in the social services, and an industrial struggle in which the British economic system would be inevitably torn to pieces. Such a policy would be sheer madness, even from the standpoint of the financiers themselves; and we cannot believe that it will be seriously pursued.

There remains, as we saw, the possibility of stabilising the pound at a new and lower gold value, perhaps a quarter, perhaps a third, lower than the pre-war value. Is this to be our policy? The answer, we think, depends on what is done in the rest of the world.

As long as the level of world prices continues to fluctuate, it is not possible for us to have both a stable internal price-level and a fixed relative value of our currency to the currencies of other nations. The gold standard fixes the relative value of our currency; but it does this at the cost of compelling us to let our internal price-level fluctuate with movements in world prices.

For, if we returned to the gold standard and at the same time attempted to stabilise internal prices, our internal price-level might be at any time either higher or lower than the world-level. If it were higher, we should lose our export trade, and be subject to an outflow of gold, as we have been in recent years. If it were lower, we should attract to ourselves a large stock of useless gold, and throw the world economic system out of gear. We could, moreover, only keep our price-level below that of other countries at the expense of our standard of living; and if such a situation arose and we had a large stock of gold, the pressure for an increased issue of currency and credit, which would raise prices, would speedily become irresistible.

Under the gold standard, then, stable foreign exchanges are secured at the cost of unstable prices at home. But, in view of the very large number of persons whose incomes are either fixed, or difficult to adjust to changes in the price-level, there is a very strong demand nowadays for stability of prices at home. If the great mass of people were asked whether they preferred stable foreign exchanges or a stable price-level at home, they would undoubtedly choose the latter.

We can get a fairly stable level of home prices if we choose, by so 'managing' our currency and credit as to keep their volume at a fairly constant ratio to the volume of things needing to be bought and sold. This is a clear and intelligible policy, which has many powerful advocates. But we can do this under present conditions only if we remain off the gold standard, and allow the value of our currency in terms of other currencies to fluctuate with changes in the level of world prices.

The reason for reluctance to do this is that it is most desirable to promote world economic co-operation and exchange, and to thwart the powerful influences at present making all over the world for economic nationalism and hostility between nations. Unstable exchanges mean unstable trading relationships; and a currency so managed as to stabilise internal prices removes the possibility of working towards a single world currency, valid equally in every country. It is therefore a serious matter to throw over an international standard permanently, in favour of the policy of stabilising internal prices.

But the fixing of the relative values of different currencies involves the instability of internal prices only because world prices are allowed to fluctuate. If the world as a whole would agree upon a common effort to stabilise the world price-level, and could do this successfully, we could have both stable exchange rates and stable internal prices without any inconsistency at all.

Could this be secured under the gold standard? It could, and it could not. It could not, under the gold standard as it has been worked hitherto; but it would be possible to work out a modified gold standard compatible with price stability.

Under the gold standard as it has been worked hitherto, the level of world prices has fluctuated broadly with changes in the supply of gold. When the gold supply has been increasing more slowly than the supply of goods and services, prices have gone down; whereas successive gold discoveries, in California, Australia and South Africa, have been followed by large rises in the world price-level. At present, the world's stock of gold bullion is certainly growing much less fast than the world's power to produce goods; and in addition a large part of the stock is laid up unproductively in America and France. This is one most potent cause of the fall of world prices in recent years. Moreover, there is every reason to believe that the production of new gold in the world is likely to fall off heavily in the future, as many of the South African mines become exhausted. Unless the world changes its monetary policy, this means that the world tendency for prices to fall is likely to be intensified, especially as the drift of gold to the creditor countries will also continue unchecked unless drastic measures are taken to correct it.

In these circumstances, it is natural to suggest that the whole world ought to go off the gold standard, and take to a 'managed' monetary system instead. Many such systems have been proposed; but the essence of them all is that the world should agree to make its issues of currency and credit depend, not on the supply of gold available as a basis, but on the needs of the world productive system. This would be no doubt a difficult matter to arrange from the technical standpoint; but there is no reason at all to deem it beyond the wit of man, if the nations are really prepared to co-operate in working out a common financial system, and to set up a really strong International Bank, based perhaps on the Bank of International Settlements, to act as a world clearing-house for their monetary dealings.

Nor is such a system really incompatible with the retention, in part, of the gold standard. For there is nothing at all sacrosanct, or even logical, about the magnitude of the reserves which bankers at present think it vital, or are even compelled by law, to keep against their issues of currency and credit. There is no reason why the ratio should not be half as much, or twice as much, or anything else—provided that the change is made by concerted action among the gold standard countries. If, in recent years, the world's gold had been better distributed, and if the world's banks had agreed to issue more currency and credit on the basis of a given amount of gold, the tendency for the level of world prices to fall could have been prevented. And world prices could, and should, be raised now, by the adoption of precisely these measures.

This amounts, indeed, to a 'managed' currency system—the management consisting in the variation from time to time of the amount of gold kept as a reserve against issues of currency and credit. It would enable currency and credit to be issued in accordance with the expansion of world productive power, and so as to keep world prices stable. And balances owing from one financial centre to another could continue, as now, to be settled in gold, if the world thought fit, or by the device known as 'earmarking' of a single centralised gold reserve kept under the custody of the League of Nations or the World Bank. By and by, perhaps, the world would wake up to the realisation that even this central reserve of gold was not necessary, and pass over to a completely 'managed' world currency. But gold has been a fetish so long that the easiest course may well be to pass away from the gold standard by stages, and even to keep the shadow of it when the substance is gone.

It is thus desirable for us at present to continue to work for an international standard of currency, based on a world policy of price stabilisation. But, if the world as a whole will not adopt the necessary measures for the successful working of such a standard, or if no adequate steps are taken to write off impossible international obligations and to put world trade once more on a reasonable basis of mutual exchange, there will be nothing for it but for Great Britain to resort to the alternative policy of stabilising her internal price-level, at the cost of allowing the exchange value of her currency to fluctuate in accordance with changes in world prices. In other words, Great Britain will have to remain off the gold standard at least as long as the working of that standard in the world as a whole continues to force world prices downwards, and to cause a persistent flow of the world's gold towards France and the United States. This is a second-best policy; but the advantages of internal stability of prices are considerable, and far to be preferred to stable exchange rates secured at the cost of persistently falling internal prices.

There is another factor that has to be taken into consideration. Not once but many times have the United States shown a tendency to upset the equilibrium of the world economic system by huge speculative booms which have been followed by disastrous panics. Now, the effect of a speculative boom in America is to send gold flying there in quest of the excessive profits that are being made, and to set up a condition of restricted currency and credit over the rest of the world. And when speculation ends in panic, there ensues in America a business slump which drives down prices and spreads trade depression over the whole world, as it has done in the past two years.

Great Britain, because of London's importance as a world financial centre, is peculiarly exposed to the effects of America's outbursts of speculation; for it is above all London that has its gold and its resources drained away to take part in the Wall Street orgy. It must be a condition of any successful attempt to stabilise world wholesale prices and monetary conditions that the United States shall set their banking system in order, and find means of curbing speculative excesses which bring disaster on the rest of the world as well as on themselves.

Unless means can be found and adopted to stabilise world prices and monetary conditions, and to keep American speculation in check, it seems clear that Great Britain will be best advised to be in no hurry to go back to the gold standard. Nor does it follow, even if we refuse to go back to it, that we need act alone. The currencies of a number of other countries, both within the British Empire and outside it, are already pegged to sterling, and fluctuate in terms of sterling rather than of gold. Failing world agreement to establish a better international method of managing monetary problems, Great Britain will be well advised to rally round her those countries with which she has the closest trading and financial relations, and endeavour to make herself the centre of a new system which will challenge the predominance of gold as a basis for currency and credit, and provide at least the nucleus of a new world order in finance. If she does this, the countries which stand out of such a system will be threatened with the disappearance of a large part of their export trade; and gold and gold-hoarding will be robbed of their power to upset the balance of the world's economic affairs.

It is not suggested that the policy here outlined will be simple to carry into effect, or that the world is yet fully prepared for its adoption. But we believe that during the next few months events will move very swiftly indeed, and exert a powerful influence on public opinion in all countries, and not least in those which adhere to the gold standard and are likely to be the chief sufferers by the developments of 1931. The population of the world is learning economics by experience at a great rate; and within a few months at the most the countries which are now unready to consider any drastic reforms are likely to change their tune. The question is whether this process of conversion will be swift enough to anticipate the logic of events; for, unless it is swift indeed, the collapse of the credit system may render the steps here proposed obsolete, and necessitate the putting forward of still more drastic projects for the restoration of the world to financial sanity and economic progress. But for the moment the right course is to make a last appeal to the world's common sense—an appeal for immediate and drastic action in relation, not merely to gold and currency, but to the whole absurd tangle in which the world's economic system has become involved. In this appeal Great Britain ought to take the lead; and, if all the world will not respond, she ought to act promptly and courageously in partnership with those who will, leaving the recalcitrant countries to bear the consequences of their folly, until they are reduced by events to a more amenable frame of mind.

### VI.—Bankers and Peoples

But can we trust our bankers and financiers to carry into effect such a policy as the foregoing sections have outlined? Emphatically we cannot; for our bankers are primarily responsible for the troubles into which we have fallen. It was on their advice that we went back to the gold standard in 1925, on a basis of pre-war parity which heavily over-valued the pound, and thus put a severe strain on our exchanges and disastrously hampered our export trade. It was their action in locking up in long-term loans sums borrowed from abroad which we were liable to repay at short notice that contributed largely to landing us in the financial crisis of 1931. They have been convinced deflationists almost to a man; and, though they have for the time acquiesced perforce in the suspension of the gold standard, they are deflationists still—witness the high bank rate imposed on the morrow of the suspension, when the danger of a further loss of gold had been removed. They are hankering still, not merely after the gold standard, but after a return to it at pre-war parity, and after the drastic cuts in wages and social services which such a return would involve. They have let us down again and again since the war; and now they are eagerly waiting their chance to let us down once more.

It is out of the question to leave the banks free to dictate to Governments in the future as they have dictated hitherto. If we are to pursue a courageous policy of leading the world back to financial sanity, or even to safeguard the interests of our own industries and our standard of living, we must convert the banks from the agents of a narrow financial group into responsible instruments of public policy. This involves socialisation, in some form, not only of the Bank of England, but also of the

Joint Stock Banks which, with it, occupy the key positions of the financial system. We must socialise the Bank of England in order to pursue an expansionist monetary policy on the basis of a managed currency, and in order to be free to negotiate with other countries under conditions which will enable our Government to implement, through its control of the Central Bank, whatever policy may be agreed upon with other nations. Nor can we, if that proves to be the best course to pursue, possibly stabilise our own price-level without full control of the operations of our Central Bank.

So far there will be a wide measure of agreement. But many people who favour socialisation of the Bank of England still boggle at the socialisation of the Joint Stock Banks. This is, nevertheless, equally indispensable. Broadly, in our present financial system, while the Bank of England chiefly controls the total volume of currency and credit available, the Joint Stock Banks control its distribution among the various classes of potential borrowers. The Bank of England can, in the main, limit their total lendings; but it has far less power to cause expansion than contraction, and very little power indeed of regulating the flow of credit in this or that direction.

This power is, however, indispensable for the effective control of prices as well as for a co-ordinated policy of national economic planning and development. Largely for want of it the policy of price stabilisation pursued by the Federal Reserve System in the United States broke down; for no means were devised of preventing the flow of the available credits, through the member banks, into stock speculation, instead of the financing of increased production and employment. Moreover, if the Bank of England, under public control, were pursuing one policy, while the directors of the Joint Stock Banks believed in another, we should have a situation of pull devil, pull baker, in which each would be able to thwart the other, and the result would be a deadlock worse for industry than almost any positive policy.

It is, moreover, very necessary, if we are to inaugurate a new financial policy, to have effective control over the doings of the numerous private financial institutions of the City of London—

discount houses, acceptance houses, issue houses, investment agencies, and, last but not least, the stock and produce exchanges. Now, many of these—and especially the discount houses and the Stock Exchange—are at present related closely to the Joint Stock Banks, from which they draw the loan money with which they carry on their operations. We are not suggesting that we ought to socialise these private institutions—that would be at this stage far too complex a business. What we suggest is that the requisite control over them can be ensured if, and only if, the State has in its hands both the Bank of England and the great Joint Stock Banks.

Socialisation, of course, does not mean nationalisation in the old-fashioned sense of taking the banks over, and running them on Civil Service lines under a responsible minister and a Government department. Almost no one, we take it, wants that. Socialisation means rather the reconstitution of the Bank of England and of each of the Joint Stock Banks as a publicly owned corporation, with directing bodies appointed and removable by the Government, and subject in matters of high policy to Government control, but free from day-to-day political interference in their ordinary business. The precise implications of this form of socialisation need working out; but we are already in process of working them out in the case of such institutions as the Central Electricity Board and the B.B.C.—both public bodies whose employees are not Civil Servants and which are not tied down to Civil Service methods or subject to detailed Treasury control or interference by Parliament. There are already the models to be followed in the impending socialisation of the banking system.

The aims of a socialised banking service should be threefold. The first should be to secure a management of the issue of currency and credit that will promote industrial expansion and increase employment, without allowing inflation to occur—for emphatically an increase of currency and credit accompanied by a corresponding increase in production is not inflation, but only legitimate and necessary expansion. The second object should be to use the credits thus made available so as to secure the maximum increase in production and employment, and to

## II. THE CRISIS 55

check speculative activities, by their right distribution among the various industries and services asking for loans. And the third object should be to regulate overseas investment of capital, and to direct home investment into the right channels, both by controlling the operations of private concerns in the capital market, and by setting up new public institutions—and especially a National Investment Board—and so to avoid the colossal waste which has been characteristic of the new capital issues of recent years. The Macmillan Committee on Industry and Finance has recently pointed out that investors in the last investment boom in Great Britain lost practically half the sums they invested within less than two years. This is insane waste of capital, which is badly needed for the reorganisation of our basic industries and the employment of our workers.

Any full discussion of these three objects would, however, go far beyond the scope of this booklet, which is concerned only with the causes of the present crisis and a general indication of the appropriate remedies. We have put forward two things as the indispensable conditions of averting a complete world collapse in the very near future. These two things are, first, a drastic revision of all international claims, including a complete cancellation of War Debts and Reparations, and a determined attempt to stabilise prices at a satisfactory level by world action, and to ensure for the future an adequate supply and a right distribution of currency and credit to meet the world's needs.

These objects, we have further suggested, cannot possibly be secured without the thorough socialisation of the banking system; for if States are to agree on a new financial policy they must have in their own hands the means of carrying that policy into effect. We would add that the country must have as well a strong Government, thoroughly aware of what it is attempting to do, and prepared to stand up courageously to the opposition of financial and *rentier* interests, and to put up with no nonsense from obstructionists either at home or abroad. What is wrong with the present Government is not that it has demanded emergency powers, but that it is putting these powers to the wrong use.

## VII.—The Alternatives Before Us

For what does the policy of the present Government amount to? It came into office with the declared intention of maintaining the gold standard at the old parity. It knew that this policy involved not only drastic retrenchments on the social services and a total stoppage of all large schemes of national economic development, but also the cutting down of insurance benefits to the unemployed, and the handing over of a million or more of them to the mercies of the Poor Law authorities, and also a great capitalist offensive to bring down wages in every trade, until British costs had been reduced to the level dictated by the starvation wages of foreign workers. This was the policy to which the members of the present Government stood committed when they assumed office; and the object of it all was to preserve the gold standard intact. Yet they have persisted in carrying it out, although the conditions have been entirely changed by the suspension of the gold standard.

To what do they stand committed now? They are still busy cutting down the salaries of teachers and civil servants, combing out the unemployed, and cancelling plans for housing, road-making, and every other form of national development. But the gold standard, which these violent measures were designed to defend, has gone already; and with it has disappeared any case there ever was for the policy which they are still attempting blindly to follow. The unemployed are still to be condemned to a winter of cold and hunger; the teachers, the police, the soldiers and sailors, are still to have their wages reduced; progress in housing, in education, in the health services, and in every form of social and economic development is still to be put back. And all—for what?

In order to balance the Budget, and to restore confidence in Great Britain's financial position, we are being told. But have the countries whose confidence we are courting balanced their own Budgets? America has a far bigger Budget deficit than we are faced with. The way to get both balanced Budgets and world confidence is by stimulating trade, and not by a panic cancellation of productive expenditure that is certain to make unemployment and depression worse. And the world is most unlikely to have confidence in us if we run round and round like terrified sheep, bleating at bogies of our own imagining. Moreover, we could have balanced our Budget without these false 'economies'. We could have suspended the Sinking Fund, paid for the maintenance of the unemployed by an emergency levy on all classes of incomes, and readjusted taxation so as to put a larger burden on the *rentiers*, who have profited by the fall in prices.

There is no case, in a world teeming with productive power, for cutting down the standard of life. There is, on the contrary, a strong case for advancing it as fast as our power to produce increases. But the gods of capitalists are scarcity of goods and cheapness of labour. They want wage reductions, not in order to preserve the gold standard, but because they believe in cheap labour as the means to higher profits. They want to take away the incomes of the unemployed, because they believe that is the surest way of forcing wages down. Never has there been a clearer class issue than there is today in Great Britain, never a clearer call to the workers to rally to the defence of their standard of life.

But, if they are to defend that standard with success, it is not enough to take up a merely negative attitude—to object to, and fight against, the cuts which the 'National' Government has already imposed, and intends still further to impose if it remains in office. For a falling standard of life is inevitable unless drastic measures are taken here and now both for the complete reorganisation of the financial system and for a rapid advance towards Socialism over the whole field of economic policy. This booklet has been confined to the question of financial policy, both because that is the immediate matter raised by the political crisis, and because the reorganisation of the banks is a necessary condition of any effective measures for putting industry on its feet.

But banking reform is not enough. It is only an indispensable first step towards the reorganisation of industry on Socialist lines. We are by no means to be numbered among those who believe that a few adjustments of the financial machine, or even the most far-reaching changes in financial policy, will rid us of all our troubles; for the causes of the present world depression lie deep down in the capitalist system itself—in its determination to create artificial scarcity in place of the plenty that ought to exist. We need, as the alternative to the present Government, with its demand for a free hand to do it knows not what, nor with what object, a Government of determined Socialists who, having made the cleaning up of the financial mess their first task, will then advance promptly to constructive Socialist measures in the industrial field.

The only possible source of such a Government is the working-class movement. Labour has decisively rejected the policy of wage-cutting, unemployed-baiting, and putting back economic and social progress that is advocated by the self-styled 'National' Government and the financial interests behind it. But it cannot successfully defeat that policy unless it is prepared to advance at once to the determined enforcement of a constructive Socialist policy of its own. The first step towards that policy is the thorough reorganisation of the financial system on a basis of full public control. The next is the rebuilding of the essential industries as great public corporations working directly for the service of the people.

But our advance towards these objects must be international as well as national; for the cause of the workers is one everywhere, and no country can hope to prosper in a world diseased. The causes of the present world depression lie deep down in the capitalist system, of which the banks and the financial agencies of the world are the central machine. An indispensable step towards world Socialism is the social control of world finance.

It may indeed be too late, even now, for the measures outlined in this booklet to save the world from an economic collapse beside which the troubles we have been through will seem as nothing. For everywhere the very survival of the structure of world credit is precarious. Not only in Germany, but even in the United States, for all their wealth, the banking system is in imminent danger of insolvency and ruin. No one knows what the next few months, or even weeks or days, will bring forth. But the measures outlined in this booklet are at least a workmanlike attempt to promote an orderly transition from Capitalism to Socialism instead of a plunge into chaos. The programme we have set forth is a *minimum* programme; and every day that action upon it is delayed creates a need for yet more drastic measures. For it is certain that any policy will be built upon sand unless it begins a thoroughgoing reorganisation of world finance, based on a far-reaching socialisation of the banking system.

# APPENDIX

## Some Facts and Figures

We have kept figures out of the text of our booklet in order to make it more readable. But it seems desirable to add, in an appendix, certain of the more important figures on which our arguments and conclusions are based.

### I.—The National Debt

On the average of recent years, the service of the National Debt has been costing Great Britain over £360,000,000 a year. We have spent, on the average, well over £50,000,000 a year in repaying the debt; and yet our total indebtedness has only fallen from £7,829,000,000 in 1920 to £7,413,000,000 in 1931. In interest alone, we have been paying at a rate of over £300,000,000 a year; and even in this year of low interest rates the estimated interest charge alone amounts to £289,500,000.

Meanwhile, there has been a huge fall in the price-level between 1920 and 1931.

Measured in terms of the change in retail prices since 1920, every £100 paid in interest on the debt has gone up in the past ten years by over two-thirds in purchasing power, and in terms of wholesale prices has much more than doubled. The real income paid to the *rentier* class as interest on the debt is at least two-thirds greater in 1931 than in 1920.

We are spending at present more than three times as much on the service of the National Debt as on benefits to the unemployed.

### II.—The World's Gold

At the end of 1930, before the last phase of the world crisis had begun, France and the United States between them already held 57 per cent of the total gold supply of the world, whereas in 1920 they held only 43½ per cent. Thus, the world's gold is silting up uselessly in France and the United States. Great Britain has less than one-fifth as much gold as the U.S.A., and less than one-third as much as France. Here are the actual holdings in 1920, and at the end of 1930 ($ millions):

|  | 1920. | *Percentage of Total.* | 1930. | *Percentage of Total.* |
|---|---|---|---|---|
| U.K. | 763 | 10·5 | 718 | 6·6 |
| U.S.A. | 2,451 | 34·6 | 4,225 | 38·8 |
| France | 686 | 9·4 | 2,100 | 19·0 |
| World Total | 7,206 | — | 10,872 | — |

Great Britain is the next largest holder of gold after France and the U.S.A., and her losses of gold are nothing beside those of the debtor countries, which are having their entire gold supply steadily drained away. Thus, Australia's gold stock dwindled from £49,000,000 to £18,000,000 between 1928 and 1930; and the gold reserves of such countries as Brazil and Chile were almost wiped out. Between the beginning of 1929 and the end of 1930, the share of creditor countries in the total stock of gold rose from two-thirds to three-quarters, and that of the debtor countries fell from one-third to one-quarter. At the rate at which gold has recently been flowing out of the debtor countries, it would only take a few years to deprive them of all their gold. (See the *Report of the Macmillan Committee on Finance and Industry*, p. 134.)

### III.—CREDITORS AND DEBTORS

Great Britain is a creditor country. As we have seen in the text, she imports more goods than she exports; but in normal times she is able not only to pay for the excess by means of her 'invisible exports'—interest on overseas investments, receipts from shipping and financial sources, etc.—but also to have a large surplus available for fresh investment overseas. This surplus British investors do actually invest—indeed, the tendency is for them to invest overseas more than the surplus available rather than less. We set out below the Board of Trade estimates for recent years of the British balance of payments, together with the figures for new capital issues made in the London market. These last do not fully correspond to the volume of new investment overseas, but they suffice to give a general indication.

GREAT BRITAIN'S BALANCE OF PAYMENTS
(£ million)

|  | 1924. | 1928. | 1930. |
|---|---|---|---|
| Excess of imports of Merchandise and Bullion | 324 | 358 | 392 |
| Government receipts from Overseas (net) | −25 | 15 | 21 |
| Net National shipping income | 140 | 130 | 105 |
| Net income from Overseas Investment | 220 | 270 | 235 |
| Net receipt from Short-term Interests and Commissions | 60 | 65 | 55 |
| Net receipts from other sources | 15 | 15 | 15 |
| Total | 410 | 495 | 431 |
| Estimated total credit balance on above | 86 | 137 | 39 |

OVERSEAS CAPITAL ISSUES (1924–1931)
(£ million)

|  | 1924. | 1928. | 1930. | 1931 (to June 30). |
|---|---|---|---|---|
| British Empire | 73 | 86 | 70 | — |
| Foreign | 61 | 57 | 39 | — |
| Total | 134 | 143 | 109 | 43 |

It will be seen that the balance available for investment overseas shrank greatly in 1930; and it is estimated that it has disappeared altogether this year, and been turned into a debit balance. Nevertheless, considerable new overseas capital issues have been made in London not only in 1930, but also in 1931; and this is one source of the exceptional strain on British credit.

The United States are also a great creditor country. Unlike Great Britain, they export more goods than they import; and they have also large masses of capital invested abroad, and claims on Europe for interest on War Debts.

Here is an estimate, from the Report of the Macmillan Committee, of the U.S.A. balance of payments up to 1929:

|  | 1924. | 1928. | 1929. |
|---|---|---|---|
| Excess of Exports | 882 | 850 | 734 |
| Excess of Invisible Imports | 80 | 200 | 250 |
| Net Surplus available for Investment | 802 | 650 | 484 |
| Net Long-term Lending Overseas | 733 | 708 | 386 |
| Net Short-term Lending Overseas | −216 | 226 | −13 |
| Net Investment Abroad | 517 | 934 | 373 |
| Net Import or Export of Bullion— | | | |
| Import | 236 | — | 120 |
| Export | — | 272 | — |

It will be seen that America has each year a huge surplus available for overseas investments. Unless she invests the whole of this surplus, or lends it on short-term overseas, gold is bound to flow to the U.S.A. from other countries. But if she does lend it the effect is to increase the amount payable in interest in future years, and thus to swell still further the American balance. This process can only end in default by the debtor countries, unless steps are taken to cancel international debts which have become an impossible burden in face of the fall in prices.

France is also a creditor country, though, like Great Britain, she imports more goods than she exports. She receives a considerable sum in interest on her foreign investments, and also gets large receipts from the tourist traffic. Here is a rough estimate of the French balance of payments for 1930:

### FRANCE'S BALANCE OF PAYMENTS IN 1930
(Millions of francs)

| | | | |
|---|---|---|---|
| Excess of Imports | 12,973 | Increase from Shipping | 2,700 |
| Debt Service (including repayments) | 5,398 | Tourist Receipts | 8,500 |
| Other Loan Payments | 919 | Interest on Foreign Investments, Insurances, etc. | 5,500 |
| Sums repatriated by Immigrants | 2,500 | Reparations and Young Loan | 7,034 |
| | 21,790 | | 23,734 |
| Foreign Capital Issues | 1,400 | Sales of Foreign Exchange | 4,140 |
| Imports of Bullion | 11,530 | Sales of Short-term Foreign Bills, etc. | 6,800 |
| | 34,720 | | 34,674 |

It will be seen that France had a balance on the right side, and that she actually received in gold and precious metals more than the amount of this balance. This was partly because the French did not lend abroad nearly as much as their current surplus, and partly because they actually called in during 1930 a considerable part of the sums which they had lent abroad on short-term in previous years. These are the reasons why gold has been silting up even faster in France than in the United States.

Germany is a great debtor country. It has been officially estimated that she owed abroad in July 1931 about 14·5 milliards of Reichsmarks net (over £700,000,000 at gold parity). By far the largest amount was owing to the United States, with Great Britain next, and France a long way behind. Here are the estimated figures (million Rm.):

|  | Long Term. | Percentage. | Short Term. | Percentage. |
| --- | --- | --- | --- | --- |
| German Debt to U.S.A. | 5,626 | 55·2 | 1,629[1] | 37·1 |
| German Debt to Great Britain | 1,100 | 11·5 | 1,051[1] | 23·9 |
| German Debt to Holland | 1,174 | 12·3 | 336[1] | 7·6 |
| German Debt to France | 475 | 5·0 | 297[1] | 6·8 |

But in addition to these debts Germany is being called upon to meet heavy payments for Reparations. These amounted to over £88,000,000 in 1931, or would have done so if there had been no moratorium.

Clearly, the only means of payment available to Germany is an excess of exports over imports; for she has but little gold (and had lost a good deal even of that little in recent months until she prevented its export). But Germany has to import both raw materials and foodstuffs in considerable quantities. It is hard for her to build up an export surplus at all, and utterly impossible for her, especially in face of falling prices and the world slump, to pay anything like the sums demanded of her. Here is an estimate of the actual German balance of payments in recent years:

---

[1] These figures refer to a specimen enquiry covering only 85 per cent of the total short-term investment.

## GERMANY'S BALANCE OF TRADE
(Milliards of Reichsmarks)

|  | 1924. | 1928. | 1930. |
|---|---|---|---|
| Excess of Imports over Exports | 1·8 | 1·3 | — |
| Excess of Exports over Imports | — | — | 1·5 |
| Gold and Foreign Exchange— | | | |
|   Imports | 1·3 | 0·9 | — |
|   Exports | — | — | 0·1 |
| Reparation Payments | 0·3 | 2·0 | 1·7 |
| Revenue from Shipping and Services | 0·3 | 0·5 | 0·2 |
| Interest on Investment | 0·2 | 0·6 | 0·8 |
| Deficit on above | 2·9 | 4·3 | 0·7 |
| Capital Movements— | | | |
|   Long-term invested in Germany | 1·0 | 1·7 | 1·6 |
|   Short-term invested in Germany | 1·5 | 1·4 | — |
|   Other movements | 0·4 | 1·2 | −0·9 |
| Total | 2·9 | 4·3 | 0·7 |

It will be seen that Germany had, by tremendous efforts, built up an export surplus in 1930, but still on nothing like an adequate scale. The attempt to meet her obligations in 1931 confronted her with bankruptcy, and compelled the granting of a moratorium. Clearly, she will be unable to resume payment next year—or ever, until her obligations are drastically scaled down.

## III

## FREE TRADE, TARIFFS, AND THE ALTERNATIVE

GREAT BRITAIN is by instinct and tradition a Free Trade country. It was led to the adoption of Free Trade mainly by its interests as a producer; for the effective drive towards Free Trade came far more from the captains of industry, who wanted to lower costs of production, than from the consuming public. And it remained, until yesterday, faithful to Free Trade by consent of the main body of consumers and producers alike, but with the emphasis passing gradually from the producer to the consumer. In the mid-nineteenth century, the captains of industry fought and won the consumers' battle; in the twentieth, when the industrialists were no longer united, the consumers became the protagonists of the Free Trade doctrine.

This is somewhat remarkable; for through most of history the producers have been instinctive protectionists. Each group of producers has usually an instinct to get protection for its own trade, and, while it has no instinct to extend protection to others, it does tend to look at the entire problem of economic policy from a producer point of view. The producer is usually an instinctive monopolist; for he believes by instinct in the virtue of selling in the dearest market, and feels that the dearest market will be that in which there is least competition. The consumer, on the other hand, wants to buy in the cheapest market, and is usually well aware that cheapness is likely to depend on a wide area of supply.

How, then, did it come about that, in nineteenth-century England, the most influential representatives of the producers were not protectionists, but stalwart free traders? It happened because every producer is a consumer as well, and will, under certain conditions, be more concerned with buying cheap than with selling dear. This was the position of the Lancashire cotton lords in Cobden's day. They became the allies and protagonists of the consuming interest because, as producers, they had nothing to fear from foreign competition, provided only that they could buy their raw materials, and their employees' provisions, reasonably cheap. The advantage over the foreigner, in terms of industrial efficiency, was unquestionably theirs. They could be held back from conquering in world markets only if raw materials and foodstuffs were made artificially dear.

The almost universal endorsement of Free Trade in Victorian England, except by the dwindling agricultural interest, was thus a consequence of the superior efficiency of British industrial enterprise. Temporarily and for quite special reasons the producers abandoned their instinctive protectionism, and rallied the consumers on behalf of Free Trade. But it was always certain that, if at any time British industry should lose its superiority in productive efficiency, the instinctive protectionism of the producer would be speedily and strongly reasserted. The agricultural interest, which never enjoyed the same advantage over all competitors in productive efficiency, remained throughout protectionist in outlook, though its voice was almost silenced amid the clanking of the machines. The captains of industry remained free traders just as long as they felt no fear of foreign competitors; but as soon as that fear did overtake the producers in any trade, the demand for protection promptly reappeared, gaining ground with the progressive industrialisation of other countries, and the gradual narrowing of the margin between their productive efficiency and our own.

But, though the triumph of Free Trade was secured far more by the captains of industry than by their consumer followers in the Anti-Corn Law League and the Liberal Party, when Free Trade had been once established the consumer interest rallied to its defence. The extension of the franchise was one factor in increasing the political influence of the consumer; and another was the growth of a large middle class depending rather on fixed incomes or professional charges than on the variable profits of industry. The old *rentiers*—the landlords—had been strongly protectionist; for they wanted to give land the largest possible monopoly value. The new *rentiers*—holders of fixed interest-bearing investments or of other fixed claims to income—were free traders; for they wanted their money to buy the largest possible quantity of goods. So it came about that, even if the majority of industrialists turned again to protection, as a defence against foreign competition, they were certain to find powerful forces arrayed against them, both in the consumer attitude of a wide electorate and in the growing influence of the new *rentier* class.

There can be no doubt that, for a long time past, the British employers have been slowly reverting to a protectionist attitude. But there has been, and is even now, no general agreement among them. For Great Britain depends, more than any of her leading competitors in world trade, on imported foodstuffs and materials; and even her manufactured imports are largely means to further production, such as fuel, or materials for her finishing trades. It needed a special emergency to provoke anything approaching a general demand for protection from British industrialists; and, even so, there remained among them a large body of hesitant or antagonistic opinion. Only as the loss of exports has caused the home market to assume an added importance in the eyes of the producer has he reverted to type, and set up once again the familiar cry for protection against the foreigner.

As the Victorian producer's belief in Free Trade was an assertion of strength, the present business demand for protection is a confession of weakness. It implies a loss of confidence on the part of the industrialist in his power to compete abroad, or to retain the home market without artificial help. It is accompanied, as the demand for protection has always been, by accusations of dumping and unfair commercial practices on the part of the foreign producer, and by complaints that either British wages are too high or foreign wages too low. It is, indeed, certain that the margin of industrial efficiency between British and foreign producers has narrowed of late years, so that differences in wage standards have become more formidable to the British employer. The trouble is far less that wage differences have grown wider than that differences in efficiency have become less. But the effect is the same. It is to drive one body of British employers after another to give up the hope of expanding their foreign sales, and to seek compensation in a protected monopoly of the home market.

But they would stand no chance of getting this, under present political conditions, unless the attitude of the general body of consumers had also changed. In the nineteenth century, it was broadly true that the bulk of the British working class, as well as of the middle class, tended to think politically as consumers rather than as producers. This attitude was a natural outcome of the triumph of *laisser faire*; for as long as it was not regarded as the State's business to regulate industry, the defence of the producers' interests seemed to be a matter for voluntary bodies such as the Trade Union, and the function of politics in relation to economic affairs was confined to the prevention of anti-social monopolies and nuisances, which might adversely affect the general body of consumers. The Trade Unions sought higher wages and improved conditions for their members, and endeavoured to some extent to erect a monopoly of labour; but not until the rise of the New Unionism under Socialist influence in the eighteen-nineties did they seriously attempt to use the State as an instrument for achieving their ends.

The influence of Socialism was, indeed, to shift the emphasis back from the consumer to the producer; for Socialism became politically important by drawing the Trade Unions into politics. But Socialism, as it took political shape in the Labour Party, also inherited much of the old Radical tradition, which was deeply imbued with the consumer attitude of mind. Consequently, the British Labour Party has been always an ideological hybrid, regarding industrial policy primarily from the producer standpoint, but adopting in commercial policy the standpoint of the consumer. It has demanded the regulation of industry; but it has desired to leave trade 'free'.

To state this difference of outlook is not necessarily to condemn it; for under the prevailing conditions a hybrid view may have been right, as a practical compromise with the facts. But the double position is theoretically weak; for whereas the demand for the regulation of industry foreshadows Socialism, Free Trade is essentially an individualist doctrine. It may be right for the State to bring the productive system under an increasing degree of control, but to leave the operations of commerce free and unrestrained; but it is not easy to explain why this should be so, or to bring both policies under the banner of a single philosophy of society. It is, moreover, evident that, if the Socialists were ever to reach their goal of the socialisation of industry, they would, in effect, have socialised commerce as well; for the State, having taken over production, would have to provide for the marketing of its products. Free Trade would be a term without meaning in relation to a completely Socialist community.

As long as the Labour Party was only a Socialistic party, without being definitely Socialist, collectivism and Free Trade were able to dwell side by side in its policy without serious jostling. Labour made its appeal to the producers with its demand for the regulation of industry, while it appeared before the consumers as the upholder of the Free Trade system. But the more the Labour Party became Socialist, the harder it grew to sustain this double rôle; for it became evident that a planned national economy meant a planning of foreign trade—imports and exports—as well as of home production for domestic use. It was at this stage that proposals for Import Boards and other non-tariff methods of regulating overseas trade made their tentative appearance in the Labour programme—tentative, because of the strength of the Free Trade tradition, but inevitable as a logical outcome of the Socialist doctrine.

Meanwhile, Free Trade was losing its hold, not only on British employers, but also on the general body of the electorate. The chief reason for the weakening of Free Trade convictions was the prevalence of unemployment, with its correlative of unused capital resources and loss of profits in the depressed trades. Year after year since the war Great Britain has been faced with a large mass of unemployed labour; and this has entailed heavy public expenditure upon maintenance and relief. No doubt the volume of unemployment has seemed larger since the war because of more complete registration; and until the coming of the world slump it was not really so much more severe as it appeared than pre-war unemployment. But it was a good deal more severe, even after full allowance for this factor; and there has been in fact, ever since the war, a chronic surplus of labour, largely concentrated in the industries most dependent on selling their products abroad.

Naturally, the first reaction to the consciousness of this surplus was a demand for energetic action to revive the export trades, especially as a rise in the standard of living had made Great Britain more dependent than ever on imported supplies. But it was gradually realised how formidable were the obstacles to a recovery of the pre-war volume of exports, much more to an expansion in proportion to the rise in imports. Other countries had become more self-sufficient, and foreign competition more intense, in the staple industries on which British exporters had concentrated mainly in the past. The cotton industry was faced with the growing competition of Japan, India and China, and with the growth of production for the home market in the Southern States of America. The woollen industry met with increasing competition all over Europe. The coal industry had to face the effects of economy in the use of fuel and of the growing rivalry of oil and water-power, as well as the competition of the German and the Polish mines. The iron and steel industry had been stimulated all over the world by war demands, and possessed a productive capacity far ahead of possible consumption. Engineering and the lesser metal trades had undergone a similar expansion. In all these industries the margin of technical efficiency in favour of the British producer had narrowed, and the competition of up-to-date plants operated by cheap labour had become more formidable. But at least as serious as this was the rising level of world tariffs upon manufactured goods, the multiplication of tariff frontiers, and the tendency of countries to make their markets close preserves for the home producers even at a sacrifice of economic gain. All over the world the desire to buy in the cheapest market seemed to have grown weaker, and Economic Nationalism to have gained ground as a result of the war.

Consequently, it was gradually realised in Great Britain that the expansion of the export trades by a recovery of pre-war markets was not going to be at all an easy matter, even if it were possible at all. The cutting down of wages, though it was carried to considerable lengths, produced most disappointing results in the expansion of sales—in the coal trade and in the metal industries, for example. It was, indeed, widely argued for a time that all troubles could be cured if only our industries could be thoroughly 'rationalised'; but the panacea of rationalisation, though it was not in fact tried, soon ceased to carry much conviction. Rationalisation might be thoroughly desirable; but few even of its advocates expected it to bring back British exports to anything like their pre-war position. For it came to be realised that the expansibility of exports was not wholly a question of price, that if we lowered our wages so would our competitors lower theirs, and that a good many countries were determined to offset any lowering of our prices by raising their tariffs to new record levels for the protection of their own producers.

It is no wonder that, in face of the failure to regain exports, men's minds began to turn towards the alternative of increased production for the home market, in order to absorb unemployed workers and utilise idle resources. At first, there was nothing specifically protectionist about this change of front. The demand was mainly not for a tariff to keep out foreign imports, but rather for an expansionist policy in the sphere of credit, and a courageous scheme of national development to be inaugurated and financed directly by the State. The unemployed were to be employed upon useful public works; and the indirect demand generated by this means was to act as a stimulus to industry generally. This policy involved credit expansion and a great national development loan. In varying forms, it became the policy of the Labour Party, of the Lloyd George Liberals, of Sir Oswald Mosley, and of Mr. J. M. Keynes and the younger economists. The Conservative Party, it is true, had already set up again a loud cry for a tariff; but there were serious hesitations among the Conservative leaders, and at this time the tariff idea had certainly not captured a majority of the electors.

It needed the world slump to bring a majority over to the side of protection; for I think there is undoubtedly a protectionist majority in Great Britain today. The world slump killed absolutely for the time being the prospect of an expansion of exports. It involved a serious further fall in their volume, without a corresponding fall in imports. Indeed, though the prices of imports fell far more than those of exports, the so-called 'adverse visible balance of trade' grew substantially wider. Under these conditions, projects of rationalisation mostly faded away; for the capital expenditure involved in them was less likely to yield a satisfactory return in face of the shrinkage of demand. Contraction of revenue and increased cost of unemployment led to budgetary difficulties, which stood formidably in the way of State-aided schemes of national development. The fall in the yield from overseas investments and shipping services diminished the flow of 'invisible exports' that could be used to pay for imports, or applied to new investment abroad. The difficulties of other countries led them to withdraw funds which they had held on deposit in the London market, or locked-up funds which London houses had lent abroad on short term. These factors diminished Great Britain's power to invest or lend abroad, on long or short term, and thus exaggerated world depression; and they also finally put such a strain on the exchanges as to force Great Britain, after futile attempts to rectify the situation by borrowing in New York and Paris, off the gold standard.

In these circumstances, tariffism was bound to make rapid headway; for it seemed to many that, as we could neither expand our exports nor get from our depreciated investments the means of paying for imports on the existing scale, the one remaining course was to cut down the volume of imports by the imposition of a tariff, and so restore the lost 'balance of trade'. I am not saying that this was a justifiable or logical conclusion, in this form. But it was the conclusion which made the most obvious and plausible appeal.

Of course, the experts were all the time well aware that the British crisis of 1931 arose mainly, not from the size of the import surplus, but from the movements of short-term capital. It is true that, altogether apart from these movements, Great Britain would probably have had, for the first time in a century, an adverse balance of international payments, due mainly to the shrinkage of income from international investments and loans—for there was, before we went off the gold standard, no increase in the amount of the adverse money balance of trade over the previous year. But this adverse balance of payments, though serious, would not by itself have been enough to cause any crisis. It could have been met by the sale of a tiny fraction of our past overseas investments, or by temporary borrowing of short-term funds on quite a small scale. Continued over a series of years, it would have led to trouble; but there was nothing in it to account for the sudden crisis of the summer of 1931.

That crisis was due, above all, to the withdrawal by foreigners —and especially by American banks—of short-time funds from London. These withdrawals began, not because of loss of confidence in Great Britain, but because the foreign depositors had lost confidence in themselves and wanted to increase their liquid resources at home. The loss of confidence in London was a result, and not a cause, of the earlier withdrawals. But these withdrawals showed how open to attack Great Britain's financial position was, and so led to further withdrawals on an ever-increasing scale. At this point, the appearance of the May Committee's scare-mongering report on our national expenditure aggravated the situation; and events moved swiftly to the crisis which drove Great Britain off the gold standard.

When the crisis had once arisen, it was obviously impossible to meet our temporary adverse balance of payments by borrowing from abroad; for what we had already borrowed was being rapidly withdrawn. It was impossible, on the other hand, to rectify the situation by calling in our own large volume of short-term advances abroad; for this would not only have brought trade to a standstill, but also caused widespread bankruptcy and default in foreign countries. It was difficult to meet the situation by selling foreign investments; for, in order to offset the withdrawal of short-term funds, we should have needed to sell on a very large scale and at a heavy loss. There remained only the course of going off the gold standard, and thus transferring to the foreign depositor the loss involved in the withdrawal of his money.

The suspension of the gold standard was calculated to ease

the situation in two ways—first by checking the removal of foreign money from London, and secondly by altering the conditions affecting the balance of trade. For obviously, as sterling depreciated, British exports could be sold more cheaply abroad, in proportion to the alteration in the rates of exchange with other currencies. To some extent, this bonus to exports was bound to be counteracted by some increase in our costs of production, wherever foreign materials from a country with a less depreciated exchange entered into our exports; but there was no reason why this should offset in most cases more than a small fraction of the exporter's advantage. On the other hand, as we should have to pay more for imports of all kinds from countries with less depreciated currencies, the effect on the 'visible balance of trade' would depend on the extent to which the higher cost of imports reduced the quantities actually imported.

In other words, the depreciation of sterling had the same effects, up to a point, as would have been produced by Mr. Keynes's plan of a revenue tariff coupled with a subsidy to the export trades. But there were two important differences. First, these effects would both be partly neutralised to the extent to which other countries followed our example, and related their currencies to sterling instead of gold. When this was done, we should not have to pay more for imports from such countries, but we should retain the advantage in exports to them in competition with countries which remained on the gold standard. So far, then, the net advantage was likely to be substantial, though the effect of currency depreciation in checking imports was liable to be lessened by a diversion of purchases from the countries which remained on the gold standard to those whose currencies fell with our own.

But, secondly, our departure from gold increased the sterling cost of all debts we had promised to pay in gold, or its equivalent, and especially of our War Debt to the United States, whereas it did not increase the nominal, and decreased the gold, value of debts payable to us in sterling. This was a factor of some importance on the debit side of the account.

In fact, a large number of countries have followed us off the gold standard. Indeed, there are today very few which remain effectively upon it. Consequently, the bonus upon our exports has been lessened or wiped out, except in relation to the gold standard countries; and these countries, feeling the effects of our policy upon their own exports, have been inclined to retaliate either by raising the general level of their tariffs or by imposing special duties on goods consigned from this country, and from others with depreciated currencies. Some bonus to our exports remains; but it is not so great as was expected, and the expansion of our export trade has been disappointing. This, however, is partly due to a further intensification of the world depression and a further fall in gold prices throughout the world. Our exports would certainly have fallen off a good deal more if we had remained upon the gold standard.

On the other hand, it is difficult to see that any diminution at all in imports has taken place as a result of our currency policy. The money cost of British imports was actually higher in November 1931 than in November 1930 by 5 per cent, and that of manufactured imports alone by 30 per cent, though for the two years taken as a whole there has been a substantial fall. The position in November was, however, certainly due to a great extent to the abnormal importation of foreign goods in anticipation of our adoption of a tariff policy; and it is impossible to conclude from it what the position would have been if there had been no question of a British tariff, or of equivalent measures of protection. Almost certainly, apart from abnormal imports due to this cause, the total value of imports would have been lower than a year ago, despite the increased cost of imports from countries whose currencies are less depreciated than ours. But it would hardly have been much less. And, on the other side, despite the bonus to our exports, their total value in sterling was more than a quarter less in November 1931 than in November 1930, and for the whole year nearly a third less. Even if there had been no abnormal imports, the adverse visible balance would have been greater in 1931 than in 1930. Actually, for the first eleven months of the two years, it was £341,000,000 in 1930 and nearly £370,000,000 in 1931. For November alone it was £28,500,000 in 1930 and £46,400,000 in 1931.

## III. FREE TRADE AND TARIFFS

If the return upon British investments overseas, shipping services, and other 'invisible exports' were still as large as it was a few years ago, and if, further, there were no problem of a shrinkage of foreign balances in London, even an adverse visible balance of this magnitude would present no serious difficulty. It would diminish the resources available for fresh overseas investment; but it would still leave a surplus available for this purpose. But in fact the fall in 'invisible exports' has been heavy. In 1928 and 1929 the Board of Trade put our net income from overseas investments at £270,000,000. In 1931 it was probably at least £100,000,000 less; and there was a corresponding fall in the other 'invisible' items. Probably we had about £190,000,000 less credit from 'invisible exports' to offset the adverse merchandise balance. In 1928 and 1929 our surplus available for new lending or investment abroad was probably between £120,000,000 and £130,000,000. In 1931 this had plainly turned into a deficit, even apart from the adverse movement of short-term capital. But the real difficulty arose far more from the shrinkage of 'invisible' exports than from the rise in imports. In other words, the source of our troubles lay mainly in the world depression of trade.

It was, however, plausible to argue that, of all the factors which go to make up the balance of payments, the only factor this country was able to influence was the volume of imports. For exports we had done what we could by going off the gold standard; and our new foreign investment had already been cut down to a minimum. We had no means of getting more for our shipping services, or from our investments overseas, unless world trade were to revive. The plain truth, then, was that we could no longer afford to import so much as before, even though foreign exporters were offering us their products at very low prices, in terms of gold. We must cut down imports, as the one available way of rectifying the balance of payments.

There were, if this logic was accepted, four possible lines of approach to the effective restriction of imports. The first was to reduce wages, salaries and any other incomes that could be reduced, either directly or by way of taxation, and so to cut off the demand for imports at the source. This, however, could not be done without depressing the demand for home products as well as imports, and so intensifying the depression; for it was not really possible to believe that the pursuance of this policy would bring such a revival of exports, through lower costs, as to offset the decline in purchasing power. Moreover, this deflationary policy would probably have caused sterling to rise, and so cancelled, in part at least, the bonus on exports. And, above all, it would have meant a bitter and prolonged industrial struggle, which most employers, even, were by no means eager to face.

The second possible line of approach was that of inflation. It was possible, by inflationary methods, to cause so great a rise in the British price-level, and so great a fall in the external value of the pound, as to force a contraction of imports through our sheer inability to pay for them. This policy would also have involved an additional subsidy to exports; but it is doubtful if this would be of any advantage, even to the export trades, in view of the reprisals which it would be certain to provoke. It would, moreover, have caused further loss in the real value of the return from our foreign investments, and a big addition to the sterling burden of the American debt.

The third and fourth lines of approach were both aimed at the direct restriction of imports. It was possible, by means of a high and extensive tariff, to reduce imports at the cost of a rise in prices to the consumer; for it was certain that British producers of competitive goods would take advantage of a tariff by raising their prices. Or it was possible to aim at the exclusion of imports by prohibitions, quotas, and similar arrangements, worked on the basis either of bulk purchase through Import Boards, or of a licensing system.

Of these four alternative policies, only one was of such a nature as to be readily explained to the general body of the electorate. Familiar already with the long controversy between tariffists and free traders, the electors were perfectly prepared to listen to fresh variations on the accustomed theme. Many who had been doubtful before were won over to tariffs when the case for them appeared to be strongly reinforced by the need for measures to restore the 'balance of trade'. Other alternatives were barely considered; and the issue seemed to the ordinary man to be between those who advocated a tariff and those who had nothing at all to suggest beyond waiting helplessly for a problematical recovery in trade. Naturally, the tariffists won; for, if these were the only alternatives, the weight of the argument seemed to be wholly on their side.

Vainly the free traders demonstrated that the advantages to be derived from any practicable tariff, even in relation to the immediate balance of trade, were very doubtful and certain only to set up awkward reactions. Vainly they showed that even our manufactured imports consisted largely of materials in a semi-finished state, vital to the finishing trades producing for export, or of oil-fuel and other goods which could not possibly be produced at home. Vainly they raised once more the ancient cry 'Your food will cost you more', only to discover that it seemed to have lost its terrors for a large section of the electorate. Their position appeared fatally weak, because in face of an admittedly serious emergency they were, in effect, proposing to take no action at all.

The advocates of tariffs, with the perturbed aid of free traders *manqué*, who recognised the need for doing something, but knew not what to do, therefore swept the country; and, as I write, Great Britain has already imposed almost prohibitive duties on a small range of imported manufactures and 'luxury' foodstuffs, and seems to be heading straight for a high general tariff. Tariffists are grumbling at the Government for not moving faster; but they are really exultant that it has moved so far and so fast. In the pause, then, before the plunge is finally taken, it is worth while to enquire what the actual effects of a general tariff are likely to be.

A general tariff, I have written; but let us begin by considering a general tariff on manufactured articles only. Such a tariff may be either high or low. If it is kept low, it is unlikely, in view of the present pressure on world exporters to make sales, to have much effect in excluding imports. It will lead rather to a rise in prices less than the amount of the duty, with the foreigner paying a part of the tax, and the British producer raising his prices by the remaining part. Such a tariff will do little either to stimulate home production or to rectify the balance of trade. A very little it may do, but not much. On the other hand, a very high tariff, such as we have already imposed on a narrow range of goods, will undoubtedly exclude a large quantity of imports, but is also likely to bring about a very considerable rise in home prices, unless stringent measures are adopted for their control by the State.

A general tariff on manufactures, whether it be high or low, is bound to react on our export trades. Iron and steel furnish, of course, the outstanding example. Our imports of iron and steel goods are very largely semi-manufactures, which are the materials of our finishing trades. It is not even suggested that, with a monopoly of the home market, our manufacturers could produce many of these goods as cheaply as they are being bought from abroad, though the depreciation of sterling has added considerably to the cost of imported Belgian and German steel. The steel-makers want a tariff, not only because it would give them a wider home market, but also because it would enable them to charge more. They might, indeed, keep export prices down while raising their prices in the home market; but this would only shift the loss of exports from the steel industry to the steel-using trades, such as engineering.

I do not deny that the loss of exports might be less than the contraction of imports, and some effect be produced on the balance of trade. But, in the absence of stringent price control, this result would be secured only at the cost of a considerable rise in domestic prices.

The larger the home market for any particular commodity is in relation to the export market, the easier will it be to retain exports by means of differential prices. But, where this is done, the aggregate effect in raising home prices will also be larger.

If, now, the tariff is extended from manufactured goods to raw materials, the adverse effect on exports will obviously be still more marked, whether the materials are capable of being produced at home or not. Again, something may be done to keep exports by means of differential prices, but only at the cost of raising prices at home.

Finally, if the tariff is extended to foodstuffs—beyond a

narrow range of luxury goods—the cost of living, which has been raised already (and is likely to rise more) because of the depreciation of sterling, will be increased again. This will certainly lead to a chorus of demands for higher wages; but it is possible that the employers in general will successfully resist these, provided that the increase of prices is kept within bounds. The effect in that case will be to lower the standard of living, just as if wages had been lowered. This will lessen the demand for imports, no doubt, but it will also lessen the demand for home-produced goods, and so intensify depression. Nor can it even be argued that such a reduction in real wages will benefit the export trades, by reducing their costs.

It will, however, be urged that a tariff on foodstuffs need not raise prices, because it will not be applied to Empire products, and accordingly its effect will be to divert demand from foreign to Empire countries. But, if Empire countries are given a protected market, they will assuredly be able to charge more. Why else, indeed, do they want the protection? Partly, it may be said, in order to get an assured market for as much of their output as we are able to take, even at the world price; but not only this. Under a preferential tariff system, they would assuredly charge us more.

That is presumably why, in the case of wheat and possibly other products as well, a quota system is being put forward as the alternative to a tariff. The British Government now seems to be pledged not only to a quota arrangement for home-grown wheat, but also to offer a much larger quota to the Dominions. It is not yet clear whether this quota is to be accompanied by a guaranteed price in any form, or whether the price is to be left to settle itself by competition. If a price above the world price were guaranteed, obviously the effect would be to raise the cost of bread to the British consumer. But even without a price guarantee, a quota fixed at a higher level than our normal importation from the Dominions is likely to give their producers a bargaining advantage, and so enable them to charge more. The effect on prices may be less than the effect of a preferential tariff; but there will be an effect, which will fall upon the British consumer.

I am not saying that it may not still be worth while, if there is a sufficient *quid pro quo* in Empire markets. But the *quid pro quo* outlined in Mr. Bennett's offer at last year's Imperial Conference is certainly not sufficient. It is of scant advantage to British producers, and bad for world trade, to be given larger preferences, not by reduction of existing duties, but only by raising them still higher against foreign goods. But will the Dominions be prepared to consider actual tariff reductions? They are determined to accord their own industries high protection against British as well as foreign goods; and they too are busy rectifying their trade balances by exporting more and importing less.

In general, it seems clear that, while a tariff policy may lessen the adverse balance of trade, it will do this only by restricting imports in such a way as to raise home prices. But what will be the effect of allowing our domestic price-level to rise? It will either directly hamper exports, or lower the standard of living; and, if it does the latter, it will shift depression from the export market to the home market, on account of the loss of home purchasing power. It may be urged against this view that a rise in home prices will stimulate production and investment, by making industry more profitable; but, while this may be in some degree its initial effect, can that effect last if the power to buy goods is decreased? And, if wages are raised to meet the rise in prices, depression will be shifted back again from the home market to the export trades.

There is another consequence of a rising level of prices to be taken into account. Now that Great Britain is off the gold standard, sterling has no fixed value in relation to other currencies. Its value, then, depends principally on two sets of forces —on the fluctuation in the balance of payments resulting from current transactions and from the movements of capital. A rise in prices due to the imposition of a tariff is bound to affect these fluctuations. It will tend to offset the effects of the depreciation of sterling by making Great Britain a less good place to buy in; and it will thus discourage such invisible exports as foreign tourist expenditure. And it will also tend, in some degree, to encourage further withdrawals of short-term funds.

On the other hand, it may serve to some extent as a stimulus to foreign manufacturers to set up works in Great Britain inside the tariff wall, and thus help to attract long-term capital. Altogether, the effects are exceedingly difficult to predict; for they depend mainly on the extent to which prices rise. A small rise might have little net effect on either the balance of payments or the external value of the pound; but a large rise would certainly involve a vicious spiral of inflation, with the inevitable outcome of a flight from sterling that could not be easily checked, and a further fall in its external value that might go so far as to endanger the supply even of necessary imports.

The risk is at any rate serious enough to make it right to be very wary of any course which is certain to aggravate the effect on prices of the existing depreciation of sterling. Accordingly, it seems indispensable, if we are to have an extensive tariff on imports, to institute at the same time a stringent control of domestic prices. But no workable mechanism at present exists for this purpose; for we have nothing in Great Britain at all corresponding to the control over cartel prices which exists today in Germany. Nor does it seem at all likely that the present Government, or the present Parliament, will be disposed to institute any such control, which most of their members would presumably regard as a pernicious instalment of Socialism. It is to be feared that, if an extensive system of duties is introduced, as seems likely, it will be brought in without its due complement of conditions, as an unsafeguarded present to the protected industries.

A tariff is, in any case, an awkward instrument to combine with a system of price control; for its effects are inevitably uncertain unless it is raised to a quite prohibitive level. What is needed, if we are to restrict imports at all in order to lessen our adverse balance, is an instrument that will be certain in its operation, and at the same time flexible as needs and conditions change. The Government, or some more expert body acting on its behalf, ought to be able to negotiate with the British producers, offering them an assured market for a definite quantity of products of this or that sort, provided they will undertake to market them at a reasonable and agreed price. The importation of the kind of goods in question could then be prohibited altogether, if the British producers were able to promise an adequate supply, or restricted, by a licensing system or through an Import Board, but without tariff duties, to the quantity needed in order to supplement the domestic production. The quantity of goods admitted from abroad could be rapidly varied in order to meet changes in home demand, or in the British supply; and any tendency to profiteering on the part of the home producers could be instantly countered by allowing free importation to be resumed. This method would have just the flexibility that a tariff system, as ordinarily operated, notoriously lacks; and it would afford neither excuse nor opportunity to the British producer to raise his prices by something approaching the amount of the duty.

A system of this sort—protection without tariffs—could be worked in either of two ways: by prohibitions, quotas and licences if the import trade were left in private hands; or by a public Import Board actually buying and marketing the entire imported supply. For the present, at any rate, the second of these methods would be suitable only for bulk imports of a standardised sort, such as wheat, some sorts of meat and dairy produce, raw textile materials, and perhaps crude iron and steel. For the more diversified types of foodstuffs and manufactures the first method would probably be easier to work, and would involve less disturbance by its introduction. And, even in the case of bulk imports, I think the first method, while inferior to the second, would be preferable to a tariff, or to a rigid quota system like that now apparently projected for Empire wheat.

It is objected to this proposal that it runs counter to existing commercial treaties and conventions—to the League of Nations Convention (signed by only a few countries), which binds the signatories to abstain from prohibiting or restricting imports, with certain specified exceptions; to the present Anglo-German Treaty; and to one or two minor commercial treaties with lesser countries. This is true. If we wanted a free hand to prohibit imports, or to restrict them by licence, we should have to denounce the Convention mentioned above, and to revise the Anglo-German and certain other treaties. This could be done, though it would take time. But the Convention and the treaties do not prevent us from establishing public Import Boards with sole power to bring in particular classes of goods, provided that the Boards are made public bodies exercising a monopoly on behalf of the State. Indeed, the creation of such monopolies is explicitly authorised by the Convention and the Anglo-German treaty.

How would Import Boards, of the type here contemplated, work in practice? Their task would be to buy enough abroad of the commodities with which they dealt to bring the total supply into balance with the needs of the market. They would aim at giving British producers the first chance of supplying the market at a reasonable price; but they would at once counter profiteering by the bringing in of additional imports—or by the threat to bring them in. They would be free, in buying abroad, from Empire or foreign countries, either to buy from day to day at the market price, or to enter into forward contracts for bulk supply. Probably they would in fact do both, contracting in bulk for a minimum supply, and meeting additional needs by ordinary market purchases. Their bulk purchases could be made either at a fixed price, or at a price fluctuating with the world price. And they would presumably sell again in the home market at prices calculated to cover their average costs, and to eliminate disturbing short-term fluctuations. Their effect would thus be to steady prices; and, if they were managed with reasonable skill, they should be able to lower them also, both from the strength of their position as bulk buyers able to exact favourable terms and from the economies which they should be able to achieve in the field of wholesale distribution.

An Import Board, as I understand the term, is essentially a public body wielding a State monopoly. A system of prohibitions and licences, on the other hand, implies that actual buying of imports is still left to the private importer. Under such a system there would have to be a board or committee deciding, or advising, about the types of goods to be prohibited or admitted freely, and about the quantities and varieties to be admitted in cases of restriction. This system is already being worked under the Dyestuffs Act in the case of one type of imports; and the experience of that Act, while it has not been wholly satisfactory, because there has not been enough pressure on British producers to keep down prices and supply an adequate range of dyestuffs, has proved the method to be entirely practicable. It is suitable at this stage, where the types of imports to be controlled are too diverse to be either purchased in bulk or satisfactorily handled by a public Board directly importing and marketing on behalf of the State.

The method of prohibitions and licences is, of course, essentially protective. It is designed, like a protective tariff, to limit imports and offer the home producer, on terms, a guaranteed market. Import Boards, on the other hand, are not necessarily protective, though they may be so in any degree desired. An Import Board could, if it thought fit, bring in as many foreign goods as private importers would bring in under a Free Trade system, or indeed more; or it could, on the other hand, decide to bring in none at all, if it could strike a satisfactory bargain with the home producers for meeting the entire home demand. Its object would be to consider not the interests of producers or consumers as such, but the interests of society, and to expand, contract, or cease importation as seemed best for the general welfare.

Obviously, a system of Import Boards—with their correlative of Export Boards as well—would be the only possible way in which a Socialist community could carry on its external trade. They are fully as much an integral part of the economic structure of Socialism as the public Corporations or concerns proposed by Socialists for the conduct of productive industries or services. And they are the only means by which a comity of Socialist communities could build up, as the complement to national planning of their industries, a reasonable and orderly system of international exchange. They are, in fact, the necessary instruments of world trading under Socialist conditions.

But it may be questioned how far they are appropriate to a community which is not yet Socialist, and has not advanced far towards the socialisation of its internal industries and services. Some people hold that to begin now by socialising any part of international trade would be to begin at the wrong end, and that the State organisation of overseas commerce should come last and not first in the transition to a Socialist system. I do not agree; for the present chaos in world trade seems to show that there is the greatest need in this sphere to begin building up agencies for constructive world co-operation, strong enough to counteract the present tendency towards Economic Nationalism, based on the raising higher and higher of obstructive tariffs over the whole world. There is need today for organised methods whereby the countries of the world can exchange their products far more freely; and Import Boards and Export Boards could be the means of fostering this exchange by way of reciprocal transactions and even of simple barter of goods for goods. The Import Board is not, as some of its critics suggest, merely another project for the strengthening of Economic Nationalism. On the contrary, it is a positive contribution to the cause of international economic co-operation.

But it will be replied that I myself have put forward the Import Board as a possible method of restricting imports, and not of promoting them. It is true enough that Import Boards would restrict imports—in certain directions; but that is no reason why they should not promote imports in others, on a basis of exchange for exports. For no one who is more than half-witted supposes that restriction of imports is desirable for its own sake. The more imports a country gets the better—provided it has the means of paying for them. The world needs for its economic health more imports and not less, and of course more exports also, for every import is an export from somewhere.

The creation of Import Boards is, then, the logical policy not only for Socialists, but for all who believe in organised international economic co-operation, to pursue. And it is also, over the field of bulk imports, the best means of providing for any restrictions that may be needed, for a Board will be in the strongest position for the prevention of profiteering and for keeping the supply flexible in response to changing conditions of home production and demand. It will obviously not appeal to believers in *laisser faire* as still the best of economic systems, in both industry and trade. It may, however, provide a solution for those who have so far clung to Free Trade, not from any passionate belief in *laisser faire*, but rather from a positive dread and dislike of tariffs. For, all the world over, tariffism has not merely failed to cure unemployment, but left a nasty taste in the mouth. Its sole function, apart from the raising of revenue, is to obstruct trade: it has no constructive aspect or potentiality. The world needs an instrument, not for the obstructing of trade, but for its orderly government and promotion on principles of mutual exchange; and that a tariff system can never provide.

The case for Import and Export Boards, as an alternative policy to both tariff protection and Free Trade, rests, then, not on the present financial emergency of Great Britain—though that emergency strengthens it—but on the need for constructive means of international collaboration to draw trade out of its present depression by a revival of mutual exchange. The emergency compels us to reduce our adverse balance of payments. But that does not mean that we must import less, if only we can find means of exporting more by way of exchange. Tariffs do mean importing less, and thereby depressing our national standard of living. Free Trade means restricting imports either by cutting down wages directly, or by letting the value of the pound sink until we can no longer afford to buy. Public control of trade, designed not only to restrict but to promote, offers the only reasonable hope of an escape from our difficulties that will both preserve our domestic standard of life, and lead the way towards an orderly revival of world trade and production.

# IV

## PUBLIC OPINION AND MONETARY POLICY

It is strange to remember how little, in those far-off days before the war, banking policy was a subject of public controversy or discussion. There was some discussion even then—a speech from Sir Edward Holden throwing doubts on the literal inspiration of the Bank Charter Act of 1844, a suggestion by Mr. Sidney Webb that the State might do a good stroke of business for itself by nationalising the banks, and Mr. Arthur Kitson's *Open Review*, attempting vainly to arouse a public demand for a credit policy based on productive capacity instead of gold. There were too, as there are always, mere currency cranks, announcing panaceas to an inattentive world. But, in the view of most intelligent people, monetary policy was not a question of urgent practical importance; and the man in the street and the daily newspapers had never heard of it at all. Bimetallism had been forgotten in Great Britain; and since that controversy died, no major issue centring round money had appeared. Things were different in America, where the memory of the 1907 smash was still fresh and the Federal Reserve system in process of construction; but in Great Britain nothing disturbed the opulent repose of Lombard Street and the 'Old Lady'.

Men always talk most, and most confidently, about currency and credit when things are going wrong; for money has at least the merit of being a very convenient scapegoat. The absence of monetary controversy in pre-war Britain was a clear sign that, in the business world at all events, things were going well. Equally, the revival of monetary discussion since the war shows that, in most people's opinion, things are going very badly indeed. For hardly even in the years that followed the Peace of 1815 were controversies about currency and credit carried on with such intensity as today. And this has occurred though we have had no Cobbett—no great demagogic figure with a bee in his bonnet—to rouse us all to fury over the iniquitous behaviour of the money interest. Mr. Keynes is too intellectualist to be a demagogue; and Mr. Lloyd George has never understood enough about money to devote more than an *entr'acte* to denunciation of the bankers.

Nevertheless, we are in these days all talking about monetary policy, and almost everyone who professes opinions about politics has some strong views upon the subject. Professional economists spend a great deal of their time disputing whether gold, or banking policy, is or is not really at the bottom of the world slump. The battle over inflation and deflation is joined, not only in City counting-houses and the offices of industrial magnates, but in the workshop and the home, and in buses, trams and tubes as men go to and from their work. The newspapers are full of it; and people with no interest in investments have taken to reading the City columns. For everyone realises now that, whether or no money is responsible for the great slump, monetary policy touches him very nearly indeed.

The Socialist movement and the Labour Party have naturally been affected in the highest degree by this changed aspect of the money question. Socialists used to think mainly in terms of the public ownership of the leading productive industries and of such services as transport and the supply of power. They desired to nationalise the banks, no doubt, as part of their policy of bringing all the vital services under public ownership. But they had not, in fact, thought very much about the subject. Certainly, they had never put it in the forefront of their programme, or considered it until recently as one of the first steps to be taken in the advance towards a Socialist system. Railways, mines, electricity, and probably a good many other productive and distributive services, were to come before banking in the order of transference to national ownership.

But then, as the post-war controversy over monetary policy developed, Socialists began to realise that the nationalisation of banking might mean not merely the taking over by the public of a single vital service, but the acquisition of a power to influence the policy of all other industries and services, and perhaps to determine the prosperity of the entire economic system. They saw that, in the light of modern technical improvements, the problem of producing wealth was well on the way to being solved, and that the real difficulty of modern societies was to find markets for the goods which they were technically able to produce. This perception focussed attention on the question of money, because demand is a question of people having enough money to buy. Mr. J. A. Hobson, who had been reiterating his doctrine of under-consumption vainly for decades, suddenly found his views taken up; and new writers went far past him in alleging the existence in modern communities of a standing deficiency of purchasing power. Major Douglas in Great Britain, and Messrs. Foster and Catchings in America, were widely read, and enlisted much support because they seemed to be laying their fingers on the sore spot when they alleged that the real source of trade depression was lack of money to buy the goods that were waiting to be sold.

It was mainly with the idea that the banks, which are all over the world endowed with the function of issuing money, ought to issue more of it, and so enable more goods to be produced and sold, that a discontented generation turned to the demand for a revision of monetary policy and banking control. Some of the reformers had simple formulæ by means of which everything could be put right, if only the bankers could be persuaded to act upon them; while others stressed the need for a change in the control of the banking system, and wanted it either reofficered by captains of industry, or taken over by the State and run as a public service. Practically all the reformers wanted more money to be issued, in one way or another; but it was clearly essential to their plans that this must happen without a corresponding rise in prices, or no more goods would be sold. Major Douglas audaciously promised to halve prices as well as increase the supply of money—and some people believed him. Others, less daring, said only that more money need not mean higher prices if arrangements were made for a corresponding increase in the supply of goods and services.

But, while these plans were being eagerly debated, men had before them the object-lessons of inflation in Germany, France,

Italy and many other countries, to tell them that an increased supply of money could not be all that was needed. The effects of inflation in these countries scared some back to a complete acceptance of the old monetary policies of pre-war days; and in spite of the reformers' protests, the world, under the auspices of the bankers, was led gradually back to the gold standard, under promise that the return to gold would bring back the old security. But hardly was the last of the leading countries back on gold—a return not accomplished without a great deal of difficulty and hardship—than fresh troubles set in. Getting back to the gold standard had meant for all countries one of two things—deflation or devaluation. Deflation had involved unemployment on a large scale, wage-cuts and industrial disputes, and a great increase in the burdens of debt and taxation. Devaluation had carried with it serious loss for all those who lived on fixed incomes, including the small *rentiers* and pensioners as well as the great. It fell most heavily on the small savers and the middle classes, whereas deflation fell upon the workers and the industrial employers. Still, in one way or the other, the thing was done; and the promised result of it was financial stability.

But in fact the gold standard under post-war conditions soon proved itself inherently and persistently unstable. The world's gold silted up first in America and then in France, leaving other countries with an inadequate supply. World prices, measured in gold, persisted in falling, despite the endeavours of the United States to hold up their prices by the manipulation of currency and credit. And finally the world slump made hay of the idea that the return to gold had given all countries an assured foundation for future economic progress.

In Great Britain it is easy to trace the main phases of monetary controversy since the end of the war, or rather since 1921, when the post-war boom broke and deflation seriously began. The years that followed immediately were occupied mainly with the struggle over deflation. Those in authority, in both politics and finance, were determined to return to the gold standard by way of deflation—that is, by bringing down costs and prices until sterling could be restored to its pre-war parity with gold and the dollar. They had against them those who wished to return to the gold standard on a basis of devaluation—that is, by giving the pound a new, lower gold value—and those who did not wish to go back to the gold standard at all. But these last were disorganised, uninfluential in high places, and labelled as cranks. The real struggle was between deflation and devaluation; and the deflationists easily had their way for the time. They were not, however, then able to get back to the gold standard; and there was an interlude during which the pressure of deflation was relaxed. Soon, however, a rise in prices in America caused it to be resumed; and Mr. Churchill was able to bring us back to the gold standard, at pre-war parity, in 1925, amid the vaticinations of Mr. Keynes and others, who held that the value of the pound had been put too high.

It was soon apparent that the critics were right, and that the return to pre-war parity had been a disaster. It seriously handicapped our export trades by raising their gold prices to the foreign buyer; and it subjected our exchanges to a continuous strain. The consequent troubles of the coal trade, the desperate efforts to cut costs, and the great strikes and lock-outs of 1926 are directly traceable to our mistaken method of return to the gold standard. Equally so is the restrictive credit policy under which our industries suffered throughout the following years. Devaluation in 1921, or even at any time up to 1925, would have saved us these things, and perhaps saved us the crisis of 1931.

When, however, the return to the gold standard at pre-war parity had become an accomplished fact, most even of the critics considered that the controversy was over, and it would be impossible to go back on what had been done. Even in 1931, a few months before Great Britain was forced off the gold standard, the Macmillan Committee, including Mr. Keynes himself, dismissed devaluation as an impracticable and undesirable policy.

After 1925, then, the terms of controversy changed; and the argument came to be conducted on the assumptions of the new gold standard. The question was whether, having restored the gold standard, we were bound, in order to maintain it, to pursue a restrictive credit policy, or whether we could, while keeping it, find means of expanding credit so as to increase the volume of employment. Up to 1925, the controversy was mainly about currency and the basis on which our currency ought to rest. After 1925 it was mainly about credit. The orthodox held that any expansion of credit would send up prices, cause a fall in exports and a rise in imports, and so enforce a fresh restriction of credit in order to prevent an outflow of gold; while the critics urged that industry could be stimulated, and provided with more credits, without raising prices to any dangerous extent, if only the stimulus were applied in the right way, through State schemes of employment financed by national loans. For it was urged that there was in the country unemployed capital awaiting investment as well as unemployed labour, and that the taking up of the slack of the economic system by bringing both into use need not have any inflationary effect. This controversy became an important election issue in 1929, when Mr. Churchill's Treasury Memorandum stated the orthodox view against the buff and yellow pamphlets of Labour and Liberalism.

Labour came to authority with a Chancellor of the Exchequer more orthodox than Mr. Churchill, and plainly out of sympathy with the policy on which he had taken office. But before there had been time for him to quarrel seriously with his own followers the coming of the world slump materially altered the situation; for it was evidently far harder, though it might still be possible, for Great Britain to pursue a policy of national economic development in face of the distresses of the rest of the world. The American collapse did, indeed, ease temporarily the strain on our exchanges, which had lasted ever since 1925; and money became cheaper for a time. But its use also became far less profitable in face of the slump, and cheaper money accordingly quite failed to stimulate industrial enterprise. Moreover, the slump caused exports to shrink more than imports, though imports fell far more in price; and it also seriously reduced 'invisible exports', especially shipping earnings and the yield on overseas investments. The trouble over the balance of international payments set in, and became far more serious as the depression grew deeper. Met at first by a contraction of new overseas investments, it was soon intensified by the locking-up of British short-term loans in Germany and elsewhere, and by a withdrawal of foreign short-term balances from Great Britain, first by France and later by American bankers in need of liquid resources in order to meet their own domestic troubles of 'frozen' and depreciated assets in American business.

In face of these growing difficulties, the policy of credit expansion was less and less confidently urged in Great Britain; and by 1931 the attack on the *status quo* was coming chiefly from the opposite side—from the advocates of retrenchment at the expense of the unemployed, 'economy' in the public services, and wage reduction in industry. The Macmillan Committee's Report was a carry-over from the expansionism of 1929: the May Committee countered with the full-blooded depressionism of 1931. At this stage, the cry was that the pound must be saved by ruthless cutting down; but in fact the pound was past saving, in view of the exodus of short-term funds. The first act of a National Government whose mission was to 'save the pound' was the suspension of the gold standard.

At this, the flood-gates of monetary controversy were opened afresh; for what was our new policy to be? Were we to regard the suspension of the gold standard as a merely temporary measure, and to look forward to a restoration of the pound to its old parity at the earliest possible moment? Or were we to contemplate a return to gold on a basis of devaluation—the policy rejected in the years before 1925? Or were we to abandon gold altogether, and either adopt a purely national currency policy, with fluctuating rates of exchange, or seek to rally the world round some alternative standard not based on gold? Or, finally, were we to wait and see, deferring any decision on the general question until the world situation as a whole had become clearer, and the future behaviour of the gold standard easier to predict?

At first there was a tendency, in both financial and political circles, to lay emphasis on the first of these alternatives. My Lord Snowden and most of the bankers clearly wished it to be believed that Great Britain's lapse from financial virtue was only a matter of short-lived indisposition, and that we should be back at pre-war parity ere long. This was, of course, a convenient belief to instil; for it was calculated to check the withdrawal of funds from London. But, in the ensuing months, less and less has been heard of it; for there seems no warrant for supposing that Great Britain will be able again to afford to write up the pound's value, putting new handicaps upon her export trade, again encouraging imports, and forcing new industrial conflicts designed to bring down sterling costs. It now seems clear that if we do go back to gold at all, it will have to be on a basis of devaluation, even if the devaluation is a good deal less than the current depreciation of the pound (at the end of 1931).

But shall we go back to gold at all? The bankers at least would like to; but even they have been insisting of late that Great Britain's return to the fold cannot be unconditional. They have been asking for assurances that, if we do resume gold payments, the drift of gold to France and the United States will not be resumed. But how can it be prevented? There are only two conceivable ways. One is a cancellation, or drastic scaling-down, of the international debts which are the main cause of the drift of gold to America. The other is the maintenance by both America and France, year in and year out, of a sufficient flow of fresh foreign lending to counteract the inward movement of gold, and even to reverse it until a better distribution of the world's supply of gold has been secured. But neither of these things is easy. America is not at all inclined to cancel Europe's debts, or France Germany's Reparations; and how are the Americans to be persuaded to regulate their foreign lending by other countries' needs, rather than by the changing prospects of profit from investment or speculation at home? If we are to wait for assurances that the gold standard will behave itself in future, we seem likely to wait some time.

Devaluation, of course, implies a return to the gold standard. The pound is at present depreciated; but it is not devaluated. With the world in its present state, the choice lies in effect between the third and fourth policies, between the attempt to erect an alternative standard in place of gold, and simply waiting to see what happens before we make up our minds.

But, even between these two policies, there is hardly, as yet, a clear choice. For there is no approach to agreement about the nature of the alternative standard that we could set out to erect. There has been a good deal of talk about a new international standard based on wholesale prices, and designed to keep the level of world prices stable. But there is in fact no such thing as the level of world prices, or at all events no means of measuring a thing so abstract. Even for a single country, the general price-level is an abstraction; for the results secured by averaging a number of particular prices vary with the selection and weighting of the commodities whose prices are to be measured, with the standard taken as a basis, and with the method of averaging chosen for the purpose. Actual indices of wholesale prices measure mainly the average prices of a selection of standardised foodstuffs and raw or semi-manufactured materials. They greatly underweight manufactured goods, whose prices are far harder to measure, when they include them at all. They take no account of retail prices, which directly affect the demand for currency, or of the prices of services of any kind, though these account for a growing proportion of expenditure in modern communities.

Moreover, if it is difficult to compile a general price-index for a single country, it is in effect impossible to compile such an index for all countries taken together. There are, doubtless, a certain number of commodities in relation to which it is possible to speak of a world price; but even this can be done only by leaving the effect of tariffs on their prices in particular countries out of account. Most commodities have not a world price even in this sense, but only prices varying from one country to another. The idea of a world system of currency management, manipulating the issue of money in order to stabilise the general level of world prices, can be safely dismissed as impracticable.

There remains the idea that the world, or a large part of it, might agree to take some single national currency, such as sterling, as a standard, and to relate its currencies to sterling instead of gold. Under this arrangement, the standard currency would be itself a managed currency, not based on gold, but regulated in accordance with some deliberate policy. It might, for example, be so managed as to keep the general level of wholesale prices stable in the country concerned, in as far as this is possible for one country acting alone. Other countries would then manage their currencies so as to keep their value stable in relation to the standard currency. Or the standard currency might be managed with a view, not to price stability, but rather to the desirability of stimulating or contracting enterprise, either within the country or over the whole group of countries using the common standard.

Obviously, a single country would have to be very important in world trade to have a chance of getting its currency accepted as a standard by others. So far Great Britain, as the world's greatest market for imports, occupies a favourable position. But if Great Britain attempted so to manage her monetary policy as to stabilise wholesale prices, she could at most only stabilise her own price-level, and not those of the countries which related their currencies to hers. For within a stabilised level of general prices the prices of particular goods will continue to vary; and, as different goods are of different degrees of importance in the national economies of different countries, the general price-level would not vary to the same extent in those countries even if all particular prices varied with absolute uniformity from country to country. Accordingly, even if the country of the standard currency could succeed in stabilising its price-level—a considerable assumption—the price-levels in the other countries would still vary, though something would have been done to limit the degree of variation.

An alternative would be for the country of the standard currency to aim at stabilising, not its general price-level, but only the average of the prices of a small group of commodities having a world price, with the object of limiting general price fluctuation over the whole group of countries, without eliminating it anywhere. But this policy would be likely to involve violent monetary adjustments on account of changes in the prices of one or two staple commodities, and to react quite

## IV. MONETARY POLICY

illogically on the monetary conditions of the different countries included in the group.

On the other hand, the country which was seeking to get its currency adopted as an international standard might not adopt price stabilisation as its objective. It might work without any automatic principle, managing the supply of money in accordance with the dictates of common sense. But here again a complication arises. A country managing its currency in this way would naturally seek to adjust its monetary supply to its own national needs; but variations based on this principle would not necessarily square with the needs of other countries. On the other hand, the attempt to manage a national currency in the light of the needs of other countries, even at the cost of failure to meet national needs, would be likely to arouse a great deal of opposition within the country.

For the monetary needs of different countries do not necessarily coincide. This has been generally recognised as a disadvantage of the gold standard, to be set off against its advantage in conferring exchange stability. It is in fact a disadvantage of any standard which makes exchange stability its basis, and not of the gold standard alone. And it is so serious as to raise definitely the question whether an international monetary standard is desirable at all.

My own view, reached and expressed with considerable hesitation, is that it is not, and that it will be best for each country—or perhaps in some cases group of countries—to manage its own currency without relation to a common standard, and to allow its rates of exchange to fluctuate in order to secure greater freedom to adjust its supply of money to its own needs. This is fully compatible with a considerable degree of exchange stability in practice. Thus, it would be quite possible for other countries, without adopting definitely a sterling standard, normally to keep their exchanges at a practically fixed relation to sterling, while reserving their power to alter the relation in exceptional cases of need. In other words, day-to-day fluctuations would be kept within as narrow limits as under the gold standard, by means of monetary management; but it would be possible at any time to readjust the relative values of the currencies concerned without any such decisive step as the departure from a fixed standard involves.

There is, of course, no chance, whatever we do in Great Britain, that all other countries will be prepared either to adopt sterling as a standard, or normally to keep their currencies at a fixed ratio to sterling. But if the pound does again become the focal point for a number of other national currencies, this result is by far likelier to come about in the way just suggested—probably without any formal agreement at all. If Great Britain can pursue a reasonable and sensible policy of monetary management, based on tolerable stability of monetary conditions, a considerable number of other countries, outside as well as within the Empire, will be quite likely to manage their own currencies by keeping sterling balances in London, and relating the value of their money to the pound rather than to gold, still leaving themselves free to alter the relative value from time to time as their own monetary needs dictate. This would mean that there would be in effect two currency systems side by side in the world, with fluctuating exchange rates between them—one based on gold, with France and the United States as its leading members, and the other based on sterling, with Empire countries as its nucleus and a strong tendency to attract into its orbit other countries which have been forced off the gold standard. But it is unlikely that there would be permanent fixity of exchange rates between members of the sterling group, which would thus give away the advantage of long-term exchange stability for that of being better able to adjust their monetary arrangements to their own national needs.

I have suggested that British policy should be based on tolerable stability of monetary conditions, by which I do not mean complete stabilisation of the level of general prices. It is, indeed, very much a moot point how far stabilisation of the general price-level is a desirable thing. It is obviously impossible to stabilise the prices of particular goods, because the relative costs of producing different commodities are constantly changing. If the general level of prices is to be stabilised, this means that, whenever the price of any particular commodity falls owing to cheaper production, the prices of other things must be increased. But is there any evidence that this is desirable? It is no doubt most desirable to eliminate as far as possible monetary causes of price fluctuation; but to do this, as far as it can be done, will not result in stable prices. It will leave prices free to fall as the efficiency of production is increased. Falling prices due to monetary causes have a depressing effect upon trade; but falling prices due to increased efficiency have no such effect. They are likely to stimulate demand, and to result, on the whole, in a better distribution of income. There may be times when it is wise, by monetary action, to let prices fall only by less than the full extent justified by improved efficiency; but these times are likely to be exceptional. Normally, the objective of a managed monetary system should be, not to stabilise prices, but to interfere with their free movement as little as possible, and to adjust the supply of money to the needs of the community at a price-level whose changes are determined by the efficiency of production.

Herein lies, above all, the case for national monetary standards as against an international standard. For undoubtedly, national efficiencies increase in different countries at very different rates, and this is one cause for the unsatisfactory operation of an international standard. It is doubtless true that, under such a standard, the world found ways of adjusting itself to these different rates of change; but this had to be done either by raising wages and other incomes in the more efficient country so as to increase its costs, or by reducing incomes in the less efficient countries so as to bring their costs down to its level—or, of course, by a combination of both methods. The first method is unobjectionable in itself; but the second is difficult, depressing, and a cause of great friction. But, under an international standard, it has in the end to be adopted, unless the more efficient country does in fact completely counteract the effects of its superiority in prices by raising incomes. Under a national monetary standard, on the other hand, the readjustment can be made far more easily, and with less loss to the wage-earner, by varying the rates of exchange. This was doubtless one of the factors which determined the abandonment of the gold standard by Great Britain.

The outcome of the foregoing argument is that it may be best for Great Britain neither to go back to the gold standard at all, nor to attempt to devise any other automatic international standard as a substitute for it, but rather to seek to make sterling the rallying-point for a number of other currencies, without aiming at any assured long-term fixity of relative value. If this solution is adopted, it involves a policy of monetary management in a double sense; for whatever authority is responsible for the currency will have to regulate both its external value and its domestic supply, with the supply of credit dependent upon it. The control of banking will thus come to be a matter needing a very high degree of economic common sense, and a very intimate knowledge of the needs and working of the industrial system both at home and abroad. A managed monetary system necessarily makes greater demands than a largely automatic system on the abilities of bankers. This fact leads some people to prefer the gold standard, despite its manifest disadvantages. But under present conditions the gold standard has become clearly unworkable in this country, and ceased to be automatic in many others. We have to have a managed system whether we like it or not; and we have therefore to do all in our power to ensure that it shall be managed in the best possible way.

This involves two things—competence in the managers, and a right objective. It is sometimes suggested that these two may conflict. For it is often urged that the most competent management will be secured by making the managers completely independent of political control. But, if this is done, how is it to be ensured that they shall pursue the good of the whole community, and not of some particular class or section? If the banks entrusted with the regulation of currency (and indirectly of the volume of credit as well) are socialised, it is suggested that they will be compelled by political pressure to act unsoundly from an economic standpoint. But if they are left in private hands, will they not pursue private rather than public interests? This pursuit need not take the form of setting out to earn excessive profits for themselves. The Bank of England, for example, certainly does not shape its policy mainly with a view to its own profits. It is, however, dominated by the powerful financial interests that make up what is called 'The City'; and it is prone to think in terms of the City's interest mainly, and to identify the City's interest with the nation's. Certainly, it is less regardful of the needs of industry than of those of finance.

Any such bias will be far more dangerous under a managed monetary system, which will give the Central Bank far more discretion than it has had in framing its policy. This constitutes a new and powerful argument in favour of socialisation.

But it is also true that a managed system will allow more scope for political pressure. How, then, can a socialised Central Bank be shielded from such pressure, and so enabled to pursue economic soundness in the general interest? The Labour Party's scheme for socialisation of the Bank of England proposed to equip it with a publicly appointed governing body on a representative basis, in order to ensure that the views of all important sections of the community should be represented. But it is doubtful if such a body, representing a number of different and sometimes divergent interests, would be technically or administratively competent. It would surely be better to entrust the actual management of the Bank to a very small body of highly expert full-time salaried officers, giving them an Advisory Council representative of various interests, as is done to some extent in the American Federal Reserve system. Or perhaps the Council might have rather more than advisory powers, provided that some method were established of adjusting differences between it and the full-time board of managers.

These managers, I think, as well as the members of the Council, would have to be appointed by the Government. But it does not follow that the Government should control their day-to-day operations. It would be better for the State to leave them in the main with a free hand, subject only to the power of the Government to remove them at any time, and to resolve by its own *fiat* disputes between them and the representative Council. It is true that this involves, in the last resort, the possibility of applying political pressure upon the Bank. But it would be a power difficult to use, and probably seldom invoked. Nor can the ultimate right to apply political pressure be denied under any system of democratic government. It exists even today, in Parliament's power to legislate for the Bank, and to prescribe its policy by legislation. Moreover, the people, in a matter affecting their interests as vitally as financial policy affects them, cannot be denied the final right to say what, in broad terms, the policy is to be. All that can be done is to make it difficult for intervention to take place over small matters.

It is, however, clear that, now that banking policy has come so largely under public discussion, and is generally known as a matter deeply affecting the economic welfare of society, the education of the public in the rudiments of monetary theory has become an urgent practical task. Our educational system has at least taught most of us that, in everyday affairs, two and two make four; but many people are still inclined to assume that in banking they can be made to make five if only the bankers will let them. A man knows that he cannot, by taking thought, add a cubit to his stature; but he is disposed to think that the banker could add a great many cubits to the volume of money and credit. Perhaps he could, if he went about it in the right way. But it is very necessary to get the public to understand, in broad terms, what is possible and what is not. Nor need this be an insuperably difficult task; for, while monetary theory is very intricate and controversial in its higher regions, the rudiments are not hard to understand. At any rate, democracy has to understand them, or fail; for a country's financial policy is just as important as its economic or its political policy in its effects on the general welfare. A community that does not govern itself financially is not a democracy in any full sense.

Great Britain will have, in the very near future, to decide what her future monetary policy is to be. And this is bound to be largely a political decision; for the matter has come decisively into the area of political controversy. One question is whether we are to go back to the gold standard; a second is whether we are to bring the future regulation of our money under public control. On both these questions the public, as well as the experts, are bound to have opinions; and it is vital to get these opinions as well informed as they can be made. The plain man will never master the intricacies of monetary theory; but there is no reason why he should not be as competent to judge about money as about most other economic questions—about tariffs, for example, or State control of investment. He may not understand these matters well enough now; but he can be helped to understand them. Nor can he be denied, in fact, the right to control or influence financial policy, whether he understands or not. That is why it is so necessary to help him to understand; for otherwise he is likely to go whoring after one crank upon another—and there is no field in which cranks are so numerous, or so perverse. Popular ignorance is the crank's opportunity: so, in this matter too, we must set out to educate our masters.

## V

## WHY AND HOW WE MUST SOCIALISE THE BANKS

THE case for the socialisation of banking rests upon two grounds —the need to control in the public interest both the total volume of credit and its use. The volume of credit is a matter almost exclusively for the Central Bank, which also controls the currency. But the use of the available supply of credit is determined mainly by the Joint Stock Banks, which are the chief actual lenders of it to the business world. Accordingly, the public control of credit policy involves the socialisation of both the Bank of England and the Joint Stock Banks.

Credit is, fundamentally, of far more importance than currency; for variations in the demand for currency arise mainly out of the issue of credit. It is true that currency appears to be the basis on which the structure of credit is built, and that banks regulate the amount of their lendings mainly by the amount of currency upon which they can call. But, for all that, currency is the less important. The supply of currency ought to conform to the supply of credit, and not *vice versa*; and the supply of credit ought to be determined by the needs and possibilities of business, and not by the supply of currency. An important part of the case against the gold standard is that it makes credit conform to currency, instead of currency to credit.

The needs and possibilities of business are measured by its ability to deliver goods without increased cost, or with only such increase, if any, as is necessary in order to absorb unemployed capital and labour. Under a rightly managed monetary system, credit would be issued in quantities sufficient to meet business needs, and the relative values of different currencies would be left to fluctuate in accordance with the varying price-levels resulting from differences in national efficiency. Credit policy would be managed in accordance with national needs; currency would follow credit; and exchange rates would be governed finally by national differences in the purchasing power of money. This cannot happen under the gold standard, because it determines the supply of currency in accordance with the available stock of gold, and so compels credit to conform to currency.

Even now, when Great Britain is off the gold standard, there remains in force a fiduciary limit to the amount of currency that can be issued. Currency thus continues to govern credit. We have suspended the free export of gold; and we have in effect no gold reserve at all, for what we have is owed to France and the United States on account of the loans their banks made us in the crisis of 1931. But our supply of currency is still subject to a maximum fiduciary limit: indeed, the possible supply has become more rigid owing to the destruction of the free market for gold. This is defended on the ground that it is necessary in order to prevent inflation. But it may achieve this at the cost of preventing prosperity as well.

The danger of inflation really depends on credit policy, rather than on the supply of currency. The increased issue of currency would cause inflation, under British conditions, only if it led to an unwise issue of credit. If more credit were so issued as to increase production and sales without raising costs, there would be no inflation at all. If costs were raised only enough to absorb unemployed capital and labour, there would be no dangerous inflation, unless costs had to be raised so far as to cause a depreciation in the pound, which would make it difficult to purchase necessary imports. The object of national credit policy should be to bring into effective use all productive resources that can be used at a cost not so high as to cause a dangerous rise in prices.

Ever since the Bank Charter Act of 1844, the aim of British monetary policy has been to make the regulation of the supply of money as nearly as possible automatic. Before the war, when actual gold sovereigns formed the bulk of the cash circulation, supplemented only by a small quantity of Bank of England notes, the supply of currency was determined by the available supply of gold, which thus indirectly determined the supply of credit as well. It was held that the inflow and outflow of gold would in effect ensure satisfactory regulation; for a shortage of gold would force domestic prices down, and so cause gold to flow in, with the object of buying things cheap, whereas an oversupply of gold would raise prices, and so cause gold to flow out, in order to buy goods elsewhere, where they were cheaper. The movements of gold were thus relied on to keep British prices in equilibrium with prices in other countries, the means whereby this was done being the expansion or contraction of credit resulting from the plenty or shortage of gold.

Under these conditions, the Bank of England was conceived as having a fairly simple function. Its task was simply to watch gold movements, and to correct them where necessary by raising or lowering Bank Rate, and so contracting or expanding credit. Its function was purely passive; for it had only to respond to forces which it did not initiate. This type of reflex action by the Bank needed no very high qualities, and aroused no serious controversies, as long as the general principles of action were unquestioned. Accordingly, on this view it did not seem to matter much whether the Bank was publicly or privately owned, and amenable or not amenable to any form of political control; whether its directors were drawn from industry, or from the City, or from any other source; and whether they took up a national or an international point of view.

Of course, I am not suggesting that the Bank's functions ever were purely automatic. For even then, while it acted only as the interpreter of long-run forces arising in the business world, it did actively intervene to influence short-term fluctuations in exchange rates, and to check gold movements by other means than the raising or lowering of Bank Rate. But these activities were of secondary importance; and it remains true that before the war both currency and credit conditions were usually thought of as mainly self-regulating. There were advocates of a managed monetary system even then; but they had little influence.

The suspension of the gold standard and the introduction of Treasury Notes during the war radically altered the position of the Bank; for they removed altogether the automatic limits on the issue of currency and credit. It is true that exchange movements were still there as barometers of relative monetary conditions. But war-time foreign exchanges were largely unreal, because they were often artificially pegged, as in the case of the sterling-dollar rate. Correctives against exchange depreciation could still be to some extent applied; but their application was no longer in any sense automatic.

After the war, there was in financial circles a widespread desire to get back, as quickly and completely as possible, to the old conditions of automatic regulation; and, step by step, Great Britain, in common with other countries, went back to the gold standard. It was, however, plainly out of the question to restore the actual gold circulation; and the use of paper money had therefore to be made compatible with the automatic regulation of the quantity of currency. After the gradual scaling down of the note circulation by Treasury action over a period of years, this was finally done by handing back the issue of notes to the Bank of England, subject to a fixed fiduciary limit, beyond which all notes issued must have a pound for pound backing in gold. Power was indeed taken to extend the fiduciary issue in cases of emergency, by agreement between the Bank and the Treasury; but apart from this the system was made as nearly self-regulating as possible. The fixed fiduciary issue was to guard this country against inflation, as the use of gold sovereigns had guarded it in the past; and once more the permitted supply of currency was to dictate the available volume of credit.

In practice, however, there was under the new conditions a good deal more management of credit than before the war. The Bank had learned to use open market operations—the purchase and sale of securities—far more freely as a supplementary instrument to Bank Rate in affecting the volume of credit; and there was also far more attempt to check gold movements and to influence the movement of short-term funds by consultation among the Central Banks of the leading countries. This was made necessary by the great increase in the scale of international indebtedness, the uneven flow of French and American overseas investment, and the tendency of gold to move to France and the United States. While automatic action was still regarded as the ideal, practical necessities enforced far more interference by the Central Banks. But the Banks, even when they interfered, repudiated responsibility for doing more than interpret 'natural' monetary movements. Indeed, under the gold standard, their powers were limited for; while their resources often allowed them to counteract an inconvenient short-term tendency, they were helpless against one that was large and prolonged.

The experience, and the inconveniences, of the new conditions gave, outside banking circles, a great impetus to the demand for a more completely managed monetary system. The Central Banks had actually carried management to lengths which their protagonists had treated as impossible before the war; and their critics now urged that they ought to carry it much further, so as to make the supply of credit more responsive to the needs of the industrial system. The apostles of the Central Banks replied that this could not be done without inflation—which meant, in Great Britain at any rate, that it could not be done without setting in action forces which would drive us off the gold standard by raising prices and causing an outflow of gold. The critics answered that, in reality, no gold reserve was needed against the issue of notes, and only enough gold needed at all to meet possible demands for export. We could therefore afford to lose a good deal of gold; and there was no reason against an increased issue of credit (and of currency to match) provided that the effect was not permanently to raise prices. They held that, while there might be a time-lag before the increased supply of goods to be created by expansion of credits came into the market, and prices might tend to rise during this period, before long the increased goods would balance the increased supply of money, and prices come back to the old level. Gold would therefore flow out only for a time, and might flow back later. We could well afford to take the risk in order to stimulate industry.

The Bank of England remained sceptical. As the guardian of the gold standard, it was not prepared to take risks, or to admit that we could afford to lose gold at all. It therefore kept money rates high, restricted credit, and promptly checked any tendency towards expansion by selling securities in the market. It continued to follow this course until the world slump made the maintenance of dear money impossible, and cut down the demand for credits even below the restricted supply. And even then the Bank, in common with the Treasury, continued to oppose all plans for expansion by State action, based on a national development loan. Exchange stability and the maintenance of the stock of gold remained throughout the dominant considerations in the minds of the Bank and the Treasury.

Naturally, this policy aroused a storm of criticism; for it came near to condemning British industry to permanent depression. If other countries boomed, Great Britain had to keep her interest rates high, and so restrict credit, in order to avoid loss of gold or short-term funds. If other countries slumped, with reactions upon us, nothing must be done to counteract depression, again for fear of provoking a 'flight from the pound'.

Two possibilities emerge. Either the Bank of England was right in holding that we could not keep on the gold standard except by continuous credit restriction; or its critics were right in holding that an expansionist policy, while it might have caused a temporary outflow of gold, would not in the long run have raised prices or menaced the gold standard. If the Bank was right, its rightness constituted a very strong argument for going off the gold standard. If its critics were right, this would probably not be necessary. In either case, it seemed to a great many people that the best course was to embark on a policy of expansion, while remaining on the gold standard, and go off gold only if in the event this proved to be the necessary sequel.

The critics, of course, held that the trouble was mainly due to our wrong policy in going back to the gold standard *at pre-war parity* in 1925, as this had overvalued the pound in relation to its purchasing power. They differed on the question whether, having done this, we could afford to stick to it, and to carry through the requisite readjustments in our business costs, either by lowering wages and capital charges, or by increasing the efficiency of production. The possibility of our expanding credit *and* staying on the gold standard clearly depended on our success in achieving this.

In the event, we did not try an expansionist policy and we did not succeed in lowering our costs. Indeed, our costs rose, relatively to those of other countries, which both cut wages and increased efficiency faster than we. In the end, we were driven off the gold standard, partly because our costs were too high, but mainly because of adverse movements of short-term funds which were a result of the world slump.

The question then arose whether, in going off gold, we had freed our hands at last for the adoption of an expansionist policy. But the official view was now even more strongly hostile than ever before. We could no longer lose gold, and the Bank was no longer under a fixed obligation to maintain the exchanges; but prospective Budget deficits caused a demand that the State should restrict its expenditure at the cost of intensifying depression, and the fear of a further flight from the pound caused intense anxiety to prevent the depreciation from going to any greater lengths than were clearly unavoidable. Off the gold standard, as on it, the country had to endure a restrictive credit policy. Interest rates were raised high in order to check the outflow of short-term funds.

It is true that credit restriction, as such, was not very seriously felt; because there was little desire among business men to expand their operations. They grumbled at the high interest, rather than at the scarcity of credit. The stimulus to exports proved to be disappointing, in face of deepening world depression. Only the State could have embarked on a policy of national development; and that was the last thing the new National Government was likely to do. Both it and the local authorities were ruthlessly cutting down capital expenditure in the name of national economy.

The mere departure from the gold standard has not, therefore, either given us cheap money or led to an expansionist policy. It has actually left money dearer and made expansion far harder, wherever it needs the aid of the State or the Bank.

Either this permanent restrictive policy is inevitable, or it is not. If it is, no change in the ownership or control of the Bank of England will help to alter it; for a socialised Bank would have to behave in the same way. But, if it is not, it may require a reorganisation of the Bank to get the possible alternative policy pursued.

What is the alternative, if there is one? Under present conditions, a mere lowering of bank interest would be unlikely to produce much result; for there is little willingness on the part of business to expand its operations, even if credit were cheaper and more abundant. More abundant credit would be of use only if, at the same time, the State took action, by way of a policy of national development, to bring it into play. But the State, on its side, could not successfully pursue such a policy if the Bank continued to restrict credit. The two things go together—State action to increase the volume of business, and Bank action to provide additional credit. Credit expansion would be futile with the National Government in its present mood.

But could the State, in its present financial difficulties, afford a development policy? And could the Bank expand credit without causing a dangerous further fall in the pound? I believe the State could, because it would be more than repaid by industrial revival at home, and because it could raise the money on favourable terms, if the Bank were expanding credit at the same time. But could the Bank? In other words, would credit expansion raise prices and cause a further fall in the pound, even perhaps to the extent of making it difficult for us to pay for necessary imports?

I believe it could, but only on condition that the destination and use of the increased credit should be kept under very strict control. If the supply of credit were simply expanded, and the Joint Stock Banks left free to apply it as they chose, or if State development schemes were arranged without a very strict regard to their effects on the demand for imports, credit expansion would raise prices and would cause the pound to fall. In other words, the policy of expanded credit involves the closest coordination of policy, under unified direction, between the State, the Bank of England, and the Joint Stock Banks. The State has to set development going, the Bank of England has to ensure an adequate supply of credit, and the Joint Stock Banks have to see that the additional credit goes to the right people, and not to the wrong. Moreover, the State and the banks, with the power to give or refuse orders and credit as their weapons, have to take stringent measures in order to prevent prices from being raised.

These are the indispensable conditions of a successful expansionist policy at the present time. They are difficult conditions at best; but they are impossible as long as the State, the Bank of England, and the Joint Stock Banks are separate agencies, under different control, and without a unified policy. This is, in a nutshell, the case for comprehensive socialisation of the banking system.

Nor is this all; for there is another important factor in the situation—a fourth agency that must be unified, in matters of policy, with the other three. The State, if it is to pursue a policy of national development, must control investment as well as credit. The supply of long-term capital, as well as of short-term funds, must be brought within the scope of the development scheme; and this involves control over home, equally with overseas, capital issues. The socialisation of all the hundreds of issuing houses—many of them responsible, in years, only for a single issue—is clearly out of the question; and it would probably be wisest, in this case, to start a totally new institution, a National Investment Board, with wide powers both to invest existing public funds and to borrow new capital directly from the public, and to authorise or reject (and in certain cases promote or guarantee) new capital issues by other bodies. But I have discussed elsewhere this project of a National Investment Board; and I do not propose to deal with it further now.

I hold, then, that, unless we are prepared to envisage the permanent continuance of a restrictive credit policy, we must set to work to build up a co-ordinated organisation for the promotion and financing of a big public policy of economic development—in effect, a National Plan for Great Britain. But any such plan involves the effective public control of the banking system, as well as of the machinery of capital investment. I know that, in the past, we have been told again and again that it is vitally necessary to avoid any political interference with the banking system, which must be left free to do its highly technical work in its own way. But it is now clear that banking and politics cannot be divorced, and that, unless the State takes steps to control the bankers, the bankers will inevitably control the State. Banking policy, whether we like it or not, is a most important part of politics; and, unless the politicians and the banks pull the same way, and follow a common policy, it will be not the banker but the politician who will find his schemes brought to nothing as soon as international complications arise.

It is not necessary to attribute this situation to any deliberate and carefully matured conspiracy of the bankers against the public. The power has fallen into their hands by the logic of events, far more than they have consciously planned to make it their own. But the result is the same. Statesmen attempting to govern within the limits of a national policy are helpless in face of the vicissitudes of the world financial system, which is the bankers' province.

There are in this matter at present three distinct schools of thought among those who agree upon the necessity of drastic changes in our banking policy. One of these schools holds that the powers possessed by the State are already adequate, without any direct measure of socialisation, if they are rightly used. The problem, it is said, is to secure a management of currency and credit designed to make possible a fuller development of our economic resources through cheaper and more abundant money; and this object can be pursued with ease and safety now that we are temporarily at least rid of the ever-present fear of a drain of gold. The suspension of the gold standard is, on this showing, the opportunity for an expansionist policy; and it is urged that a Chancellor who firmly presses for this policy can secure its adoption through the Bank of England without any direct measure of socialisation. But, as we have seen, the departure from the gold standard is at present leading to a very different result—to a more intensely restrictive policy on the part of the State and to the maintenance of high interest rates by the Bank. Nor is escape from these conditions possible unless both the State and the Bank unite in following an expansionist policy under co-ordinated control.

A second school of thought urges, with the same objects in mind, the complete socialisation of the Bank of England. The Bank, it is urged, is at present a private corporation dominated by the financiers of the City of London, and prone to take the point of view of the City rather than of industry or of the community as a whole. The personnel of the Bank's directors, it is argued, needs substantial amendment; and the Bank itself, wielding so great a power for good or ill in our international dealings as well as at home, ought to be a responsible institution under full and direct public control. This has been in the past the policy of the Labour Party, which has advocated the socialisation of the Bank of England, and its reconstitution as a public corporation under the State, with a governing body representative of industry and of the consuming public as well as of commerce and finance.

But there is a third school of thought which holds strongly that such a measure will not go nearly far enough, and will largely fail of its effect unless it is extended to cover the great Joint Stock Banks as well. This school points out that the problem to be faced includes not only the reform of monetary policy, in order to secure a more abundant supply of credit, but also an effective guidance of this credit into the right channels of economic development. Under our present financial system, as we have seen, the Bank of England's policy is concerned mainly with the total volume of credit, which it regulates primarily in accordance with international considerations, whereas the Joint Stock Banks are concerned with the distribution of this volume of credit among the several applicants for bank advances. Socialisation of the Bank of England would, to a great extent, give the State control over the volume of credit; and it would doubtless also enable the State to influence, up to a point, the policy of the Joint Stock Banks in its distribution. But it would not give the State any direct or at all complete control in this sphere; nor would it enable the State to tackle effectively the problem of those 'frozen credits' which have arisen out of the banks' past advances to industries now in a state of depression.

Now, the fundamental purpose of controlling the financial

machine is not only to secure a currency system managed on expansionist principles in conjunction with a State control of investment at home, as well as abroad, but also to secure effective leverage for a concerted policy of industrial reorganisation and development. For years past we have been watching the failure of the great basic industries to reorganise themselves, or to get free from the masses of bank indebtedness that are weighing them down and keeping up their costs of production. The number of businesses virtually in pawn to the banks can be reckoned in thousands; and clearly the policy of the banks, both in dealing with frozen credits and debentures and in making fresh advances to the depressed industries, is bound to be a very important factor in the work of reorganisation.

Most people will agree that these frozen credits ought to be separated sharply from the ordinary short-term advances made by the banks, and somehow funded in the hands of a separate corporation, or series of corporations, on terms which will relieve the pressure upon industry, under the condition that industry, in return for this relief, takes effective steps to set its house in order. No less clearly, the granting of current advances ought to be closely connected with this policy, and made conditional in the same way. If the State—as seems necessary in view of the prolonged failure of business to reorganise itself—is to be the primary agent in this work of industrial reconstruction, it is surely indispensable that the State shall have direct control of that part of the financial system through which the reorganised industries will get credit, as well as of the liquidation of the frozen credits already in existence. For these reasons, socialisation of the Joint Stock Banks seems, from the standpoint of national economic planning and development, the necessary complement to socialisation of the Bank of England.

This does not mean that either the Bank of England or the Joint Stock Banks ought to be taken over and run by the Treasury or on the lines of a Government department; for, as I have long urged, that form of socialisation is out of date. What is needed is to reorganise the Bank of England as a public corporation, similar to the Central Electricity Board, with a body of directors nominated and removable by the Government, and so constituted as to include representatives of industry and labour as well as of finance. I should be disposed to favour a small full-time governing body, broadly representative of these types of experience, aided by a larger court of governors drawn directly from each of the main groups concerned in the efficient working of the Bank. Day-to-day political interference should be kept down to the absolute minimum; but there should be no doubt concerning the final control of the State through its power to appoint or remove the governors. The socialised Bank's employees would not be Civil Servants, any more than the employees of the Central Electricity Board or the B.B.C. are; but in matters of high policy it would be fully amenable to public control.

The Joint Stock Banks could be dealt with on similar lines, and reorganised in much the same way as public corporations under State control. For the present, in order to reduce changes in structure to the minimum and to avoid the creation of an instrument so large as to be unwieldy, it would be best to leave the 'Big Five' in separate existence, only equipping them with new Boards of Directors appointed by the State in such a way as to ensure the closest contact and co-operation among them and between them as a group and the reformed Treasury and Bank of England. There has been far too little contact between the Central Bank and the Joint Stock Banks hitherto. Under the new system, they ought to work as closely related parts of a single unified machine, in constant touch with the needs of industry and commerce as well as of finance.

At that point, for the time being, direct socialisation of our existing financial institutions had best stop short, though it may need to go farther at a later stage. Bill brokers can be left, as now, to borrow from the Joint Stock Banks, or, on occasions of stringency, from the Bank of England, with the assurance that, if the banks are in the hands of the State, policy in financing the business of the broker will be effectively governed by considerations of the public interest. Much the same conditions apply to acceptance houses, except that these have larger resources of their own, and therefore rather more independence. The necessary degree of control over them could, however, be secured if the banks themselves were in public hands.

Broadly, then, our aims in bringing the financial machine under effective public control will be threefold. First, we must set out to secure that our international financial transactions on short term shall be so managed as at once to keep our foreign exchange position under satisfactory control and to ensure an adequate supply of credit and currency for the needs of domestic industry and commerce—'adequate' here meaning sufficient to permit a policy of industrial expansion leading to increased employment to be pursued. This is mainly a matter of the policy of the Central Bank, to be brought under public control by the socialisation of the Bank of England. The second aim is to ensure the best possible use of the available supply of credit in order to increase production and employment in the industries capable of expansion, and at the same time to liquidate speedily the top-heavy interest burdens on industry which are a legacy from the difficulties of recent years. This is to be achieved mainly by the socialisation of the Joint Stock Banks, accompanied by a drastic writing down of their 'frozen' assets. The third aim is to stimulate home investment, and at the same time to limit overseas investment as nearly as possible to the real surplus available for this purpose, without cutting off such overseas loans (to India, for example) as are indispensable if we are to continue to receive the interest on our past lendings.

Briefly, I conclude that the indispensable first steps towards this threefold policy are the creation of a National Investment Board and the complete socialisation of central and deposit banking—that is, of the Bank of England and of the 'Big Five' Joint Stock Banks. Unless at least these things are done, and done simultaneously, chaos is likely to result. For, if we try to nationalise only the Bank of England, we shall only start a disastrous tug-of-war for power between it and the Joint Stock Banks, whereas, if we socialise both the Bank and the 'Big Five', the control of the rest of the financial machine, while it presents big technical difficulties, will at once become a manageable problem. Nor will the State be able to take effective steps towards the rationalisation of industry until it has both capital in its hands to invest in the reorganisation of business and full control over the Joint Stock Banks as the providers of credit. On all accounts, therefore, socialisation of the key positions of the banking system is the necessary next step towards an effective policy of national planning and public control over economic affairs vital to the public interest.

## VI

## THE WORLD ECONOMIC OUTLOOK FROM THE STANDPOINT OF LABOUR

IN this paper dealing with the world economic outlook, attention will be given, less to the immediate prospects of the next year, or two or three years, than to certain underlying tendencies of the present economic system, and especially of the new forms which it is rapidly assuming under our eyes. The study of trade fluctuations, which are for the world as a whole the most potent cause of unemployment and distress, is a matter of vital importance, to which many books and papers have been, and many more will have to be, devoted. I shall have little to say of such fluctuations here, except as they are germane to the narrower purpose which I have in view. This purpose is to consider how, and how far, the measures which are now being taken in every developed country for the reorganisation of industry are likely to react on the volume of production and employment.

These measures, though they take many different forms, are commonly grouped together under the name of 'rationalisation'. As far as they are relevant to our present study, they include:

1. The improvement of *productive efficiency* by the provision of more *efficient* plant and machinery; the better planning of factories with a view to the integration of related processes; the elimination of unnecessary fuel consumption and transport; the simplification and intensification of the labour process, as well as the provision of more hygienic factory conditions and, where necessary, better vocational selection and training; the improvement of the technique of factory management and job control; the standardisation of products and the elimination of unnecessary variations and processes in their manufacture; and

the more rapid scrapping of both things and men in the light of the most recent technological knowledge.

2. The elimination of such forms of national competition as are inconvenient to the organisers of business, either by complete amalgamation or by the conclusion of working arrangements between firms concerning the amount and character of the production of each unit, the prices to be charged to various types of consumers, the buying of materials or auxiliary services, the development of markets and the actual methods of sale.

3. The attempt to ration production in accordance with the economic demand both of the market as a whole, and of particular markets within it, both by the methods described in (2) above, and by the conclusion of similar arrangements on an international scale; and the consequent growth of business organisations essentially international in character, and not readily amenable to control by the nations across whose frontiers they operate.

It is not suggested that these three groups of tendencies between them comprise a full statement of the policy of rationalisation, or, on the other hand, that they are likely to be applied in all their aspects anywhere at one and the same time. But they do stand, broadly, for three very marked trends in present-day economic organisation; and they do, taken as a whole, raise certain questions of paramount importance to the working classes and of very direct bearing on the probable future course of world trade.

The first group of tendencies, centred round the processes of production, clearly leads directly and in the first instance to the elimination of 'surplus' labour and to radical changes in the labour process itself. The general effects produced by it are, in the first place, a reduction in the absolute quantity of labour used up in the production of a given quantity of commodities, and, in the second place, a change in the personnel employed. The absolute quantity of labour is reduced because more of the work of production is transferred to the machine, because the machine itself is made to run faster, and because the new plants are commonly equipped on a basis which assumes their continuous operation, so that the effect of each in 'saving' labour is spread over a larger number of workers. It is, indeed, a common phenomenon that the most up-to-date and costly plants, which have the lowest costs of production when they are running full time, cannot be made to pay at all if they are compelled to work on a part-time basis.

Besides this reduction in the absolute quantity of labour needed for the production of a given quantity of goods, the first group of tendencies described above effects a change in the personnel employed. Certain sorts of skill, which have been of 'key' importance in older methods of production, become altogether obsolete, or are needed only in greatly reduced amount. New types of machine dexterity, which can in most cases be quickly acquired, have to be developed; and there emerge here and there new really skilled trades, especially in connection with the maintenance of the new machines. At the lower end of the scale, a good deal of purely unskilled labour is eliminated by the development of highly mechanised transport within the works, as well as by new grouping of factory processes and buildings which reduces the amount of such transport needing to be done. In general, the relative quantities of highly skilled and of purely unskilled labour are decreased, while the relative quantity of semi-skilled labour grows. This tendency has, of course, been at work for a long time past; but the effect of the new forces is greatly to speed up its operation.

Now, these changes in the character of the labour force have very direct reactions on working-class conditions and on the Trade Union Movement. The reduction in the demand for certain classes of skilled work leads to the speedy dismissal of a large body of older craftsmen; and most of these are no longer adaptable enough to learn new trades, and are, therefore, liable to be flung upon the scrap-heap almost as much as the old machines which they used to tend. The younger craftsmen, who might be more adaptable, tend to be retained in their jobs when the older men are discharged, with the result that the unemployed come to include a large proportion of men who could not be readily transferred to alternative employments even if these were available.

Moreover, at the other end of the scale, the men who have become used to doing purely unskilled work are hardly more adaptable than the fully skilled. They will not, for the most part, make good machine operators, capable of staying the pace in a modern works run on up-to-date lines; and, as with the *craftsmen*, the older they are the less easily can they make the change. It is, therefore, not surprising to find severe unemployment among the older labourers as well as among the older craftsmen. The craftsman's trouble is that he cannot get a fresh job at the trade he has learnt; the labourer's is that the demand for unskilled, as against semi-skilled, labour in industry generally is on the decline.

The effect of all this is that, in the countries which have been undergoing the most rapid transformation of industrial methods, the unemployed include a large body of seriously unadaptable workers; and this undoubtedly makes harder the expansion of new industries to take the place of the old ones whose total demand for labour is no longer advancing in proportion to the growth of population. This point, however, cannot be discussed satisfactorily until we have considered the effect of the remaining tendencies in industrial organisation on the demand for labour and on the course of production. For their influence is, for the present, the all-important factor.

The saving of labour and *the making of industry more efficient on its productive side* ought obviously to be sheer gain, provided only that *greater efficiency* is secured not by taking more out of labour, but by a real reduction of the quantity of labour required to produce a given quantity of goods. Each reduction of this sort ought to be accompanied by a corresponding growth in demand, more production in one industry balancing more production in another, and creating in each either higher money wages or lower prices which will cause the same wages to command more goods. Even if productive efficiency expands in different industries at different rates, this ought not to cause unemployment, but to result, subject to some friction and to some time-lag, in a readjustment of relative prices and of the relative quantity of labour employed in each industry concerned.

The world ought as a result to enjoy the consumption of a

larger aggregate of goods; and there ought to be no limit to the expansion of consuming power save that set by the world's preference of more leisure to greater economic wealth.

But everyone is all too painfully aware that this is not what actually happens. It is true, indeed, that the quantity of goods produced in the world as a whole has continued of late years to increase; and, though the rate of increase has been very different for different countries—for the United States and for Great Britain, for example—there has been an increase of some size in practically every separate country. This increase, however, has been, especially in the older countries and above all in Great Britain, far less than it might have been. Idle plant, unemployed labour, and the part-time use of many factories and of many workers, are ample evidence of the great resources of productive power that are lying unused. Nor is this true only of the period of exceptional depression which has followed upon the American collapse of 1929, upon the steady rise in the goods value of gold and on the fall in the price of silver, with its effects in the purchasing power of the Far East. The depression of the past few months has added greatly to the numbers of the unemployed, not only by its direct effects on the volume of trade, but also by speeding up the pace of rationalisation and the supersession of older by newer works and workers. But unemployment was with the world, and, above all, with Great Britain, as an economic problem of the first magnitude long before the American collapse occurred. It is to the causes, and the probable future, of this persistent form of the disease of unemployment, rather than to the present world epidemic of under-production and distress, that I am seeking to direct attention.

This brings me to the second group of tendencies outlined at the beginning of my paper. The advocates of rationalisation are always careful to stress the point that it is a matter, not merely of reorganising the methods of production within a single works or firm, or even of the repetition of this process in the case of hundreds or thousands of firms at the same time, but essentially of treating each industry, or a large part of it, as a unit, and planning the form, methods and amounts of production for the industry as a whole. Any such planning must, of course, involve, if not actual amalgamations, at the least close working arrangements among the hitherto competing businesses within the industry or group concerned. Indeed, such amalgamations or arrangements have been so marked a feature of the reorganisation of industry in recent years that in the minds of many they are regarded as the distinguishing signs of rationalisation quite apart from any changes in the methods of actual production. Rationalisation, we are sometimes told, is simply a new name for the trustification or cartellisation of industry. The old names had a bad sound; they were unpopular with the consuming public and liable to provoke anti-trust legislation. A new name, with a compelling and virtuous association of ideas attaching to it, was therefore needed; and what could be better than Rationalisation—for who will dare to set himself up against Reason itself?

There is certainly a measure of truth in this view; but it is none the less misleading. That rationalisation leads to, and involves, the drastic limitation of past forms of competition, the creation of large amalgamations and still larger working agreements and cartels—indeed, most of the familiar phenomena associated with trusts and combines—is, of course, an undeniable fact. The distinction is that rationalisation, in idea if not always in execution, contemplates the use of combination in order to make easier the application of new labour-saving methods of production, simplification and standardisation of processes and products, better grouping of works and processes *from the standpoint of efficient manufacture*, and the rest of the technical developments mentioned as belonging to the first of the three groups of tendencies specified above.

The fact, however, remains that a feature common to most schemes of rationalisation or the like is the coming together of a number of producing firms previously in competition one with another into a group in some degree co-operative and conscious of its unity. This coming together is in many cases essential to the realisation of the productive economies hoped for from the scheme. It may, for example, be necessary, in order to take advantage of the most efficient methods of production, to equip a single factory for the making of a large quantity of a single uniform product. The making of this product may previously have been divided between a number of separate firms, each making other goods as well. It may now be agreed that one factory should specialise wholly on the production of one class of goods, while another confines itself to some other class of product, with the idea of reducing costs by turning out the whole supply of each commodity at the works best equipped for making it, and of allowing this or these works to run full time by concentrating the entire supply in its hands. Or, where a number of plants have been working short time it may seem desirable to close down altogether those with the highest costs, in order to concentrate production at those which remain, and thus allow them to obtain the increasing returns dependent on full-time working. No one will deny that these are very common phenomena of schemes of rationalised production. The closing of works and the specialisation to particular classes of products can be brought about most easily when, as in the chemical industry, the previously separate firms have been completely amalgamated into a single unified business. But they can also be pushed some way, by means of transferable output quotas, central compensation funds, and the like, even where the firms retain their separate financial basis and come together only on the basis of a limited agreement, as in a cartel.

The principal question which I wish to raise in this paper is concerned with the effects of amalgamations, or arrangements of this order, on the course of production and employment. Is it, or is it not, the case that the conclusion of arrangements designed in part to secure more efficient and cheaper production may also result in the drastic limitation of output, and accordingly in a drastic reduction in the volume of employment?

Let us consider first what happens in a free market when there are a number of separate competing producers. Let us assume that, in such a market, the price-level is tending to fall, owing to monetary causes quite apart from the conditions of production, and that this falling level of prices is acting as a check to the expansion of trade. In such circumstances competition compels each producer to bring down his prices in order to keep his accustomed share of the total trade. If this results in bringing selling prices below costs for the less efficient firms and in keeping them below costs for a substantial time, these firms gradually disappear from the market, and lose their trade to their rivals. In these days, even apart from the factor of combination, the process of squeezing out takes a good deal longer than it used to take, especially when the banks go on lending to weak firms instead of using their power to force them out of existence. But in default of combination, the process is bound to operate in the long run; and, in the meantime, prices are kept down by competition, and there is no possibility of deliberate restriction of output. Each business must, in its own interest, struggle to get all the trade it can; and production will accordingly be pressed to the limits of what the market will absorb, even if prices have to be lowered sharply in order to achieve this.

The advent of combination, and still more of the special forms of combination most closely associated with the rationalisation of industry, radically changes the situation. For now, within the national field at least (we will come to the international aspect of the problem in a moment), the question of the amount to be produced becomes a matter for concerted control by the entire industry. At any given price, a certain quantity of products can be sold, the quantity varying inversely with the price according to a formula which can usually be at any rate roughly determined.

The industry, having either output or price under its control —for it can determine either, but not both—is in a position either to fix a schedule of prices from which the amounts that can be marketed will follow almost as a matter of course, or to fix a volume of output from which the prices obtainable will follow in much the same way. High output will mean low prices; low prices will allow more to be produced, and high prices less. It is still for the consumer to say how much he will pay for a given volume of output, or how much he will buy at a given price; but the given volume, or the given price, can now be consciously settled by the associated producers, who will, of course, fix on the price or output level that promises to be most advantageous to themselves.

## VI. WORLD ECONOMIC OUTLOOK

Is it not likely, under these conditions, that it will often pay the producing firms best, or at any rate seem likely to pay them best, to sell a smaller quantity of goods at a high price rather than a larger quantity at a lower price? As long as the separate firms were in competition, this would probably not have paid them, even if they had been able to achieve it, because the sharing out of the market among them all would have caused each works to be under-employed, and would thus have raised its costs. The higher price obtained would, in many branches of production, have been more than offset by the higher costs of making the goods. But the unified industries of which we are now speaking are differently placed. Instead of running all their works part time, they can scrap or close some of them altogether, and concentrate the whole output where it can be produced at the lowest cost. The smaller number of works, running full time, can then achieve, on the basis of a smaller total output from the industry as a whole, the entire benefit of increasing return due to large-scale operation, subject only to such costs or compensation charges as have to be incurred in respect of the works which are no longer allowed to produce.

It seems to me clear beyond dispute that the growth of combination in forms which make this situation possible is likely to cause many employers to adopt the policy of restricting output and holding up prices instead of bringing prices down in the hope of selling more goods. Of course, this policy will work out differently according to the differing elasticity of the total demand for various classes of goods; but it is likely to operate most strongly in the very large group of goods for which the demand is neither highly elastic nor highly inelastic in terms of price. And, wherever it does operate, it is certain to exert a powerful effect upon the volume of employment.

I am suggesting, in fact, that rationalisation, as it is practised at present, is reacting unfavourably in two distinct ways on the volume of employment, whatever may be its beneficial reactions in other respects. It is, in the first place, diminishing directly the amount of labour required for the production of a given volume of goods, both by improving the technique of manufacture and by causing output to be concentrated in those places where least labour will be needed. And it is, in the second place, tending to restrict artificially the total quantity of goods produced, and so refusing any outlet through increased production to the labour displaced by the first method.

To the extent to which this is true, it follows that the labour which is displaced by rationalisation, as well as the great bulk of the new labour that is flowing yearly into industry, must find employment, if at all, outside the sphere of the rationalised trades. But there is no force at work likely to cause these other trades to absorb, at any rate permanently, more than their previous proportion of the national labour supply. Temporarily, such forces may have been at work. Indeed, it is probable that the very great increase in the numbers employed in distribution, due largely to changes in the exactingness of consumers' demand for delivery, wrapping, politeness in shop assistants, and so on, and the rapid development of road transport, have, for the time, diminished the effects of the discarding of labour by those productive industries which have been altering their methods of production and organisation in the ways outlined earlier in this paper. But there are clearly limits to the numbers of people who can be employed in transporting and handling as distributors a restricted volume of goods; and the recent contractions of employment on the railways, and diminishing rates of increase in the other branches of transport and in the distributive trades, seem to indicate that the point of saturation has been almost reached.

Whither, then, are the disemployed to betake themselves? It is easy enough to talk about the rise of new industries, and the need for large-scale measures of industrial transference. It is not at all easy to say what these new industries are to be, or how they are to be persuaded to grow at anything like the requisite rate. Nor is it at all clear that, where new industries do grow at present, they are more likely to represent a fresh demand for labour than a transference of demand from some established branch of production. It is doubtless true, in the long run, that industrial transference on a very large scale will be necessary; for the technical revolutions through which we are passing will entail a radical redistribution of labour between occupations.

But there are at present formidable obstacles in most countries in the way of any rapid mass transference of redundant workers.

New industries cannot grow up, without destroying old ones, unless there is a real growth in consumers' demands. But consumers' demand cannot increase (save temporarily under some form of artificial stimulus) unless wages or profits, or both, increase; for demand consists of the incomes which people have to spend. Spending takes two forms—spending in the narrower sense on consumable goods and services, and that spending on capital goods which is ordinarily called 'saving'. The advocates of the Wages Fund theory were no doubt wrong in holding that the amount of spendable income paid out as wages varied directly with the amount of spendable income saved as capital, and applied to the development of production; but most of us nowadays are prepared to admit that their view contained an element of truth.

At the present time our industrial system in Great Britain is suffering from a shortage of spendable income in both its forms. There is too little demand for consumable goods at remunerative prices to keep our existing industries employed; and there is also a shortage of 'savings', in relation to pre-war habits of accumulation. If there is not an actual shortage of capital, this is not because capital is plentiful, but because the openings for its remunerative employment are few. A revival of industrial prosperity would, of course, generate at once more wages and more profits, and thus lead to higher demand both for consumable goods and for capital goods. But whence is this revival of prosperity to come? Remember that we are leaving out of account the temporary ebbs and flows of industry connected with general fluctuations of business conditions, and considering for the time only those persistent factors which operate in periods of good and bad world trade alike.

A policy of low production at high prices may yield more profits than one of higher production at lower prices; but it is self-evident that it yields less total utility. It is also certain to yield less employment, and practically certain, in view of the inflexibility of wage rates, to yield a smaller total sum in wages. It will thus react unfavourably on the volume of demand, and therefore tend both to perpetuate itself in the industries to which it is applied and to put obstacles in the way of the growth of new industries designed to elicit new demand. Its restrictive effects will spread far beyond the industries immediately concerned, and will react on the economic system as a whole. 'Savings' are generally regarded as new resources available for the production of additional wealth. But they may in effect, under certain conditions, serve only to replace existing wealth which the things created by means of them render obsolete. Where rationalisation is advancing fast, this is likely to be true in an exceptional degree.

New capital applied to industry is likely to be used to a considerable extent, not in providing the means of creating additional commodities, but in replacing existing means of production by new ones capable of producing the same goods at lower costs. When this happens, and to the extent that it happens, the new capital goods, when once they have been made, do not lead to any creation of additional goods or to any employment of additional labour. Indeed, they are likely, as we have seen, to diminish the demand for labour, by fostering its more economical use. It is therefore clear that, to the extent to which new capital is applied to replacing means of production which are then scrapped more rapidly than of old, the available capital resources for the development of additional production are liable to be diminished. This is the germ of truth in the Wages Fund theory, in its special application to the circumstances of the present time.

I am suggesting, then, that while the new methods of production lead as a rule to the creation of goods with less expenditure of capital and effort for each unit produced, the new methods of economic organisation which usually accompany them tend to defeat the ends which make the saving of effort desirable, and to cause unemployment quite apart from that which is the familiar result of the periodical fluctuations of trade and prosperity in the world as a whole. On this account, the familiar argument that rationalisation, whilst it may cause unemployment temporarily, will before long bring about such an expansion of output as to reabsorb all those who have been displaced, appears to me to rest upon a dangerous misunderstanding of the economic tendencies of today.

I have so far discussed this problem solely upon the national plane, and in its relation to purely national combinations among business men. But, as we have seen, the processes of rationalisation and combination by no means stop short at national frontiers. We have already in the Continental Steel Cartel, in the International Rail Makers' Association, in the Nickel Agreement, and in numerous other instances, the extension of trade agreements for the regulation of output or the allocation of markets far beyond national boundaries; and it is increasingly the declared object in creating national groupings in an industry to lay the foundation for an international cartel or understanding at a later stage. The coal trade furnishes an obvious example of the prevalence of such an idea. International combination is likely to have, in the world as a whole, much the same effects on production and employment as national combination has within a more limited area. If national combines are in competition with one another, each may have a strong motive for restricting supply and keeping up prices within its home market, at any rate where that market is protected; but each is likely to pursue as far as it can the policy of low prices and large sales in such foreign markets as remain open to it. This has in recent years often resulted in what is called 'dumping', in the sense of selling in a foreign market at less than the home price. It has, especially, often enabled the countries which do not produce a particular commodity to get their supplies of it cheaper than those which do. But the effect of this competitive selling in foreign markets has been—in the case of coal, for example—sometimes to force down prices to a level unremunerative to many producers; and this condition leads to the desire for the extension of combination over the international field, with the object of keeping up export prices, even at the cost of a reduction in the quantity sold. This tendency may not yet be very far advanced; but it is undoubtedly very much in men's minds, and likely, if economic policy retains its present direction, to exert a growingly restrictive influence on world production, and especially on the production of Western Europe. We are thus confronted with the paradox that more scientific methods of production and more scientific and orderly forms of economic organisation, instead of leading to a general rise in the world standard of life, are so acting as to cause a widespread fear of over-production, despite the boundless range of unsatisfied human needs, and a new unemployment problem far more obstinate and socially destructive than that which we have learned to associate with the general fluctuations of world trade. Nor is there, while we continue on our present course, any reason to suppose that we are on the way to conquering this disastrous failure of our economic system. For rationalisation is likely to be a continuous process, spread over a long period of years; and there is every reason to fear that the restrictive tendencies which mark it now will be equally characteristic of its later stages.

Upon the transport trades, these phenomena of the productive system react disastrously. For, while improvements in the arts of transportation have again and again been the parents of economic expansion, and will doubtless be this in the future, it remains true that, in the case of any existing agency of transport, prosperity depends mainly on the quantity of goods needing to be carried from one place to another. Anything that restricts production automatically restricts transportation as well, though this effect may of course be masked by the simultaneous operation of other forces. Thus, in Great Britain of late years, the reduced rate of expansion of industrial production has reacted unfavourably on the railways and, even more, on shipping; but its effects on transport as a whole have been obscured by the contemporary growth of new services in the sphere of transportation by road. Railwaymen are apt to attribute to road competition what is in fact due to the failure of production to expand at an adequate pace. Seafarers and shipowners should see the situation more clearly; for air transport is not yet (I do not pretend to know whether it will ever become) a sufficiently powerful rival to influence the position. The index of shipping freights (though, considered as an index, it is by no means wholly satisfactory) bears eloquent testimony to the dependence of transport agencies for their prosperity on the volume of goods needing to be carried. Of course, restrictive tendencies may manifest themselves in the sphere of transport as well as in that of production. There have been, from the very beginnings of modern combination, important instances of it in the shipping trade. Indeed, the shipping conferences were for some time the outstanding examples of price maintenance by agreements transcending national boundaries. But, under conditions of restricted production, it is by no means easy to apply a restrictive policy to the shipping trade, save within a relatively narrow field. In the case of liners a good deal can be done, and is done, to keep up freight rates; but tramp tonnage presents a far more difficult problem.

In the case of land transport, again, restriction is not easy save within fairly narrow limits. Railway rates are in most countries either determined by the State itself as owner of the railways, or regulated by the State where, as in Great Britain, the railways are in private hands. States normally desire to stimulate production and trade by keeping rail charges as low as possible; and State control, as far as it has any effect at all, is more likely to keep freight rates down than to raise them. Road competition for the lighter goods, and for certain classes of the heavier goods, and the competition of canals and coastwise shipping, also serve to prevent a restrictive policy aimed at maintaining charges at a high level. Only in the case of passengers is there a wide field for restriction; and the recent fusion of interests between railway companies and road transport undertakings in Great Britain serves at any rate to show that the railway managers are fully alive to the possibilities of action in this sphere.

It remains broadly true that the prosperity of transport undertakings, and still more directly the volume of employment they are able to provide, depend on the volume of industrial (and of course also of agricultural) production. Restrictive policies in industry, therefore, hit directly at the prosperity of the transport workers. Moreover, there is a further tendency at work which makes it more than ever important to those engaged in transport that the volume of industrial production should be increased as rapidly as possible. The rationalisation of industry, we have seen, aims above all, in its productive aspects, at the reduction of costs by the adoption of the most efficient methods available. Now, the costs of transporting fuel and raw materials to the works, semi-finished products to other works in which they are to be further manufactured, and finished products to the places where they are to be used or consumed, form a very important element in the total costs of production for many classes of goods, and especially for the products of the heavy industries. Accordingly, those who set out to rationalise an industry always have their eye on the possibility of cutting down these particular items in the cost account. This may be done in a variety of ways—by building new plants nearer the sources of the bulkiest fuel or material needed, by linking up successive processes of production in a single works in order to save intermediate transport, or by carrying through the final processes of manufacture, such as assembling, in close proximity to the markets in which the goods are to be sold.

Instances of all these types are easy to find. Our iron-works have long been grouped round the coalfields, because it was, in most cases, cheaper to carry iron to coal than coal to iron. But nowadays the economy in fuel consumption in the course of production is altering the conditions affecting the most economic localisation of the industry, and causing it to settle more in the areas where the iron is found, or near the coast, to which it can be brought cheaply by sea. Again, industrial technicians have found means of employing the waste gas given off in the blast furnace as a source of power for the subsequent processes of steel production; and this is tending to bring the production of pig-iron and of steel together within a single establishment. Or again, as parts of motor vehicles can be transported more cheaply and sometimes, across national frontiers, at lower rates of duty than complete cars, assembling factories are set up in the countries in which the customers live, even if the production of the parts is carried on in bulk at a single centre.

Modern industry is seeking more and more to reduce the costs of transportation by cutting out unnecessary movements of goods. A combine is often able to supply customers with goods made near at hand, where under competitive conditions things were carried long distances, and goods of the same sort might pass each other on the railways. Much was done during the war to save unnecessary transport by regional schemes of distribution; and private business has learnt the lessons which Governments were compelled to teach it under pressure of war conditions. Economy in the use of fuel, which is one of the most marked features of recent technical progress, also reacts very greatly on the volume of goods to be transported; for coal by itself accounts for a very large proportion of the total volume of goods traffic on all the railways.

It is, of course, fully as desirable to save wasted effort in transportation as in the productive process. There is no less strong a case for rationalising transport than industry. My point is, not that the tendencies which are reducing the amount of transportation involved in placing a given volume of goods in the consumer's hands are bad, but that those concerned in the transport industries have the strongest possible reasons for objecting to any policy which tends to restrict production. The traditional faithfulness of British shipowners to Free Trade has been largely due to their feeling that anything which restricts the free flow of commodities is likely to diminish traffic. It might, indeed, have this effect without decreasing production; but we can hardly expect the shipowner to believe readily that it would.

What, then, should be the attitude of those who are engaged in the transport industries towards the monopolistic tendencies which are being strengthened by the movement of industrial rationalisation? It may be suggested, in the light of the foregoing argument, that they ought to offer uncompromising opposition to a movement which leads to these untoward results. But resistance to rationalisation is not in fact a practical policy, as the working-class movement in most countries has been quick to recognise—quicker than a large proportion of the employers. For, if industry continues to be conducted on terms of international competition, the country which rejects rationalisation will evidently run a serious risk of losing a large part of its trade; and if international combination and allocation of markets are to be the rule, the country that lags behind in bringing its methods of production up-to-date will be at a grave disadvantage in the bargaining for quotas and markets on which such co-operation is inevitably based. It is necessary to rationalise industry, because no industrialised country can afford to fall behind others in its endeavour to lower production costs.

The practical issue is not whether industry shall be rationalised or not, but whether means can be found of countering the dangerous tendency towards under-production which rationalisation, under present conditions, tends to set up. Cheaper production ought to mean more production, and not merely more production in the aggregate, but more per head of the population, so as to result in a higher standard of life. If, instead of this, it leads to serious unemployment, then there is something very badly wrong with the economic system that permits such a thing to occur.

What is wrong? In the first place, the motive to production under present economic conditions is not the total income generated by production, but only that part of it which takes the form of profit. Wages appear, in the productive process, not as incomes, but as costs, whereas profits appear as incomes. Wages, therefore, seem an evil and profits a good. But in fact both wages and profits are goods of the same sort—means of life to those who receive them. Of two possible policies, one may result in the distribution of £800 in wages and £200 in profit, while the other will distribute £1,000 in wages and only £100 in profit. Under our present system the first of the policies is almost inevitably preferred, though it creates a total economic welfare, at the most, of only £1,000 as against £1,100, and the discrepancy is probably a good deal greater than this if due account is taken of the differing marginal utility of money to different receivers of income. Moreover, if the choice of the first policy results in unemployment, someone has to keep the unemployed; and they can, in fact, be maintained only out of the £1,000, with the result that the profit-maker's £200 is considerably diminished by taxation. Secondly, the costs of production and of non-production do not fall directly upon the same shoulders. When an employer decides to produce, he pays the cost of production, and the difference between this cost and his selling price is his profit or loss as the case may be. But non-production has its costs as well as production. These, however, fall only in part on the employer. He may incur charges in keeping his plant in order even when it is not in use, and he may have interest charges on borrowed money sunk in such plant which continue whether it is used for production or not. But that large part of the costs of non-production which consists of the maintenance of those who are thrown out of work falls, not directly or mainly upon him, but upon the entire community, with varying incidence according to the provision made for the unemployed and the methods of taxation adopted in meeting the cost. If the employer had to meet the entire cost of non-production, it would often pay him better to produce than to abstain from production.

I am not, of course, suggesting that under our present economic system employers can in fact be asked directly to meet this extra cost. It would involve them, in many instances, in producing at a loss; and there is no known method, under a system of private enterprise, of making an employer produce if he does not wish to do so. It is, I think, highly desirable that when rationalisation of industry results in throwing men out of work, and the industry in question is in a reasonably prosperous condition, there should be compulsion to provide some sort of fund out of which at least the older workers who are displaced can be compensated for their loss of employment, and enabled to retire if they are too old to adapt themselves successfully to another calling. A few employers have made provision of this sort voluntarily on a limited scale. But it clearly cannot be made general, even where the industry can afford it, unless compulsion is applied.

No fund of this sort, however, even if the State as well as the employers contributed to it, could possibly meet the case of those industries in which rationalisation is being applied as the means of rescuing many of the firms from bankruptcy and the industry itself from irretrievable decline. For industries which are in this state have no ability to bear additional charges; and any attempt to impose such charges upon them would only impede and perhaps altogether prevent their recovery from their present depressed condition. Accordingly, the State must, in these cases, continue to shoulder the burden of the unemployment which is created by the adoption of new methods of production and new forms of economic organisation leading to a restrictive policy. I am not concerned with the question whether Unemployment Insurance—which is in reality not insurance at all, but a system of State payments financed by methods of taxation admitting of no theoretical defence—is the right method of providing for the needs of these disemployed workers, or whether some better method or methods could be devised. That is a different, though highly important, question; and I have certainly no space to discuss it here. My point is only that as, in one form or another, the State must bear the major part of the heavy costs of non-production, it too has a strong interest in seeing that restrictive practices shall be prevented from increasing and if possible eliminated altogether.

But what are we to do? The demand for the products of most of the industries to which rationalisation is being extensively applied or recommended is, under present conditions, fairly inelastic. A fall in prices, unless it is very great, does not bring about any considerable increase in total world demand. It may, indeed, increase considerably for a time the proportion of the total demand that is met by the producers in a particular country; but if it does this without increasing total demand to any great extent, the chief effect must be in the long run to cause competing countries to reduce their prices too. When they do this, the same volume of trade as existed before the whole movement began will tend to be shared out in much the same way as at first among the rival producing groups, unless one of these has in the meantime increased or decreased its relative efficiency, in which case it may permanently gain or lose trade in relation to the others. The only noticeable result apart from this will be that prices will have been forced down in export markets, so that all the producing countries may be worse off at the end of the process than they were when it began.

This inelasticity of total world demand is obviously the root of the trouble. Why, then, is the demand inelastic? Precisely because the controllers of production in the various countries choose, and under present conditions have to choose, the creation of a less rather than of a larger total amount of spendable income in the course of the productive process. £800 wages plus £200 profit is preferred to £1,000 wages plus £100 profit, though clearly the former produces both less goods and less demand for goods than the latter. Moreover, under our present topsy-turvy system, if by reducing wage-rates the same amount of product can be secured for £750 as was previously secured for £800, or even an amount of product less in value by anything up to £50, this will appear as a gain, because it will add to the £200 of profit, though it will usually add less to profits than it takes off wages, and thus further reduce the amount of production and of purchasing power as well as worsen its distribution from the standpoint of human utility.

Our present economic arrangements thus tend to put a premium on under-production and to make even under-production wear the appearance of over-production to the business man who has to strive to make both ends meet. Unless the world can find a way out of this tragic and ridiculous situation, the outlook for the next ten years is black indeed; for we may expect a rapid advance in the arts of production combined with a diminishing ability to take advantage of our own skill. It is, indeed, possible that a lucky accident may falsify these unhappy forebodings. If the Far East would cease from fighting and apply its full energies to the improvement of its own productive efficiency, it might become so huge a market for European goods as to set all our depressed industries working full time, and to absorb all the workers whom rationalisation could possibly displace. If the United States threw down its tariff wall and readily accepted European manufactures in payment of Europe's debts, a less spectacular but still considerable revival of European prosperity might follow. But it does not look at all likely that either of these events, or any other comparable with them in its potential effects, will occur in the near future. Moreover, even an event of this order would only counteract the effects of our economic troubles, and not finally remove their cause.

I am driven to the conclusion that, even apart from the special types of unemployment which result from the general fluctuations of trade, the capitalist system in its latest phase of development is generating a new kind of unemployment likely to be even more far-reaching and disastrous in its social effects, unless the common sense of the peoples avails to enforce a radical cure.

But is there a cure at all, however radical we are prepared to be if we can but find one? I feel sure there is, though I am far from believing that I have mastered the problem in all its complications, or know at all fully or in detail how we ought to deal with it. Broadly, I believe the answer is that in deciding whether to produce or to refrain from producing we must always take all the costs into account, including the costs of non-production as well as the costs of production in the narrower sense. We must get firmly into our heads the fundamental truth that human subsistence is a basic and unavoidable cost, attaching to non-production as well as to production, and that, accordingly, only the difference between what a man receives when he is at work and what he receives when he is unemployed, and not his total wage, can be rightly treated as a cost of production as distinguished from non-production. The fact that the cost of production and non-production falls largely upon different shoulders is irrelevant, from the standpoint of society as a whole; and the true lesson of rationalisation is that we must do our cost-accounting not only in terms of single businesses, however large, but even more in terms of the entire community.

How can this truth be practically applied? A makeshift way would be for the State to set as many as possible of the unemployed to work, making things useful to the community, even if their value in economic terms amounted to less than the total cost of producing them, according to the current business reckoning. This would, I am sure, be a great deal better than the policy of unproductive doles which most industrial States at present pursue in dealing with their unemployed.

But it would be a makeshift method, difficult to apply except as a temporary measure, and difficult even so, because of the relatively narrow range of services upon which the State can under present conditions readily embark, and the unsuitability of many of the unemployed for the execution of these particular services.

What, then, is the alternative? My answer is that, if industry cannot produce at a book-keeping profit, it ought to produce at a book-keeping loss, at least up to the point at which the loss exceeds the costs of non-production. I am well aware that Lord Melchett made, some years ago, a somewhat similar suggestion when he proposed that the unemployment benefit now paid to workers out of a job in Great Britain should be used as a subsidy in aid of wages, and paid over to employers who, in return for it, would increase their output and employ more labour. The suggestion was laughed out of court, and freely criticised as unworkable, as indeed I think it was, in the form in which Lord Melchett proposed it. But the fact remains that Lord Melchett had hold of the right end of the stick. He had at least realised the impossibility, from the standpoint of the community as a whole, of neglecting the costs of non-production, and deciding whether to produce or not to produce solely on the basis of a comparison between selling prices and total costs.

Lord Melchett's suggestion was unworkable, if it was so, not because it was wrong in substance, but because the economic system to which he was seeking to apply it was radically unsound. How, said his critics, are you to prevent employers from getting the subsidy in respect of workers whom they would have engaged even without it? The question would have been meaningless, and the objection invalid, if the employer in question had been, not a private firm, but the State itself. For there could be no possible injustice or objection to the State, or rather the whole community, subsidising itself in order to add to the aggregate of its wealth by increasing production. Lord Melchett proposed to apply a Socialist remedy while leaving the capitalist system undisturbed. His critics realised that this could not be done; and they preferred a capitalist system diseased to the application of a Socialist cure.

I should like, then, to see the State become the employer and controller of industry over a wide field, in the sense of prescribing directly the forms and amounts of production, and accepting responsibility for its financial results. In fact, I hold that rationalisation can be applied to industry, without setting up a vicious circle of under-production and under-consumption, only if Socialism is applied too, and the policy of each business directed, not solely or mainly with a view to the profit of a particular body of shareholders, but in the light of all the costs of production and non-production alike, and with a view to the general advantage of Society and the creation of the largest possible total volume of economic wealth, subject only to the claims of non-economic goods, such as increased leisure or more life-giving education.

I do not for a moment suggest that the application of this broad principle would by itself solve all our troubles, though I believe it would be found to be the key to a good many of them, and those the most obstinate and deeply rooted. I do not, for example, suggest that there are not other causes of unemployment apart from that which I have been discussing, or that these do not need handling by other methods. There is, for example, the problem of general trade fluctuations, which is responsible in Great Britain today for probably about a third of the total volume of unemployment and for most of the increase during the past six or nine months. This, as I have explained, falls outside the scope of this paper. There is, secondly, certainly a considerable body of unemployment which is the direct result of the maldistribution of economic resources, and of the slowness of our economic system in adapting itself to changing needs. Plant built to produce one class of goods cannot usually be diverted to producing another; and, as we have seen, human beings are also very apt to lose their adaptability as they grow older. There are, further, serious difficulties in the way of migration both across national frontiers and within a single country. Consequently, if the currents of demand change, it takes a long time to adapt either the human or the material factors in industry to the new needs; and the difficulty of adaptation is obviously greatest if the need coincides with and is accentuated by the dislocation caused by a world war and highly defective command of the monetary factors in the production and distribution of wealth.

These difficulties would remain, even if we were handling our problems under Socialist instead of capitalist control, and from a Socialist instead of a capitalist point of view. But I believe they would, in that case, be infinitely easier to master. For we should then be endeavouring to rebuild industry with the right proportions in view of modern needs in accordance with a definite plan, instead of trusting to the blind forces of individual profit seeking somehow to create a harmonious structure and to fit each available brick into its proper place. We should be setting out consciously to develop new industries, instead of hoping that they would somehow grow up of themselves.

Of course, the view which I have put forward in this paper is finally and utterly inconsistent with the underlying philosophy of Free Trade, in the theoretical form in which British economists have for over a century preached it to the world with a success considerable up to the third quarter of the last century, and thereafter steadily and rapidly diminishing. For, wherever protectionists may be wrong, they are certainly right when they contend that the failure of an industry to survive under Free Trade conditions cannot be taken, even from the strictly economic standpoint, as a final and conclusive argument against its utility. The total cost to the community of letting an industry die may easily be greater than the cost of keeping it in being; and only a country able, by reason of its superior economic efficiency, to pick and choose among industries fully enough to keep its population employed (apart, of course, from temporary unemployment due to general fluctuations of trade) could possibly have lost sight for long of this obvious fact. It is not always an economic advantage to buy in the cheapest market: it is a positive economic disadvantage if the result of doing so is to throw so many people out of work that the cost of their maintenance exceeds the amount by which the price in the cheapest market is lower than that at which the goods could have been made by these disemployed. Indeed, the case for a protective duty has often been put precisely on this ground. It may act as a means of keeping an industry alive when it would otherwise perish; and the cost which it involves in higher prices to the consumer may be in a particular instance less than the loss which will be incurred by the community if the industry is allowed to disappear. It is pertinent to point out in reply to the protectionist case that taxes on commodities are apt to be most unfair in their incidence, and that their desirability of keeping a particular trade alive is no sufficient reason for making the consumers of its products bear the cost of doing so. Tariffs may be an unsound way of achieving a desirable result; but the objection to tariffs does not destroy the force of the argument which underlies the advocacy of them.

What I am saying in effect is that our present method of determining the production and pricing of commodities in accordance with the total costs incurred by firms in their manufacture is radically wrong. It is wrong for a very simple reason —because it treats the wages of labour as an element in cost of production just like any other element. Wages in reality stand on quite a different footing from other costs. For, whereas most other costs are merely outgoings, wages are incomes as well.

A simple contrast should suffice to make my meaning plain. If I can make a ton of steel with less coal, the result is to achieve a real economy in production. If I can make a ton of steel with less labour, then too a real economy is achieved. But if I use the same amount of labour, merely paying for it a lower wage, or if the price of the coal I buy falls merely because the miner gets a lower wage, there is no real economy at all. Yet in ordinary parlance we shall say in all these cases that the cost of production has been reduced. It is true that in each case the money cost has fallen; but the real cost, which is from the social standpoint the vital factor, has fallen only in the two earlier cases. In the two latter it remains unchanged. And this is a vital difference, not only from a theoretical, but also from a practical point of view.

In general, British industry pays higher wages than its continental competitors. Unless the higher wages are offset by a correspondingly greater efficiency of labour, this tends to raise British money costs of production above the continental level. Similarly, German money costs tend to be higher than French or Italian, other things being equal, and European money costs than Japanese. But does this mean that real costs are also higher? In my view, it does not. The real costs depend upon the efficiency of production, and not on the amount received as wages by the workers. The workers' income is not a means to production, but, at least equally with the employers' profit, the end for which production exists. A higher wage should not, therefore, be treated as a higher cost, but rather as something to be provided, in the fullest measure possible, out of the total product of industry as a whole. It would pay Great Britain handsomely to market her steel wherever necessary at a price determined, not by its total money cost of production, but by this cost less the difference between the British wage-rates and those paid in the principal competing countries.

But this would not pay the British employer, unless he received from the State a subsidy equivalent to the difference. More than one country has at some time adopted this method of subsidy; and it has been often put forward in Great Britain, especially as a way of meeting the farmers' difficulties. In certain cases, it may even be the best way of dealing with a particular difficulty; but it is apt to result in the making of large unnecessary presents to the wrong people. The coal subsidy of 1925 in Great Britain did this. The entire situation would be immensely simpler if the State itself were the employer. For then, as we have seen, the State would only have to pay the subsidy to itself.

This, of course, would not relieve the State from the necessity of finding the money. In part, this would come from the savings on other services, such as the maintenance of the unemployed; for the object of the entire process is to increase production and get the unemployed back to work. For the rest, the necessary resources could only come out of taxation, levied, of course, not only on incomes derived from British industry, but also on non-industrial incomes and on incomes originating abroad. Only if these sources of money proved inadequate would it be necessary to conclude that British wages were in excess of Great Britain's capacity to pay. A reduction in wages would be the last, and not as now the first, resort of the industrialist in trouble.

But—and here we approach the most obvious difficulty— would not the adoption by the various nations of this policy of selling goods when necessary at less than total cost result in a gigantic development of dumping over the world as a whole? We can hardly suppose that, if one country seriously began it, others would not be impelled to follow its example. What else indeed could they do? We should have then what is now called 'dumping' on a greatly intensified scale. The policy, practised to a growing extent already by trusts and cartels, of charging in each section of the market what the trade will bear, almost without regard to production costs, would be greatly extended and intensified.

Well, why not? If more goods cannot be sold in the world at present prices, though the world has the capacity to create far more, prices will have to come down to the point at which more will be bought, and this can only be achieved on the condition that prices are not brought down by reducing wages and other incomes and so destroying the purchasing power which must be the source of the additional demand. Demand, I have said, is at present somewhat inelastic for most goods. But it will become elastic in the proportion in which we set more people to work without reducing wages, and thus call additional demand into being. Subject to one condition, any level of prices which results in under-production is obviously too high. The remedy is to reduce it until the whole volume of available productive resources has been absorbed. Actually it may be better to do this, not by reducing prices in general (a process which may set up other unfavourable reactions), but by making money more plentiful without increasing prices, which comes to the same thing. But to follow up this point would take me too far afield.

The one condition is this. There may be in the world a lack of balance in productive power. The world may be equipped for producing relatively too much of some things and too little of others. In that case, the proportions need to be readjusted; and it is not desirable to bring down the prices of the goods which are in potential over-supply to the point at which the whole potential supply could be sold. The price reduction and the supply must be cut short at the point deemed to be approximately that of equilibrium with the rest of the productive system.

Though the case that I have been arguing goes against many preconceived ideas, surely its underlying truth is plain. To reject it is to hold that there can really be such a thing as general over-production—a ridiculous and self-condemnatory conclusion. Given right economic organisation, there must be a market for all we can produce within the limits set by our desire for leisure; and it must be worth while to satisfy the whole of that demand. It cannot be true that there exist in the world large material resources and large bodies of men whose productive capacity it is simply not worth while to use.

But surely, it may be said, this talk of the need for lower prices is ridiculous in face of the happenings of the past year. Has not the world's chief trouble during this period been that prices have been falling too fast? Are not the producers of wheat, wool, cotton, tin, rubber and a hundred other commodities lamenting the disastrous fall in the prices of the goods they have to sell? Are not the manufacturers of Europe lamenting the consequent fall in the purchasing power of the countries which are mainly suppliers of foodstuffs and raw materials? That is true enough; and I am far from suggesting either that the prices of these particular commodities ought to fall further, or that a further fall in the general price-level is to be desired. Indeed, I would sooner see the general price-level rise, and the prices of foodstuffs and materials rise both absolutely and in relation to the prices of manufactured commodities.

The fall in the general price-level during recent years is, I believe, due mainly to monetary causes, and demands a remedy in terms of monetary policy. The fall in the relative prices of foodstuffs and materials is due partly to the failure of the industrial countries, which are the chief consumers, to utilise their own productive powers to the full and so raise their standard of life, and partly to the greater difficulty of combination to hold up prices in the case of foodstuffs and materials than in that of manufactured articles. A determined policy of higher production on the lines suggested above in the industrial countries would at once improve the demand for primary products, and react favourably upon their relative price. This in turn would stimulate the demand for manufactures in the countries which export chiefly foodstuffs and materials, and would thus diminish, if not wholly remove, the need for selling manufactures at less than total cost.

I am, of course, aware that the views put forward in this paper will be hotly contested, and even dismissed by many of the orthodox—in the ranks of Labour as well as among economists—as merely foolish. I am, indeed, probably wrong on many points; but I believe I am right on the fundamental issue. It is, I think, true that our present economic system is working out more and more towards a policy of limited production, and that, in view of the rapid growth of technical efficiency, this policy is certain to result in an even more serious growth of unemployment. This tendency is inherent in a system which (*a*) takes as its motive, not the creation of the maximum total utility, but only of the maximum surplus over cost; (*b*) includes the entire wage of labour as a cost, and ignores its importance as income—the source of economic demand; (*c*) ignores in its calculation the costs of non-production, or, in other words, the maintenance of those who are unemployed or disemployed by reason of its policy; and (*d*) abstains from production unless the result of this incomplete and misleading calculation makes it more remunerative for the owners of a business to produce than to abstain, ignoring altogether the question of expediency from the standpoint of the community as a whole. In other words, under modern conditions the capitalist system leads increasingly to the disemployment of labour; and there is no means of counteracting this tendency short of the adoption of a considerable measure of practical Socialism.

## VII

## WAGES AND EMPLOYMENT

THE classical theory of wages represents the employer as constantly pushing his willingness to employ labour to a marginal point determined by its productivity in relation to that of the other factors of production. The employer, we are told, is always seeking to combine these factors in the most economical proportions, in order to reduce his costs to the lowest possible point. Consequently, it appears, the cheaper labour is, the more of it will be employed, both because, at any given level of production, more of it will be used and less of other factors, such as land or machinery, and also because cheaper labour, by lowering total cost, will enable the employer to lower prices, and so produce and sell more goods. Low wages, looked at from this standpoint, appear as an unmixed blessing, and as the means to greater production and therefore to greater wealth.

Every economist, however, is well aware that this argument cannot be accepted at its face value. It involves at least three evidently fallacious assumptions. The first of these is that the productivity of labour bears no relation to the amount of wages paid to the labourer. The second is that the elasticity of demand for commodities is unaffected by the level of wages. And the third is that labour can be treated as a mere aggregate of homogeneous units, and differences of quality between labourer and labourer simply ignored.

Nor is this, in practice, by any means the total of the fallacies involved in the familiar crude generalisation that high wages mean less employment, and low wages more employment. It may often be true that a particular employer, or group of employers, could get more trade on profitable terms if they could lower wages, without any corresponding action on the part of their competitors; but it may be quite untrue that a general lowering of wages, over the whole competitive field, would have this effect. In this as in many other parts of the economic field it is fallacious in the extreme to argue directly from the particular to the general.

What, then, can we say with safety about the relation between wages and employment? We had best say nothing at all, until we have attempted to define our terms more clearly.

### WAGES

The dual character of wages is apt, unless we are careful, to introduce a great deal of confusion into the argument. For wages are, from the employer's standpoint, a cost, and, from the workman's, income—a means of life. What matters to the employer is not the rate of wages that he pays, but the return which he gets for each shilling, or mark, or franc, or dollar, in terms of productive result. And, subject to certain reservations, what matters to the worker is not the rate of wages either, but the amount of earnings he receives in return for each unit of energy he is called upon to expend. These reservations are, however, important. The worker has usually only his labour-power to purchase him the means of life. It will therefore not profit him to sell a very little of it even at a high rate: he must sell enough to give him a tolerable living. In other words, it will not pay the worker to be casually or discontinuously employed, except at a very high rate of remuneration for each unit of effort that he expends.

There is a further reservation, which applies to both parties, but does not affect them quite in the same way. What matters to the employer, fundamentally, is not the absolute cost of labour in terms of its productive efficiency, but this cost in relation to the conditions on which he is able to sell his goods. And what matters to the workman is not the absolute sum of money which he receives, but the purchasing power of this money over the particular sorts of goods and services that he wants to buy. In other words, the willingness of the employer to pay wages and the willingness of the workman to work for a given wage are both affected by the level of prices. But not by the prices of the same things, or in the same proportions. The workman is interested primarily in the cost of living, and the employer in the prices of the particular goods he makes or uses at the particular stage of production or distribution with which he is particularly concerned. It is often said, by way of contrast, that the employer is interested chiefly in wholesale, and the workman in retail, prices. But this is not a fair way of stating the contrast. Very broadly, we may measure the purchasing power of wages by means of a generalised index number, purporting to measure the 'working-class cost of living'; and this will work well enough as a rough approximation, though it will tend to break down if we attempt to apply it to the salaried and professional classes. But in the case of the general body of employers there can be no even reasonably correct approximation by means of a single index number. For each group of employers is affected quite differently according as a movement in 'general prices' results from varying movements in the prices of different commodities and services.

Moreover, labour is, from the employer's standpoint, only one among the factors of production; and his willingness to afford employment is affected by the prices of all these factors. It may be true enough that if labour becomes relatively dear, and some other factor of production that can be substituted for it relatively cheap, there will be a tendency to use more of the latter factor, and less labour. But this substitution cannot operate over anything like the whole field of productive costs. An employer cannot usually make use of less labour and more raw material, or *vice versa*; and only within certain limits can he use less labour and more machinery, or more labour and less machinery. Commonly, the employment of more of one factor involves the employment of more of others, even if the relative proportions are changed. And a fall in the relative price of, say, machinery or raw materials may, accordingly, often mean the employment of more and not less labour, even if the price of labour rises absolutely as well as relatively. Indeed, the total employment of the various factors of production commonly moves in the same direction, and not in opposite directions;

and this tendency is usually too strong to be offset by changes in the relative prices of the various factors.

The different meanings of the term 'wages' become especially important as soon as we attempt to look at the question of wages and employment from any international standpoint. For attempts to compare the wages of workers in different countries have, so far, usually been based on one of two principles, neither of which can yield a fully satisfactory answer. The first method, adopted in certain calculations published regularly by the International Labour Office, attempts to measure and compare the purchasing power of wages in different countries. It is a comparison of 'real wages', taking account of the difference in the cost of living, and attempting, by a somewhat rough-and-ready method, to allow for the differing standards and composition of working-class budgets in the various countries. The second method is to express the wage-level of each country in terms of gold, or in a dollar equivalent, without regard to differing price-levels or standards of consumption. The first of these methods regards wages purely as incomes, and thus comes nearest to the working-class point of view. The second comes nearer to regarding them, as the employer does, as costs; but it ignores the differences both in the efficiency of labour and in the amount of effort demanded from the worker in return for his wage.

There is the further difficulty that countries do not compile their wage-statistics on a uniform basis. Some countries work on a basis of wage-rates, and others on a basis of earnings; and there are other difficulties, such as the adoption of hourly, daily or weekly standards, and the classification of the available figures. Some countries have separate figures for skilled and less skilled, and for male and female, workers; while others lump all the industrial figures together into a general estimated average.

In face of these differences, and of the imperfections of the statistics themselves, it is exceedingly difficult to institute any reliable comparisons of wages on an international basis, or to reach any comparative conclusions concerning the effects of high or low wages on the international incidence of unemployment. I have spent a good deal of time in recent years in vain attempts to arrive at useful results by the comparison of the available figures; but my only conclusion is that, from this as from many other points of view, there is urgent need for further progress in getting countries both to compile and publish fuller statistics of wage-rates and earnings, and to adopt a more nearly comparable basis for their figures.

The fact, however, remains that, though the figures are capable of great improvement, no such improvement can possibly yield a purely statistical measurement of the relative levels of wage-costs in different countries. It may be possible to measure the amount of gold wage in a ton of crude steel in Germany, Belgium, France, Great Britain, and the United States; but it will certainly not be possible to present a clear picture of the relative cost of a unit of labour efficiency in general in these countries. Indeed, the very conception is highly abstract. For the wage-cost of production depends not only on the efficiency that belongs to the labourer in relation to his wage, but also on the efficiency of the utilisation of labour—that is, of the plant and machinery with which the labourer has to work, of the management that gives him his orders, of the buying and selling mechanism, and of the total economic system within which his work is carried on.

It is hardly possible to hope for complete clarity of expression about so complex a matter; but, as far as in me lies, I shall use distinct terms for the various senses of the term 'wages' that have been mentioned above. When I am speaking of the amount for which the labourer has contracted to work for a certain period of time, or (in certain cases) to perform a certain piece or stint of work, I shall speak of *wage-rates*. When I refer to the amount actually earned by the labourer over a certain period of time, with or without full employment, I shall speak of *wage-earnings*, or simply *earnings*. When I am dealing with what either of these will buy, I shall speak of *real* wage-rates, or *real* earnings, as the case may be. When I am discussing wages from the employer's standpoint, I shall speak of *wage-costs*, meaning thereby the actual money cost attributable to labour in any given unit of production. For the purpose of comparing wages internationally in terms of purchasing power, it is best to speak of *computed cost of living wages*, and when the comparison is on a basis, not of purchasing power, but of gold equivalents, to speak of *gold wages*. But it is not possible to speak with precision of *real wage-costs* either nationally or internationally; for no means exist of measuring either. Nor can we speak of *wages per unit of labour productivity*; for the intrinsic productivity of labour cannot be separated from the efficiency of plant or management.

Some of this may seem to be an instance of unnecessary splitting of hairs; but there has been so much talk about an undefined something called 'wages' that I would sooner run the risk of making too many distinctions than too few.

### Employment

Turn now for a moment to the other factor we have to consider. We are dealing with the relation between 'wages' and 'employment'. What is employment? Clearly it cannot be measured by the number of persons employed; for their employment may be more or less continuous and intensive. In one country or industry employment may be spread over a large number of persons by means of casual labour or systematic short time, whereas in another the same volume of total employment may be shared out among a far smaller number of individuals, working full time or, perhaps, adding overtime to the ordinary working week. The weekly hours of labour may be longer in one country or industry than in another. And, what is hardest of all, there may be very different amounts of labour in an hour's work, according to the intensity with which the labourer is driven, and to his own habits of industry or the reverse. This intensity of labour, be it noted, is something different from its productivity, as Marx long ago realised. A workman is more productive if he produces more, under given conditions, with less expenditure of effort, but not if he produces more in an hour by working harder than before. Or, at all events, the term 'productivity' means two quite different things in these two cases. It is better, therefore, to use two different terms, and to speak of the productivity of labour in the first case, and of its intensity in the second.

It follows from what has been said that the amount of employment and unemployment cannot be measured simply by deducting from the available population the numbers totally unemployed. Account must be taken of short time as well—as both Germany and Great Britain do, in varying degree, in their systems of unemployment insurance. But much discontinuity of employment escapes measurement, even in these countries, and far more elsewhere. Over the world as a whole, unemployment statistics are still in their infancy; and in some great countries, such as the United States, it is not even possible to make an approximately reliable estimate of the numbers in and out of employment, much less of the extent of short-time and casual working. Moreover, such a country as France, which imports labour in prosperous times, cannot have unemployment statistics which measure the real variations in its demand for labour. The unemployed of French industry are in part dispersed over the countries from which they would have migrated to France if there had been a better demand for their services.

In these circumstances, the size of the wage-bill, corrected for any variations in the rates of wages,[1] may furnish a better measure than the numbers out of work or the volume of employment. Better statistics of total wages paid, collected at more frequent intervals, are therefore greatly to be desired as a means to the more satisfactory correlation of industrial phenomena.

In the following pages, when I speak of unemployment generally, I shall mean the total amount of time lost by available workers owing to the lack of opportunity to work, whether this takes the form of total or partial unemployment for the individual; and when I speak of employment, I shall mean the total number of man-hours worked, whether by a larger or smaller number of workers. It will not be possible to find a phrase that will denote the effects of an increased or decreased intensity of labour within the hour of sixty minutes; but it will be made clear when this factor is being brought into the account.

Having thus done something to clear the ground, I can now return to the main problem before us. Our object is to determine, in general terms, what relation, if any, exists between

[1] And for longer periods for the migration from one trade to another.

'wages' and the volume of employment. Let us begin by looking at the question from the standpoint of a single manufacturer.

For our hypothetical manufacturer, the question of the worthwhileness of production—or of more or less production—presents itself in the shape of a relationship between estimated costs and expected sale prices. Any reduction in cost makes it worth while to produce at a lower sale price or more worth while to produce at the same sale price. This applies equally to wage-costs and to any other element in cost, such as a reduction in the prices of materials, or in the rate of interest payable on bank overdrafts. Now, a reduction in wage-rates is fairly certain to result, immediately, in a reduction in total cost; for even if the lowered wage-rates lead to a fall in the efficiency of labour, this is unlikely, at least in the short run, to be equal to the fall in the rate of wages, unless this rate was exceptionally low before the reduction took place, or unless it provokes a resentment resulting in deliberate 'ca'canny' by the workers. To the individual employer, then, a reduction in wage-rates is apt to appear as a ready means to more, or to more profitable, production.

This, however, does not apply universally. Certain employers deliberately pay relatively high wage-rates in order either to secure their pick of the most skilled labour, or to persuade their workers to stand a pace of work more intense than the ordinary. Such employers may, or may not, welcome a general fall in wage-rates which will enable them to reduce their wage-costs while preserving the same relative superiority as before; but they will not desire to reduce this superiority, for fear of losing their comparative advantage in skill or pace of work. A reduction in wage-rates, applicable only to their own workers, will accordingly not attract them. But such employers, it must be admitted, are still the exception.

Let us now widen our example to embrace, not a single firm, but the whole of a trade or industry within a given area of collective bargaining. The body of employers within this area will be likely to see much the same advantage in a reduction of wage-rates as we supposed would appeal to a single employer, especially if their products are in competition with those of other employers outside the range of the collective bargain in ques-

## WAGES AND EMPLOYMENT

tion. Thus, if the employers in a particular trade in Lancashire, or in Germany, can reduce their wage-rates in comparison with competing employers in London, or in Great Britain, they are apt to see in this an advantage which will lead either to more, or to more profitable, production. For they can hope that the lower wage-rates will not, in the short run at least, be offset by decreased productive efficiency; and they can look both to capturing some of their competitors' trade, if they choose to reduce prices, and perhaps to securing the benefit of an increased total demand, or, even if they leave prices unchanged, to driving their previous amount of trade under more profitable conditions.

Some of these expected benefits clearly turn on employers in other areas of bargaining not being able to make, or not making, corresponding reductions in wage-rates. If the reductions become universal, there is no reason to suppose that the trade will be shared out in different proportions than before, except to the extent to which wages form, in the different areas, a different proportion of the total costs of production. But even if the proportions of trade are unchanged, the total amount may be increased; and this will clearly happen if prices are reduced when costs fall, and the commodity in question is in elastic total demand. The extent of the gain will then depend on the degree of elasticity in the total demand, except in so far as wages form differing proportions of total cost in the case of the various producers.

But we must now widen our example still further. We have been speaking so far solely of the conditions affecting a single product, and assuming a change in the wage-rates of the industry producing the product without any corresponding change in other industries. We have now to see what will happen if the change in wage-rates becomes general over the whole field of employment, or at least over a large number of different occupations.

Where wage-rates are reduced in a single industry, the effect may, or may not, be a reduction in the total wage-bill. This will depend on the policy pursued by the employers in the industry, and on the elasticity of demand for the product.

Where the employers concerned choose, and are able, to leave prices unchanged, the result will always be a fall in the total wage-bill; for they will certainly sell no more than before, and they may sell less in consequence of the fall in the purchasing power of their own employees. This latter factor is likely to be relatively unimportant if the change is confined to a single industry, unless the industry is largely localised and sells most of its product in the local market. But clearly more will not be sold; and accordingly the total wage-bill is bound to fall.

If, however, prices are reduced, this does not follow. But, normally, the total wage-bill falls in this case, unless the elasticity of demand is greater than unity—*i.e.*, unless purchasers are willing to spend an increased total amount of money in buying the goods in question at the reduced price. This is not likely to be often the case, except where trade is gained at the expense of competitors. When this condition applies, a powerful stimulus will be applied to these competitors to bring down their prices either by reducing the wage-rates of their workers or by other means, with the result that the gain secured by the original wage-reduction will be inherently unstable. Only when the elasticity of total demand is greater than unity is the total wage-bill likely to be durably increased. And this, in the case of a single industry, is likely to be a very rare occurrence.

As soon as we think in terms, not of a single industry, but of a wide group of industries, or of industry as a whole, a fresh set of considerations presents itself. For it is no longer possible to ignore the direct loss of purchasing power due to the fall in wage-rates. This will be offset only if, over the whole range of employment affected, the elasticity of demand proves to be greater than unity, in face of the fall in individual incomes. In other words, prices must be reduced enough to persuade those in employment, though their wage-rates have been reduced, to buy enough more, not of one commodity, but of all those affected taken together, to cause enough additional employment to bring the total wages-bill up to the old level, after allowance has been made for the demand of those brought back into employment by this means. But this is a most unlikely supposition; for a general fall of wage-rates, even accompanied by a corresponding fall in prices, is likely only to leave demand at the old level as far as wage-incomes are concerned.

There remains, of course, the possibility that demand will be increased by larger purchases out of incomes other than wages. But, unless prices are reduced, there is no reason to anticipate any increased demand except from one source—the profits which have been increased at the expense of wage-rates. And it is most unlikely that the increased demand from this source, being merely the result of a transference of income from wages to profits, will exceed the loss of demand from the reduction in wage-rates; while, if prices are reduced, it is again unlikely that, over the whole range of industry, the increased demand from incomes other than wages will exceed the reduction in demand from wage-incomes, unless the fall in prices is considerable.

May it not, however, be considerable enough to achieve this result? Here we meet again the vital distinction between different sorts of prices. The only change in prices that will affect ultimate total demand is a fall in retail prices. But the change in wage-costs will react largely on the prices of materials and manufactures at the wholesale stage. It will doubtless, if it is generally spread, react on retail prices as well; but all the evidence goes to show that it will not react upon them as strongly or as swiftly as upon wholesale prices of materials and manufactures. Accordingly, it is likely that only a part of the fall in wage-costs will be reflected in retail prices, and that there will be a time-lag before even this part is fully so reflected. It is therefore probable that the elasticity of retail demand (upon which other demand ultimately depends) will be less than unity, and that the total wage-bill will fall. This is not to say that there will be no increase in employment, but only that the increase will not be enough to make the total wage-bill as large as before.

It appears to follow that, save in very exceptional circumstances, a fall in wage-rates over all occupations (or over a wide group of occupations) in an area will be likely to lead to a reduction in the total wage-bill, unless the reduction is made in one area and not in others, so that the area in which wage-rates are reduced is enabled to capture a large share of its competitors' markets, and by this means to achieve an elasticity greater than unity in the demand for its products.

It is thus not denied that one country, or economic area, can increase the amount of employment within its borders, under certain conditions, by bringing about a fall in wage-rates which does not extend to its competitors. It may even, under exceptionally favourable conditions, increase by this means the total amount of its wage-bill, provided that the whole reduction in costs is passed on to the consumer in reduced prices, and not retained in order to raise profits or eliminate losses. But the realisation of this condition depends on a number of circumstances which are by no means safe to reckon upon. The capture of trade from competitors must be large enough to offset and counteract a fall in demand which will otherwise, owing to the difference between wholesale and retail prices, tend to occur in the home market, and still to leave enough surplus to make the net expansion greater than unity. And success, even so, depends on a passive acceptance of defeat by the competitor countries or areas, without any success on their part in either cutting down their own wage-rates, or by other methods reducing their prices.

In fact, of course, the cutting down of wage-costs in one area tends to set up a powerful movement towards their reduction in others. This is true, whether the reduction is achieved, in either case, by cutting down wage-rates or by other means. If one area cuts its wage-rates, other areas will try hard either to follow suit, or to reduce their costs by improved mechanisation, better selling methods, or even bounties or subsidies in the last resort, or perhaps by higher tariffs designed to protect their own home markets and give improved opportunities for export dumping at their home consumers' expense. Commercial gains secured by stealing the trade of rivals are always precarious; and they are most precarious of all when they are secured by reducing wage-rates, both because the policy is likely to react adversely on the home market and because, in the long run, it is likely to lead to inefficient production. While, therefore, it may, in certain cases, lead immediately to an increased volume of employment, or even, in very exceptional circumstances, to an increased

## WAGES AND EMPLOYMENT

total wage-bill, it is far more likely in the long run to lead to diminished employment as well as to lower earnings. It is, moreover, from the international standpoint, a most disastrous policy, in that it is calculated to give rise to a world movement for lower wage-rates, without any compensation in an increased world-total of employment.

Throughout the foregoing argument, the question of the effect of reduced wage-rates upon efficiency has been touched upon only in an incidental fashion. It is, however, vital. Wage-rates react upon efficiency in two ways: through their effects upon the workers and upon the employers.

In the case of the worker, reduced wage-rates need have no adverse effect, provided that they are accompanied either by a rise in earnings enough to offset them; or by an equivalent fall in the prices of all the goods and services which enter into the expenditure of the workers concerned. But reduced wage-rates will lead to increased earnings only if they lead to further employment of those who were previously under-employed. The realisation of this result clearly depends upon the achievement of a larger demand. It is exactly the same case as we have been examining already; for we have defined increased employment to mean either the employment of additional workers or the fuller employment of the same number of workers. It may be—in my opinion it is—usually a better thing, both from the standpoint of the workers and from that of the efficient conduct of industry, to concentrate a given volume of employment upon a limited number of workers rather than to share it out among a larger number at the cost of systematic under-employment. But this question is not germane to our present argument; for this concentration, or its opposite, can take place at any level of wage-rates. The reduction of wage-rates cannot increase earnings unless it leads to an increase in the volume of demand; and the conditions under which this can, and cannot, happen we have examined already.

We are left, then, with the second alternative, of a fall in the prices of all the goods and services which the worker buys sufficient to offset to the full the fall in his earnings. But this is most unlikely to be secured, not only because of the tendency of retail prices to fall less than wholesale prices, but also because there are important fixed items of working-class expenditure which are not likely to fall at all (*e.g.*, insurances, and rents under present conditions), and others likely to fall much less than general commodity prices (*e.g.*, taxes and rates, and probably a good many services). Even, then, if a fall in wage-rates produces no considerable immediate reactions on working-class efficiency, it is likely to react on it in the long run, by reacting upon the standard of living—unless, of course, the fall is more than offset by an increase in the social services provided by the State out of general taxation raised largely from non-wage incomes.

Under modern conditions, however, the effect upon the employer is likely to be more direct and disastrous than the effect upon the worker. For there can be no doubt that, all the world over, high wage-rates, wherever they have been enforced, have been a most powerful stimulus to industrial efficiency. The mechanisation of industry has been pushed furthest, and the total cost of production most reduced, whenever, over a considerable period of time, employers have been compelled, either by State or Trade Union action, or by scarcity of labour, to pay high rates of wages. It is at least plausible to suggest that, in the United States, high wages have been the most powerful single factor favourable to intensive mechanisation, and that, in Great Britain during the nineteenth century, the pressure of the Trade Unions for higher wages was an outstanding cause of the superior efficiency of British over continental methods of production. It is sometimes suggested that these relatively high wages were purchased only at the cost of a larger volume of unemployment than would have existed if wages had been lower. But there is absolutely no evidence in support of this view; for there is nothing to show that countries with high wage-rates have had more unemployment than countries whose wage-rates have been lower. I am not asserting dogmatically that this is not the case; but I do affirm that there is no body of evidence to show it to be so.

Indeed, on the face of the matter, the opposite view has a good deal more to support it. In general, countries with high wage-

## VII.   WAGES AND EMPLOYMENT

rates have increased their production and trade most rapidly, and have shown the greatest capacity to absorb an expanding population. This is true of Great Britain, of the United States, and of Germany; and, if Belgium appears to be a case on the other side, the exceptionally low cost of living in that country must be taken into account.

Now, a reduction of wage-rates presents itself to the employer as a means of reducing his costs without using his brains. It removes a powerful stimulus to improved plant efficiency and business organisation. It may, in the short run, enable a business to survive without adapting its methods to the most modern technical improvements; and it almost always presents itself in the first instance to the harassed employer as the easiest way out of his difficulties. The call to scrap obsolete plant is often unwelcome; and improved business organisation often presents itself to the employer as the painful necessity for learning a new and difficult technique, or at least for an unwonted use of the faculty of imagination. In modern times, it often demands as well some sacrifice of the independent isolation of the individual firm; and business men, cradled in individualism, are often exceedingly reluctant to co-operate, or to sink their rivalries, or to abandon a tradition of secrecy and self-sufficiency that is out of tune with modern industrial conditions. The alternative of reducing wage-rates is apt, in practice, to be far less unpleasing to the business mind; and it has the additional attraction of offering the more immediate results. For, as we have seen, reduced wage-rates within a restricted field will often produce, in the short run, higher profits or more production, or even both, at the cost of ultimate loss, whereas the results of business reorganisation and improved plant efficiency take longer to harvest, though they are far surer in their lasting effects.

There is, accordingly, on all counts a very strong balance of argument against any attempt to combat unemployment by the method of reducing wage-rates. The case against doing this is strongest of all from the international point of view; for a successful campaign to reduce wage-rates in one country is exceedingly likely, under modern conditions, to usher in a general campaign for their reduction in all countries. A far better way of combating unemployment would be an international agreement to raise wage-rates, and so increase the volume of purchasing power in accordance with the modern expansion of productive capacity. This, of course, does not mean that money rates of wages can be, under all conditions, absolutely sacrosanct. Workmen would be even less ready than employers to agree to a permanent stabilisation of existing money rates; and there are also bound to be changes in the relative levels of wages from trade to trade as methods and fashions change. There is, moreover, the changing value of money to be taken into account. Thus, during recent years, a fall in prices throughout the world has caused the real value of any given wage-rate, fixed in terms of money, to appreciate. In some cases, where wage-rates have been regulated automatically under a sliding-scale based upon the cost of living, the purchasing power of earnings (in default of fuller or less full employment) has been only maintained; while in other cases, especially in trades dependent on export, wage-rates have sometimes been reduced by more than the cost of living has fallen. But, over industry as a whole, the effect of falling prices has usually been to increase the purchasing power of the earnings payable for a full week's work. In face of increased unemployment and under-employment, this has often happened without any increase in the actual real earnings of the individual, or been accompanied by a fall in these real earnings; and it has certainly not involved an increase in the aggregate real earnings of the working class as a whole, or at least in real earnings per head. It has, however, tended to increase effective costs of production to the employer, by exacting from him a wage-rate which absorbs a larger proportion of the total selling price of his goods. He has, other things being equal, to give a larger quantity of his goods in return for a given quantity of labour.

Other things, however, are not usually equal; for, largely under pressure of these wage-rates, the employer has in most cases been making considerable efforts to improve his utilisation of the labour which he employs. He has pushed mechanisation further than ever before, has sought means of cutting down redundant business expenses, and has succeeded in increasing the amount of production quite out of proportion to any increase in the quantity of labour employed, and often while actually using a greatly diminished quantity, and so causing what has come to be called 'technological unemployment'. When this has occurred, it is to a considerable extent actually the result of high wage-rates; and it is nonsense to suggest that the same rate of productivity could have been secured if wage-rates had been lower. Nor can it be stated at all positively that there would have been less unemployment; for that would have depended upon the extent and intensity of competition, and on the elasticity of demand for the commodities in question. Failure to make industry more productive might have entailed so great a loss of trade as to throw quite as many workers out of employment as are thrown out by the technical developments of productivity, or caused so great a loss of potential demand as to have the same effect.

There can be no doubt that in every country since the war the technical efficiency of production has greatly increased, though it has not done this at anything like a uniform pace over the world as a whole. Any difficulties in paying wages at the present rates (or indeed at higher rates) arise, not from any defect in productive capacity, but solely from a failure of the world economic system to provide for the full utilisation of the capacity that exists. Neither of foodstuffs nor of raw materials nor of manufactures is there any shortage, or lack of ability to produce more. Rather do men speak again of over-production, and go short in the midst of a plenty they cannot control. It is surely manifest that the reduction of wage-rates is a most inappropriate remedy to apply in such a situation as this; for it is bound to accentuate the factors making for a limitation of markets and a shortage of total world demand. Any rigidity introduced into the wage-structure by collective bargaining or State action has been, therefore, on the whole, a blessing, in as far as it has helped to save the nations of the world from plunging into a competitive struggle to capture one another's trade by the method of reducing wage-rates.

Nevertheless, if and as far as this struggle is allowed to go on, it may become impossible for a particular country to maintain its wage-rates without loss of trade and consequent unemployment. This may be so either because its competitors have reduced their wage-rates, and so, in the short run at least, lowered their costs, or because they have, without lowering wage-rates, improved their relative efficiency. Equally, a particular country may lose trade to others either because it has raised its wage-rates, and so, in the short run, raised its costs, or because it has become relatively less efficient. Where the loss of trade by a country is due to a fall in its efficiency, or to an increase in the relative efficiency of its competitors, there are three courses open to it. It can take steps to increase its efficiency, and so regain its lost trade. Or it can lower its wage-rates to correspond to its lower level of relative efficiency. Or it can withdraw in part from the world market, and seek to become more self-contained, and to compensate for what it loses by securing through an assured home demand the fuller utilisation of the productive resources and man-power at its disposal. This may involve the using of these resources in directions in which a given expenditure of effort yields a less return; but the loss involved in this may, in certain circumstances, be more than balanced by more employment. But to pursue this last point further would take me much too far afield—into the entire question of Free Trade and Protection, which has an important bearing on the matters under discussion, but one that considerations of space forbid me to consider here.

My present point is that it is disastrous for a country to be compelled to lower its wage-rates by pressure of world competition—disastrous not so much for the country concerned, though its fate is bad enough, but above all because of the reactions of the disaster upon world economy as a whole. For if one country lowers wage-rates in order to capture trade, the countries from which the trade is taken will be under a strong temptation to lower their wage-rates in order to get it back. The result, no doubt, will be cheaper commodities, especially in the free markets of the world. But it will be also decreased purchasing power of working-class incomes, because the cost of living will not fall in proportion to the fall in general commodity prices.

Let us now pursue the point a little further. Low prices are a benefit only if they are combined with high production at high wages, or, in other words, if they are not balanced by a fall in purchasing power through low wages or unemployment. Low prices can well be combined with these conditions; but falling prices cannot, save under quite exceptional conditions. Now, falling prices may be due to several causes. They may arise from a restriction in the supply of money and credit, resulting in a disproportion between the transactions needing to be financed and the means available for financing them. Falling prices due to this cause always tend to cause industrial depression and unemployment, because the producer's costs always include rigid elements that do not fall with the prices of the goods he sells.

Secondly, falling prices may be due to competitive selling, intensified by changes in the relative efficiency of production between one area and another. Area A reduces its cost through increased efficiency, and other areas, B, C, D, in which efficiency has risen less, have then to bring down their prices, or to lose their trade. Such a situation is obviously, for the time, unfavourable to areas B, C and D, and likely to cause depression in them in proportion to their dependence on foreign trade, or exposure to foreign imports. It will continue to affect them until they either bring their efficiency up to the new level, or cut down their wage-rates, or adapt their industrial systems to the changed world conditions.

Thirdly, falling prices may be due to competitive selling, intensified, not by changes in efficiency, but by changes in relative wage-rates without a change in relative efficiency. If area A reduces its cost, not by improving its efficiency, but by reducing its wage-rates, areas B, C and D will suffer heavily in the same way as if the change were due to a change in relative efficiency. And the same choice of alternatives will be open to them.

Now, of these three causes the first, a change in the monetary supply, is clearly preventable as soon as the nations of the world acquire the sense to act together for its prevention. But, as this matter is now under discussion by the League of Nations, which has recently produced a useful preliminary report upon the gold situation, I do not propose to discuss it here, except to say that, as long as the monetary factor is allowed to remain uncontrolled, it is clearly impossible to devise any entirely satisfactory means of adjusting wages, or to deal with full effect with the problem of wage-rates in relation to unemployment. The control of monetary fluctuations is, for the immediate future, by far the most important of all world economic problems. Until we can prevent prices from fluctuating *as a result of changes in the supply of money and credit*, we shall not be able to advance far along the road of international regulation of the remaining factors.

The second cause, improved economic efficiency in one area as against others, is one we can neither hope nor wish to control, though we may desire to cope with its adverse reactions. For we obviously want the world's productive efficiency to increase, and we cannot expect it to increase everywhere at the same time and pace. What, then, ought we to do in order to prevent the adverse reactions which such an increase is apt to set up upon the areas in which the advance is less rapid? The only sound way of dealing with the situation is to allow incomes, and especially wage-incomes, to advance as fast as productivity increases, so as to meet increased efficiency by raising incomes and not by lowering prices. This involves an expansion of money and credit within the area concerned sufficient to finance the growing volume of transactions at the existing level of prices —a condition which can only be assured if the world devises means of securing an adequate expansion of total monetary supply.

Even this, however, will not wholly meet the situation; for the increase of productive efficiency will not be evenly spread over all commodities produced within the area in question, and even the stabilisation of the general price-level will not carry with it the stabilisation of any particular price. Particular prices cannot be stabilised in face of changing relative costs of production as between commodity and commodity. Accordingly, the stabilisation of general prices will not prevent those goods whose costs have fallen more than the average from entering into the world market at a lowered price, and so competing with the products of countries whose efficiency has risen less, or not at all. General price stabilisation would, however, greatly mitigate the effects of this competition, and reduce the problem of relative levels of efficiency to manageable dimensions.

There remains a further and more serious difficulty. Even if, in the country in which efficiency has improved, the internal price-level is stabilised, this does not imply stabilisation in the price of exports. Under modern conditions of production, it often pays, with an assured home market, to produce additional goods for export at a comparatively low run-on price; and this is likely to apply most of all to those countries which have increased their efficiency to the greatest extent. There will therefore be a strong temptation for such countries, even if their domestic price-level is stabilised, to engage in a form of export 'dumping', in the sense of selling abroad at less than the domestic price. But even this tendency will operate less if internal prices are stabilised, because their stabilisation, based on the policy of raising incomes to balance increased productive efficiency, will tend to raise costs, or rather to prevent their falling in correspondence with the rise in productivity.

Within the limits set by a policy of internal price stabilisation, and by such measures for the prevention of export dumping as the world may wish and be able to devise, the inconveniences resulting from a different rate of advance in productive efficiency in different areas must be accepted as part of the inevitable friction of the economic system, at any rate until international trade has been placed firmly on a collective, or Socialist, basis of exchange. But the disadvantages arising from the third cause of falling prices demand a more drastic and complete remedy; for in this case there are no compensatory advantages from the world standpoint. It is bad for the world as a whole when any country reduces its wage-rates, not because its productive efficiency has fallen off, but as a means of capturing trade from its rivals. For this course tends to create the conditions which lead to diminished purchasing power, and therefore to under-production and unemployment, in the world as a whole.

Now, it may be taken for granted that there is no important country in the world in which productive efficiency is actually falling. Every important country has in recent years been rapidly increasing its efficiency, though not all have been advancing at the same pace. There ought, therefore, to be no need for any reduction in wage-rates in any country; indeed, they ought to be everywhere advancing rapidly. Actually, in most countries, real wage-rates have been rising, even where money wage-rates have fallen; but the advance is certainly not in most areas as great as the advance in productivity. Moreover, there is now a strong world movement towards the reduction of wage-rates to an extent corresponding to the fall in prices in recent years. What prices (wholesale, or retail, or prices of manufactured goods, or 'general prices' including them all) are meant is none too clear; but the attempt to bring money wage-rates down is unfortunately plain enough. It is, however, evident that it would not pay any country to reduce its level of money wage-rates *if it knew that its competitors would do the same*; for each country thinks of wage reduction as a means of stealing some of its competitors' trade. Surely, in this situation, the appropriate remedy is an international agreement not to reduce money wage-rates at all, just as the Washington Hours Convention is the appropriate remedy for attempts by one country to steal a march on others by working longer hours. There is indeed this difference. It would be impossible to enforce uniformity of wages, or even a uniform minimum, in all countries, or even in Europe, whereas it is quite possible to enforce a uniform maximum working day. But it should be at least possible to secure a common agreement among States to countenance no movement designed to bring about a general reduction in wage-rates in any one country, and to do their best to prevent any such movement from occurring. And it should be possible, if this were done, for the International Labour Organisation to promote among employers and Trade Unions international agreements for particular industries stabilising the existing level of money wage-rates as a minimum for the future, subject to any general adjustments that might thereafter be made by consent on an international basis. Goods made in any country at less than the wage-rates thus approved as minima should be regarded definitely as sweated goods. It would be necessary to include in any such conventions or agreements a provision allowing money rates to be altered, to a uniform extent for all countries, if the value of money could be shown to have risen faster than the efficiency of production. But, in fact, this would not be likely to occur, and ardour to secure wage reductions would be greatly diminished if they were to become operative simultaneously in all the main competing countries.

Even as I write down this proposal, I am convinced that it may be regarded as Utopian. If the world cannot even combine to deal with the gold situation, is it likely to combine to deal with the far more intricate question of wages? I confess that at present it is not; for the world has shown in these last dozen years abundant evidence of its collective economic insanity. But there is really no logical objection to the proposal; for the sole reason for wishing to reduce wage-rates, or for regarding their reduction as anything but a calamity, is the hope of stealing, by means of lowered costs, some part of a competitor's trade. It is simply not possible to argue that there is any need to reduce wage-rates because they are too high to be afforded on the basis of present productive capacity, if only that capacity can be fully used. And, as we have seen earlier in this paper, reduction of wage-rates is far more likely to decrease than to increase the effective utilisation of the productive resources that are at the world's command.

In short, the idea that high wage-rates and a high level of employment stand in an antithetical relation is as far from the truth as it is possible for any superficially plausible idea to be. Low wage-rates may conceivably, in the short run, add to the amount of employment within a particular economic area; but they will always tend to diminish the total amount of employment in the world as a whole.

There remains, however, another aspect from which it is possible to approach our problem of the relation between wages and employment—that of the supply of capital for the development of production. The familiar argument in this connection runs as follows: Under the present economic system, new capital for the development of industry is supplied chiefly out of the savings of the richer classes—that is, out of profits and interest. Anything which tends to restrict the amount of profits therefore tends to restrict savings and the supply of capital for industry. High wages tend to leave less for profits out of the selling price of the product, and therefore tend to restrict savings and the supply of capital. Thus the familiar Wages Fund theory makes its reappearance in a fresh guise.

It is undoubtedly true that under the present economic system new capital for the new issue market and the development of industry is supplied mainly out of profits and interest. This is the case whether developments are financed out of profits placed to reserve or by means of new capital issues. But, whereas in the former case the new capital is drawn solely from profits, in the latter it is drawn from profits and interest indifferently. The narrowing of the profit margin therefore reacts most directly on that part of the accumulation of capital which is derived from reserved profits, and tends to limit the power of industry to finance itself in this way more than it limits the power to raise money by means of new capital issues. High wage-rates do not directly affect the amount of interest payments—which, in a time of falling prices such as the present, tend far more than wages to absorb an increasing share in the national dividend. Interest, indeed, tends under present conditions to provide an increasing volume of saved money available for reinvestment; and the drift of this money into new fixed interest-bearing securities is a marked feature of the present trend of investment. Under normal conditions, this pressure would result in a fall in interest rates; but these tend to be kept high by the continued existence of large-scale Government borrowing, both for conversions and for new expenditure, and for such exceptional purposes as the settlement of international debts. These high interest rates naturally make it harder to secure money for risk-bearing industrial enterprise; and the difficulty of offering the prospect of a high-profit yield under the existing conditions of industry tends to hold back the reorganisation of industry and its re-equipment with new capital goods capable of producing at the lowest level of costs. But this shortage of capital for industrial development is at least as much due to high interest rates for fixed interest-bearing securities as to any other cause; and it is by no means evident that a fall in wage-rates would contribute materially to ease the position. It would do so only if the lowered wage-rates did actually lead to higher margins of profit; and we have seen that the prospect of their doing this is by no means so well assured as it appears on the surface to be.

In fact, there is not at present much evidence of an actual shortage of capital in relation to the effective demand. Capital for industrial reorganisation is not in great demand because industry is depressed; and it is not at all likely that a fall in wage-rates would either increase greatly the supply of capital or open up more profitable opportunities for its use. It would be more likely to perpetuate obsolescent methods of production and, by decreasing the pressure on employers to re-equip their works with more up-to-date plant, to lower the demand for risk-bearing capital rather than increase it.

This is not to say that more capital is not needed. It is; but the condition of its effective use is the maintenance of a high level of purchasing power among the members of the community, and especially among the workers, who are the main repositories of the demand for consumable goods. For capital can be profitably employed only in providing, in the last resort, for the needs of the final consumer; and any attempt to increase the supply of capital at the expense of consumers' demand is therefore initially suspect. It is true enough that, if all the productive resources of society were being fully employed, capital could be increased only at the expense of final consumption, and final consumption only at the expense of capital. But this antithesis does not hold good of a society in which the existing productive resources are being under-employed. In such a society there is an unused potential supply of productive power, which can be directed to the increase of capital resources so as not to diminish, but actually to augment, the income devoted to the purchase of consumption goods. In fact, consumption and saving, so often represented as antithetical, are likely, in most of the conjunctures of the modern economic system, to vary together and not inversely. It is, of course, possible for a community to spend so much of its income as to make inadequate provision for the future, just as it is possible for it to try to save too much—*i.e.*, more than is required to keep pace with the demand for consumable goods. But it is a fallacy to suppose that high wage-rates are likely to lead to the former condition unless they are pressed up more rapidly than the advance of productive efficiency admits.

Moreover, as Mr. J. A. Hobson has pointed out, it is a mistake to regard saving as being solely a function of the surplus incomes of the richer classes in society. High wage-incomes not only react directly on the efficiency of labour, but also lead, through better nurture and education, to the upbringing of a more efficient new generation of workers. Nor are the money savings of the workers negligible, apart from those which are put into education and training. They supply the accumulated resources of the Trade Unions, Co-operative Societies and friendly societies, a large part of the capital of industrial insurance companies and of that devoted to housing, and considerable further sums made available for use as capital through savings banks and thrift institutions of many kinds. The importance of working-class saving is apt to be under-estimated because it does not appear directly in the ordinary capital market, and is controlled indirectly through the various agencies which undertake its reinvestment. A society which relied mainly on the small saver to provide industrial capital in the narrower sense would doubtless need to adopt different methods of capital issue from those hitherto in vogue; but there is no reason to believe that it would go short of necessary capital for economic growth.

I conclude, then, in general that there is no substance behind the opinion that unemployment is largely caused by the maintenance of wage-rates at an uneconomically high level. Such a view is, indeed, highly paradoxical in view of the events of the past year. For the crisis through which the world has been passing is, on the face of the matter, a clear case of the failure of demand to keep pace with the development of productive power, whereas, if high wages were at fault, it would be more natural for the demand for consumers' goods to outrun the supply, and for prices to rise than to fall. In the world as a whole, there is manifestly need for a larger amount of income available for spending on consumable commodities, and not for a contraction of consumers' demands. Such a contraction would assuredly reduce, instead of increasing, the supply of capital for investment.

The desire to reduce wage-rates arises from a perverted and mistaken form of economic nationalism. There are in each country persons who hope to steal a march on the rest of the world by reducing wage-rates and costs of production, and so capturing prosperity at the expense of the adversity of others. They would do well, however, to remember that more than one can play at such a game, and that the game is rendered useless if everyone plays it. Nor should they be allowed for a moment to forget the simple fact that reduced wage-rates are bound to react adversely upon the home market, whereas their reaction on the export market is highly problematical and dependent upon the action of competitors. Reduction of wage-rates ought therefore to be the last, instead of the first, resort of any economic system; and we should be wise, instead of flying to this way of escape from our difficulties, to seek out and correct the real causes of world depression, which are to be found in a shortage of world demand rather than of the world's power to supply, in a lack of co-operative action designed to stabilise the price-level or economise in the use of gold, in the rigidity of our industrial structure from the standpoint of business organisation and mobility of labour, and above all in our failure to use our brains to good enough purpose in facing squarely the realities of the post-war economic world. If the world would only co-operate in order to increase the purchasing power of the workers, instead of competing to reduce it, there would be far more hope that depression would be overcome, and productive power be fully employed on a reasonable basis of mutual international exchange.

### A Note on Relative Trade Wage-Rates

I have discussed in the preceding paper the case for a general reduction in rates of wages, but not the special case that is put forward for the reduction of wage-rates in the 'sheltered' trades. It is, of course, true enough that in recent years the workers in industries and services sheltered from international competition have tended to improve their wage-position relatively to the workers in the exporting industries. Especially, there has been a marked improvement in the wages of distributive workers and of those engaged in many of the public utility services. Workers in the exporting industries, on the other hand, have suffered large wage reductions during the years of industrial depression. It is accordingly suggested that if wage-rates in the sheltered occupations were brought down to the unsheltered level, the effect would be to reduce the cost of living so as to bring it more closely into conformity with the fall in wholesale prices, and also, by cheapening finished goods to the consumer, to create more elastic markets for the producing industries.

It cannot be denied that there is some force in this view. But it has to be remembered, first, that the workers in such services as transport and distribution were, in most cases, very poorly paid, in relation to the main bodies of productive workers, before the war, and that the absolute level of their wage-rates, though it has risen more than the average, is still in most cases not high; so that it can hardly be easy to force these workers back into the old position of relative inferiority from which they have but lately emerged. Secondly, we must not forget that wage-rates in the exporting industries have in many cases been pressed down to a very low level, defended only on grounds of sheer necessity; so that the demand that sheltered wages should fall to the unsheltered level amounts in fact to a demand for a general reduction in wage-rates, and is open to the objections described in my paper.

Moreover, no one has suggested how the reduction of sheltered wage-rates is to be brought about, save as part of a general campaign to reduce wage-rates over the entire field. But such a campaign would almost certainly be more effective in bringing down wage-rates in the unsheltered than in the sheltered trades, low as the former rates are already. For the main pressure of competitive forces is still playing upon the unsheltered trades; and wages in the sheltered trades have been maintained chiefly because the bargaining power of the workers is greater in these trades than it is elsewhere.

Accordingly, an attempt to reduce wage-rates in the sheltered trades alone would hardly succeed, while an attempt to reduce them in all trades would probably but exaggerate the existing disparities between the sheltered and unsheltered groups. The real need is that wage-rates in the unsheltered occupations should be increased, rather than that those in the sheltered occupations should be cut down.

### A Note on the Efficiency of Labour

The efficiency of labour in production is the result, we have seen, of two forces: productivity and intensity. Both these forces are compound, and depend partly upon the labourer and partly upon the utilisation of labour by those responsible for its direction. There can be no doubt that, in recent years, both productivity and intensity have tended to increase, and to do so in a dual fashion. Labour has become more productive, both because its quality has tended to rise with improving education and physique, and because it has been given the aid of more powerful and efficient machines, and of better business administration and control. But at the same time the intensity of labour has tended to increase, both because the fear of unemployment has induced harder work, and because modern machinery and factory discipline have tended to set a hotter pace. Both tendencies have been to some extent offset by the reduction of working hours; but in spite of this reduction the average product per man-day has certainly been increasing fast.

This factor must be borne in mind when we are comparing present-day wage-rates with those of a decade or two decades ago. Hourly, and even weekly, wages are not being paid for the same amount of expended effort as before, but often for a larger amount. If wage-rates rise in proportion to production per man-hour, this rise takes account of the increase in both productivity and intensity of effort; but where a man whose weekly wage in 1914 was $x$ is now being paid $2x$, it must not be inferred that his money remuneration for effort expended has been doubled. This tendency to increase the intensity of production is naturally accompanied by a tendency to throw the older and weaker workers upon the industrial scrap-heap. There is an abnormally large proportion of older men and women among the unemployed; and what is called 'technological unemployment', due to the increasing mechanisation of industry, tends to add most of all to the numbers of older workers discarded from employment in favour of those who will stand a hotter pace.

# PART II
ECONOMICS IN THEORY AND PRACTICE

# VIII

## TOWARDS A NEW ECONOMIC THEORY

WHAT things should the economist study, and from what point of view? It is not helpful to answer that he ought to study economic things from the economic standpoint; for that answer only pushes the question back a stage, or asks for its restatement in a different form. What are economic things, and what is an economic standpoint? we have next to enquire.

The economist is tempted to answer that economic things are those which can be measured in terms of prices, and no others. For he has usually a keen desire to introduce as much precision as possible into his subject, and to make it as susceptible as possible of quantitative statement; and, in the world of wealth production and distribution with which he has to deal, price appears usually to afford the only means of bringing many different things under a common standard of measurement. It is possible to state the number of tons of coal raised, or yards of cotton cloth manufactured, in the world or in any particular country or area, provided that the trouble is taken to collect the necessary figures. But it is not possible to measure the coal in comparison with the cotton cloth, under the conditions of modern industry, without invoking the concept of price. It is possible to determine the number of men employed in mines or cotton factories; but it does not seem possible to compare the amounts of human productive energy used up in producing the coal or the cotton goods except in terms of the wages paid—the price of labour. All the most familiar economic terms—rent, wages, interest, profits, costs, margins, capital, credit and a host of others—are thought of most easily as sums of money or rates of money return, or somehow in terms of money as prices or values; and this seems to be the only way in which they can be thought of *together*, and made the subject-matter of a study embracing the economic system as a whole.

It is true that the economist does think of each of the things which he studies in another way as well—as long as he is studying them one by one. Thus, after Ricardo, he thinks of rent as a quantity of produce, depending on the differential productive capacity of a parcel of land, and treats this real rent as underlying its expression as a sum of money. He thinks of real wages, as well as money wages; real wages being the quantity of goods secured by the labourer in return for his work. He thinks of both interest and profits, not only as sums of money, but also as shares in the real product of society as a whole, or of a particular industry or enterprise. He thinks of costs, not only in terms of money, but also as the using up of scarce real factors of production; of margins in terms of the different quantities so used up; of capital as a stock of buildings, machines and other physical productive assets, and not only in terms of shares valued in money; and of credit as the advancing of goods or of the right to goods as well as of money. Indeed, he is conscious all the time that the prices of which he treats are only worth discussing because they are the prices of real things, material or immaterial; and that production and distribution matter because they secure a flow of real goods and services to the consumer.

But while these real things appear plainly in the separate statement of the conditions underlying each part of the mechanism of prices, they drop right out of sight when the separate factors have to be brought together, and marshalled into a general theory of production or distribution, or even into a sectional theory involving the comparison of one thing with another. For how, asks the economist, am I to compare one thing with another except in terms of its money value, or price? Is not this the most realistic way of comparing things—the way in which they are being compared every day in the course of ordinary economic transactions? How else are they to be compared? What other possible standard is there?

The earlier economists thought they had found another and a more real standard, when they attempted to measure value, as distinct from price, in terms of the amounts of labour expended on the production of different goods. This value seemed to be a real standard, based on the real amounts of scarce factors of production used up in placing the commodity on the market, and therefore expressing the real social costs of its production. But in fact neither Ricardo nor anyone else ever found a way of measuring the amount of labour apart from the wages paid. As long as the subsistence theory of wages held the field, this did not seem to matter; for the wages could be held to express directly the actual goods consumed by the labourer. But as soon as the subsistence theory was given up, the amount of labour became a purely hypothetical and unmeasurable concept. Marx attempted a complex restatement of the amount of labour theory on the basis of the subsistence doctrine; but this is admitted to be the least digestible part of the Marxian system. Marx's doctrine of surplus value does not stand or fall by his acceptance of the amount of labour theory of value or the subsistence theory of wages.

With Mill we pass into the realm of 'price of production' instead of 'amount of labour'. Clearly the attempt to get at real value apart from money has been abandoned, and we are in the realm of prices, with only an endeavour to abstract from short-term market fluctuations, effects of monopoly, and other disturbing factors. Value is still thought of as determined by the conditions of supply, with demand in a quite secondary position; but it has come to be thought of in terms of money and not of quantities of the real agents or factors of production.

From this time onwards, Economics passes over thoroughly and completely to the study of prices; and the old distinctions between prices and values are either discarded, or kept only as two names for the same thing in its phenomenal and noumenal forms. Economics is trying to become the study of prices, and to concentrate its attention directly on the working of the price-mechanism in modern societies. It keeps, to be sure, in its opening chapters and scattered here and there through its treatment of particular subjects, some stale metaphysic and some very crude psychology. But, when it cuts the cackle and comes to the horses, it is of prices that it speaks. The metaphysics of wealth, and the psychological generalisations about the relation of wants and desires, satiety and diminishing satisfaction, mental discounting of the future, disutility of labour, and all the rags and tatters of the hedonistic calculus, are irrelevant to its serious work, which is the study of the prices of goods and consumers' services, of money and credit, of land and capital and labour—in short, of everything that enters into the working of the economic system as it is.

I confess to finding this conception of the scope of Economics fundamentally unsatisfactory. This is not because I am at all disposed to deny the importance of price calculations, of supply schedules and demand schedules and the rest of the marginalist stock-in-trade, of the careful statistical analysis of actual price data, of the studies of trade fluctuation, currency questions, and schemes of stabilisation that are being largely pursued by this means. Much less do I deny the importance of measurement in some form, or its central place in any scheme of economic study. But the limitations of these quantitative methods using money as their measure, and their tendency to mislead unless these limitations are kept firmly in mind, seem to me to need constant emphasis; and especially I want economists to be on their guard against attaching undue importance to, and drawing unsuitable and incongruous conclusions from, either actual or, still more, purely theoretical data concerned with the behaviour of the price system.

It is easy enough to understand how the tendency to draw such conclusions arises. Price is so convenient a measure, and does so appear to answer the economist's demand for precision. It is, moreover, so omnipresent a fact of existing economic relationships that to study it seems above all else the way of being realistic and practical as well as precise. Since price is for producer and consumer alike both the dominant consideration and the only point of contact over a wide field of economic activity, it seems as if, by studying it, we should get down most quickly and easily to the roots of the economic problem.

But do we? It is, indeed, obvious that, for many special purposes, study of the price relationship is essential. It is necessary for the consumer, trying to make both ends meet; it is necessary for the business man, studying his prospective money costs and yields in every productive operation on which he embarks; and it is necessary for a Chancellor of the Exchequer or a City Treasurer, seeking to make his budget balance. The price relationship seems to be by far the most characteristic relationship of the economic world; and a recent economist even goes so far as bluntly to label Economics as 'The Science of Prices'.

And yet—how many of the questions that sensible people want to get help from Economics in answering can be answered purely in terms of this 'science of prices'? That considerations relative to prices will be involved in many of the answers I fully admit; but are they all the questions, or even always the principal questions involved? It is, of course, possible—and even fashionable—to say that these other questions are non-economic, and to push them aside in the hope that some other 'science' or study will be kind enough to deal with them. But is this a satisfactory way of meeting the plain man's desire for help? It may be true—it is true—that the answer to almost every big practical question involves non-economic as well as economic considerations; but are we to say that all considerations which cannot be reduced to terms of price are non-economic? I at any rate do not think we can; for there are many problems, incapable of complete expression in terms of prices, that I can see no way of referring to any other study. They are economic problems essentially; for they deal with the supply and use of goods and services which need effort to produce, and take away, if they are produced, from the supply of productive resources and energy remaining for other uses. If problems of this order are not economic, what are we to call them? And, if the economist is not to attempt to play his part in answering them, who is?

I am saying, then, that while price considerations are admittedly important, they are no more important, and no more economic, than many considerations which cannot be expressed at all in terms of price. Perhaps an instance will help to make plainer what I mean. It may be quite possible for a steel manufacturer to say exactly what the coal and the labour used up in a particular operation cost him—in other words, to know their price. But we cannot take the price which he has paid for these factors of production as representing necessarily their 'cost' to the community. The conditions under which the coal was mined, the conditions under which the ironmaster employed his labour, have all manner of social reactions which we certainly cannot assume to be accurately represented in the purchase price of either. And, even if these reactions are described as being 'social' rather than economic in character, my argument is not affected; for even if they are, in their totality, social, they certainly include elements which no one will deny to be economic —as, for example, the cost of any poor relief given to the coal-miner or any subsidy to his employer, and the cost of the medical treatment which may become necessary if work in the iron trade is carried on under unhealthy conditions.

Here, of course, I am saying simply that, distinct from the actual cost to himself which the buyer calculates in any transaction, we must admit a conception of 'social cost' differing from this market cost, and having in it at the least economic elements which the market cost does not accurately reflect. This is a vitally important difference. But I think my point goes even deeper than may at once appear; for it is clear that, whereas the business man measuring market costs is dealing with prices, any estimate of social cost involves getting behind prices to the realities which they in some part represent, but in some part also distort.

It is indeed true that even the business man seldom or never makes his most vital decisions purely as a result of a calculation of prices. He has also mentally to weigh up factors which cannot be reduced to terms of money costs, and to weigh these in the same scale as his money costs before arriving at his judgment. He has to do this as a business man, apart from any purely 'social' consideration which may affect him, business man though he is, as a citizen or a human being. There are in his own costs, as distinct from the costs of society, elements which do not respond to the price valuation, though they have to be related to it in his act of judgment. Obvious examples are to be found in his decisions about the amount of hard work he is prepared to put in himself in order to make his business a success, or as to the worthwhileness of a particular contract in relation to the toil and trouble, as distinct from the money cost, in which it is likely to involve him. Let us agree, however, that his aim is to express all possible factors in terms of price, because it is in terms of price that his balance has ultimately to be struck.

The social point of view is essentially different, since its concern with prices is only incidental. The social valuation of the 'costs' of any service has to be made ultimately in terms, not of its prices, but of the amount and quality of the labour and real capital resources which it uses up, the quality of the life which it affords to the labourers, the real value of the product to the consumers, the indirect effects of the particular uses to which the labour and capital are put—*e.g.*, such effects as pollution by smoke, the promotion or destruction of the employees' intelligence or vitality, the disturbance of amenities as well as values caused by a particular localisation of an industry, and a hundred other considerations which will not directly admit of money measurement. The earlier economists from Ricardo to Marx, with their 'amount of labour', as distinct from 'cost of production', theories of value, were certainly nearer to measuring social costs than any later school has been. As soon as 'amount of labour' was discarded in favour of 'cost of production'—that is, a real in favour of a money measurement—the social element was in effect jettisoned. Political Economy became 'Business Economics', and the way was opened, *via* the Jevonians and the Austrian subjectivists, for a mere 'Science of Prices' instead of an attempt to understand the principles governing the wealth of nations.

More and more since then the economist has ploughed his business furrow, allowing 'Economics of Welfare' to intrude only as a half-alien metic in his beautiful City of Prices. That he has achieved along these lines certain substantial and very desirable results I have no wish to deny. But let us pause for a moment to enquire just how much he has achieved.

Economics, as it is ordinarily taught, has two main branches —production and distribution. Its study of production is in fact mainly concerned with the theory of value—that is, of prices—as determining what shall be produced or not produced. In the forefront of the current presentation of the subject is consumers' demand, conceived as the final determinant of the productive process. This demand is expressed in a number of demand schedules, representing the total market demand for each commodity at various prices, and made up by disintegrating the individual and household budgets of a large number of separate consumers. Over against this conception of consumers' demand is set the willingness of the producers—that is, of business *entrepreneurs* in the main—to supply the various goods and services which the consumers want, in varying quantities and at varying prices in accordance with the conditions of demand. These supply schedules, whose interaction with the demand schedules results in the actual production and consumption of such and such goods and services at such and such prices, are conceived in terms of costs of production varying with the quantity produced. We thus get a theory of prices, worked out initially in terms of the relations between buyers and sellers of finished goods and services, and then applied by analogy to the buying and selling of producers' goods as a case of 'derived' demand; and this is offered to us as a theory of production.

The typical text-book of Economics then passes on to Distribution, by which it means primarily the division of the national income arising out of production among the various 'factors of production'. These shares in income are again regarded as prices, arising out of the relation between the demand for varying quantities of various kinds of land, labour, capital and business ability at varying prices, and the willingness of those who control these factors to supply them in varying quantities at different prices. But whereas the theory of production, which is also the general theory of value, deals in the main with all commodities together before proceeding to a discussion of the differing elasticities of supply and demand in the case of various commodities, in the theory of distribution most of the time is spent in dealing with the separate characteristics of rent, interest, profits and wages, and very little is usually done towards formulating any general theory of distribution. Perhaps it is held that this has been done already, under the head of Production, in stating the general theory of value, and that the various forms of distribution are only special cases in the working of this theory. If that is so, there are not really distinct theories of production and distribution at all, but a single theory of prices or values which embraces both. Nevertheless, the twofold arrangement commonly persists.

The weakness of this method of treatment is surely clear enough. It begins, in the statement of the theory of the value of commodities, by assuming that consumers' demand exists independently of supply, whereas in fact people get the incomes which make up the schedules of demand only if production takes place, and as a function of the productive process. For either their incomes come to them directly from production, as wages or salaries or profits or rents or certain kinds of interest, which are shares in the product accorded to 'factors' of production; or, if their incomes come to them in any other way, they must take the form of deductions from the incomes accruing to these same 'factors'. There is no source of income except production; and if production slows down or stops, the flow of income must slow down or stop as well.

Of course, everyone is well enough aware of this; and it even appears plainly in the statement of the theory of distribution, which is represented as a sharing-out of the product among the several factors. But the theory of distribution takes the production for granted; for has not that been dealt with already, in the opening treatment of value? But in that opening treatment we have not really been given a theory of production at all. Instead, we have been offered a very different theory—a theory of the response of producers to a demand which is assumed to possess an independent, and even a prior, existence. For the traditional statement of the theory of value makes demand its starting-point, and then studies the producers' reactions to it; whereas in reality there can be no demand, in the economic sense, save as a result of production.

In saying this I am not, of course, attacking what the economists have to tell us about the working of their schedules of demand and supply. It is perfectly true that, other things being equal, more will be demanded of a commodity as its price falls, the degree of elasticity varying greatly from one type of goods to another. It is no less true that producers, or rather *entrepreneurs*, will be willing to supply different quantities of goods at different prices, though in this case their response cannot be so simply stated because of the complications of increasing and decreasing costs. But the demands to which the supplies are conceived as responding do not exist independently of their response, and can be taken as a starting-point for analysis only because the economist is studying a process already at work, and a situation in which incomes are being generated as a result of actual production.

But even so the theory fails to supply a satisfactory analysis of production. It proceeds on the assumption, sometimes explicit, but often unspoken, that we can take demand for granted, subject only to temporary frictions in the working of the economic mechanism, because the logic of the interacting forces will result in a situation in which the available productive resources will be fully employed. Demand will exist because production will exist; and production will exist because the forces of demand will adjust the prices of the factors of production to levels which will cause them to be fully employed. For consumers' demand, from which the demand for producers' goods is derived, will determine the total income to be distributed among the factors of production; and the 'factors' will have to take what they can get, as a result of their several pulls or relative productivities, out of the total income thus determined by consumers' demand.

What is ignored in this analysis is that the producers' unwillingness to use all the available productive forces at the prices offered by the consumers can at any time, and must, if it is exercised, result in a contraction of consuming power. If supply is contracted, demand is contracted as well, because the incomes of the consumers arise out of the productive process. Since this is the case, if once for any reason the powers of production come to be incompletely used, the means of getting them back into use is destroyed at the same time, through the fall in real consumers' demand. It does not matter whether the goods that are still being produced are sold cheap or dear; for in either case no more income is being generated in production than will suffice to buy those goods. There is no consumers' demand available for the goods that could be produced in excess of the current production.

I am not now raising any of the questions—vitally important as they are—which arise out of the possibility that at certain times, owing to a kink in the economic system, there may be either an excess or a deficiency of purchasing power in relation to the supply of goods on the market, or that relative over- or under-saving may produce a deficiency or excess in the demand for consumers' goods. These are quite separate problems. My point is simply that, under existing conditions and apart from such special disturbances, the system by which incomes are generated in the course of production, while production is a voluntary act which producers are free to undertake or to refuse, provides no ready means of getting from a situation in which under-production has actually arisen back to a full utilisation of the available resources, even if the producers, chastened by under-employment, become willing to sell their goods more cheaply. For a mere cheapening of supply will not widen the market: it will cancel incomes as well as lower prices, unless it is achieved by a lowering of the real, as distinct from the money, costs of production.

Of course, a cheapening of supply by one group of producers, from whatever cause it arises, may cause a transference of demand to them from other supplies; but this may only transfer unemployment of productive resources, and not prevent it. The point is that there exists, under present conditions, no economic law, and even no tendency, making for the full use of all the available productive resources. Unemployment of men and resources may be, not a merely temporary result of disequilibrium, but a permanent feature of the economic system, incurable by means of any mere readjustment of the prices of the factors of production. Indeed, unemployment, whereas it causes a redundancy of labour, may actually shorten the supply of new capital available for productive use, both by diminishing the inducement to the *entrepreneur* to embark on production and by lessening the supply of new savings owing to the decrease of the flow of profits out of which such savings are largely made. A shortage of new capital available for industry may coexist with a redundancy of old capital resources already embodied in factories, plant and other productive assets, which may be unusable for want of new capital to bring them up to date, and to effect a fall in the real costs of production.

Thus, unemployed men and resources can exist under the present economic system, and while they exist there can be a perfect balance between the actual supply and the actual demand, which both arise out of the production that does in fact occur. It follows that, while the analysis of the interaction of these forces is a very necessary part of economic study, it cannot constitute a theory of production. It assumes the existence of production, which is implied in its first postulate, the existence of demand.

A theory of production should begin with the analysis of production itself, since production is logically prior to demand, and therefore to the interaction of supply and demand. It is true that production, to be of use, must deliver the kinds of goods which the consumers want, and that production which does not achieve this is sheer waste of effort. But under the present system, the analysis of production must come first, because out of it and in no other way does demand arise. This is as true of State demand, or of demand which appears to be independent of production, like the demand of *rentiers*, because this demand has to come out of taxes or other claims ultimately charged upon production.

But how are we to begin with an analysis of production? I should have said rather that the logical starting-point for Economic Theory is an analysis of productive powers. There is in any community, or in the world as a whole, a certain supply of productive resources, human and material. The economic problem is so to organise the life of society as to use these resources for the creation of the greatest utility. But this cannot be merely a question of the total quantity of resources available; for the resources themselves are highly differentiated already. They include potential workers possessing many different kinds of skill and aptitude for both manual and mental work, and natural resources and capital goods capable of being used to turn out many different classes of finished commodities and services. Some of these resources are fixed absolutely to a single use, and cannot be used at all in any other way; others are usable in a variety of ways. There are fixed resources and adaptable resources; so that society has always the choice up to a point between different kinds of production, but cannot rapidly change the character of its production beyond this point without rendering some of its resources valueless, and involving itself in expense of materials and effort for the adaptation of others. To some extent, certain things must be produced, or productive resources left unused; but the possibility of changing the forms of production by a redistribution of free resources is always considerable enough to allow a good deal of adaptability.

These facts suggest a twofold problem—first and most obviously, the direction of the new and more readily transferable resources into the branches of production in which they will be of most use; and secondly a wise discrimination in the scrapping or retention in use of those productive resources which can be transferred either not at all, or with greater difficulty. But how is the community, or the economist, to judge to what forms of production free or transferable resources can be most usefully applied, or whether resources of the second sort should be scrapped or kept in use? The orthodox answer is that this is not a matter either for the economist or for the community as an organised body, but for the market—the free demand of the countless individual consumers. They, it is assumed, will by their demand schedules transfer production steadily to the most useful applications, and settle the fate of existing resources by either providing or not providing a sufficient profit incentive to those who order their working.

But is this good enough? If consumers' demand is withdrawn from existing undertakings and transferred elsewhere, the result will be to throw workers previously employed in these undertakings out of work and to cancel profits and other incomes dependent upon them. It is not true that the result will necessarily be only a transference of demand: it may be a reduction in total demand through the cessation of the incomes of those who are thrown out. The new incomes generated in the course of the new production made possible by the changed current of demand will to some extent replace these lost incomes; but they need not replace them to the full extent, and a new balance may be struck at a lower level of production. Whether this happens or not will depend mainly on the scarcity or abundance of free or easily transferable resources that can be applied to the new types of production. If these are deficient, and the new balance is struck at a lower level, that lower level will tend to perpetuate itself, just because it does rest on a balance between supply and demand.

Nor can we assume that the free play of consumers' demand will either evoke a full use of new productive resources, or direct new and transferable resources into the most useful forms of production. If it takes some time to bring the new resources effectively into play, the destruction of incomes through the disuse of the old resources may so contract demand in the interval as to make new development not worth while from the standpoint of the *entrepreneur*. The strength of monetary demand cannot, moreover, be accepted as a valid test of usefulness, in face of the inequality of incomes and the different utility of money to different purchasers. And, thirdly, the possessor of income may elect not to apply it at all in the form of consumers' demand, but to hoard it, or use it in some other way which will upset the balance of the economic system.

I conceive it to be the economist's function, in his study of the productive possibilities of society, to work out precepts for securing the maximum of useful production. If it were in fact enough to leave this to be seen to by the free play of consumers' demand, there would be no more to be said, and the economist would be free to pass on to the next subject—the study of the supply and demand relation in its interaction with the system of prices. But if the free play of consumers' demand is not enough, both because there is no guarantee that it will be adequate to elicit the greatest possible production, and because it will not necessarily lead to the best kinds of production, the economist has to be kept prisoner for a while until he can tell us what complementary or supplementary criteria we can use.

I am not for a moment suggesting that free consumers' demand is an unimportant criterion, or one that ought to be superseded. But I am urging that it needs to be supplemented and, on occasion, corrected. It cannot really be economically right for a community to leave usable productive resources unused, as long as there is *any* unsatisfied demand for the goods they can be used to produce, even if their employment will not yield a profit. For all income, and not profit income alone, is from the social standpoint a gain, and all usable products that people want at any price are worth producing, if the alternative is to produce nothing.

The attainment of maximum production is, indeed, commonly stated at the beginning of treatises on Economics to be, *par excellence*, the economic objective. But, apart from assumptions that the free play of consumers' demand will in fact secure this, the methods of getting maximum production are usually no further discussed. As we have seen, however, the method of beginning with consumers' demand as the initial datum means that, at the most, the securing of production can be discussed only within the limits set by this demand, and not in relation to the capacity of the available productive resources.

While, therefore, there is every reason for leaving the consumer free to choose what he will buy from among the goods offered for sale, it does not follow that the supply of goods offered, or the prices at which they are offered, should be left to be determined by the response of the *entrepreneur* to consumers' demand.

Indeed, this is very far from being a true picture of what happens under the present economic system, or has ever happened in the past over the whole field of industry. Price-fixing is, in the case of many classes of materials and manufactured goods, nowadays a function of the productive organisation rather than of consumers' demand. Of course, the productive organisation can act only within the limits of demand, in the sense that the level of prices fixed is bound to react on the quantity sold; but the price is actually set, in a great number of cases, by the *entrepreneurs*, and consumers' demand left to act on output rather than on price. Nor is this merely a result of the growth of monopoly in the modern world. Two centuries ago, prices were on the whole a good deal more rigid than they are today, partly through the action of guilds and corporations, but also because tradition was a far stronger element in economic life. It was not only the breaking down of privileged corporations and the growth of commercial competition, but even more the destruction of traditions in the Industrial Revolution, that made price highly elastic in response to consumers' demand. The conditions depicted as typical in the text-books were perhaps typical of the nineteenth century: they were not typical of the sixteenth or the seventeenth, and they are not typical of today.

But a system under which price-fixing tends again to become a function of the *entrepreneur* is no more calculated—indeed, it is even less calculated—to elicit maximum production than one in which prices respond readily to consumers' demand. For this system not only fails to escape from the limitation of demand which arises from the fact that incomes are generated only in the course of production, but also adds to it in many cases the deliberate restriction of output in order to maintain prices. Under either system, the determining factor between production and non-production is worthwhileness from the standpoint of the *entrepreneur*. That is to say, the form of income which we call profit provides the sole incentive to production, and the other forms of income, though they are equally valuable from the standpoint of the community, appear as costs or deterrents, and not as incentives.

If, then, we desire to discover the conditions likely to lead to the full use by society of its productive resources, we have clearly to question the assumptions on which the present system of production rests, and especially the existing relations between income and production. But we can cut clearly away from these assumptions, without putting new ones in their place, only if we begin by studying the productive system in itself, as distinct from its relations to the processes of distribution and exchange.

A realistic Economic Theory based on this principle will set out from a study of the character and organisation of the available productive resources of modern societies, from the standpoint of production itself. It will study the general technological conditions of modern industrialism in relation to the sources of power and the developing forms of power production. It will survey the available material resources of modern communities, and the changing relations of the human labour power to the machines and the power equipment at its disposal. Of course, the special techniques of the various branches of production, as such, are not its business; but it is essentially its business to consider the forms of economic organisation most appropriate to the technique of modern industry, and best calculated to promote a full use of the available resources. It will therefore proceed from a survey of the underlying technological conditions to a study of the actual and possible forms and methods of industrial and economic organisation—the structure and working of joint stock companies, cartels and combines, the development of co-operative production in agriculture and industry and of the consumers' Co-operative Movement, the forms and operation of public enterprise, State and municipal, and of statutory public and semi-public concerns. It will deal also with the growth of planned economic organisation, both national and international, with the international action of trusts and combines, with State planning schemes as they exist in Russia and have been adumbrated elsewhere, and with Socialism as a theory of the right method of organising the productive powers of society on both a national and a world-wide scale.

So far, this revised Economic Theory will be considering its problem solely from the standpoint of production. It will be dealing with the relative merits of large-scale and small-scale economic organisation, of public and private enterprise, of mass production and its alternatives, entirely as questions of productive efficiency. It will have, of course, to include in its survey the economic effects of different forms of production on the workers as producers, but only the economic effects, and only those as far as they react upon production. So far, no question of demand or distribution arises; for the question is not how the product is to be distributed, but how to make it as large as possible, and we are for the present leaving demand out of account, and assuming that whatever can be produced can also be consumed.

This, however, is an assumption which, as we have seen, cannot be sustained, in relation to the present economic system. The next point, accordingly, is to enquire why it is that the mechanism of distribution breaks down. But in passing to this branch of Economics we find ourselves under the necessity of redefining its scope. The classical theory of distribution is concerned with showing how the relative shares in the product of the various factors of production are determined. It takes for granted both the volume of production and its correlative, the amount of income available for distribution, and considers only how the rival claims of the different factors are adjusted. This, however, is just what an Economic Theory which aims at laying down the conditions for the maximum production as well as the best possible distribution of the product cannot do. Its first task is to discover the conditions necessary to ensure a total distribution of income on a scale which will make possible the full use of the available productive resources.

It will therefore concentrate first of all on expounding the present relation of the productive system to the distribution of wealth, and try to discover why it is possible for unused productive resources to coincide with need for precisely the kinds of goods which they could be employed to make. This will cause it to enquire whether it is really desirable to make the distribution of income, as it is now, a function of the productive system, or whether there is some way of escape from the vicious circle of under-production and deficient demand. Why, it will ask, should not incomes be assured and distributed on a basis of available productive power, instead of actual production, so as to ensure the maintenance of a sufficient total volume of effective demand?

This enquiry will inevitably take the economist into deep waters. It will mean asking in the first place how, under existing conditions, a deficiency of demand in relation to productive power can actually arise. This raises at least three outstanding questions. The first has to do with a possible unevenness in the flow of goods and of purchasing power, due to the accumulation or reduction of stocks, the irregular flow of income into the hands of the consumers, and the time-lags in the effect of reduced or increased production on the flow of goods and incomes. Since this essay was first written, this question has been discussed at length by Mr. P. W. Martin in his book, *The Problem of Maintaining Purchasing Power*.

The second question has to do with the double relation of incomes to producers' and consumers' goods. Money can be used to buy either; but an addition to the effective supply of producers' goods is of value only if the demand for consumers' goods also expands enough to absorb the additional supply which results from bringing the new producers' goods into productive use. If, then, the possessors of income, in an endeavour to increase their future incomes by saving, apply so much money to buying producers' goods that there is not enough left to absorb the available consumers' goods, some of the available productive resources are bound to go out of use. Under-consumption will thus lead to under-production and unemployment. It is the familiar thesis of Mr. J. A. Hobson that the maldistribution of incomes in capitalist societies tends to produce this result.

The third question relates to international competition as a cause of under-production. Costs of production differ from country to country in accordance not only with differences of productive efficiency, but also with higher or lower wages, interest charges, taxes, rents. A country with low costs in any particular branch of production can undercut its competitors in such markets as are not closed by prohibitive or discriminating tariffs or restrictions on imports. According to the classical theory, the countries with higher costs ought then to abandon the trades in which they are being undersold, and find others in which they enjoy a comparative advantage. If they cannot do this, it is a sign that their general level of costs is too high; and they must reduce their standards of living until equilibrium is reached. But this classical doctrine is not easy to apply in practice; for attempts to reduce the standard of living are resisted and lead to friction, which lowers efficiency, provokes retaliation from other countries, and, above all, tends to destroy purchasing power in the home market wherever the fall in retail prices lags behind the reduction of producers' incomes, as it almost inevitably does. Friction arising out of international economic intercourse has therefore to be considered as a third factor making for a deficiency or redundancy of purchasing power.

It is the first business of the Economics of Distribution to consider these flaws in the working of the present system, and to suggest means of ensuring an adequate and regular flow of incomes in relation to goods. The first set of questions—those discussed by Mr. Martin—suggests the need for a regulation of the growth or diminution of stocks, which involves in turn a regulated flow of new production. It suggests, further, a regulation of the even flow of incomes, involving consideration of methods and times of paying dividends, interest, wages, and of the conditions under which credit is expanded or contracted. And, finally and most fundamentally, it suggests a regulation of the total amount of income to be distributed, so as to bring it into the right relation to the available supply of goods and services.

Mr. Hobson's contention about relative over-saving raises a quite distinct issue. It suggests that the system under which income can be used, at the recipient's choice, for buying either producers' or consumers' goods may be radically wrong, and that there is much to be said for distributing as incomes to the members of society only as much as society can afford to spend on consumers' goods, and providing in a different way for the necessary amount of capital accumulation. There is a foreshadowing of this method in the practice of business concerns of financing developments out of reserved profits. But this method involves no *collective* regulation of the relative amounts applied to 'saving' and 'spending'. This collective regulation seems, however, to be the only means by which the accumulation of capital can be kept in the right relation to the volume of spending. It is not suggested that there is an economically right relation, and only one; for a society may decide to spend or save more or less, just as an individual can. But a society which has saved so much in one period must release enough spending power to absorb the new consumers' product at a later stage, or make its saving sheer waste.

The third problem—that of international friction—suggests obviously the need for a far closer international regulation of the world's economic affairs, for a correspondence of the standards of income in different countries to their relative efficiencies in production on a basis of the full use of their productive powers, and for an organised interchange of goods and services in place of the present unregulated competition.

Problems of this order, and not a mere discussion of the relative shares of the different factors of production in a total product assumed as a datum, should be the chief preoccupation of the Economic Theory of distribution. Until they have been discussed, and the means of providing for an adequate and even distribution of incomes thoroughly examined, it is of little advantage to make a study of wages, or profits, or interest, or rent in their separate manifestations under the existing system. For, without the necessary prolegomena concerning the relations of production and distribution, such a survey can be merely descriptive and analytical of things as they are, and can possess no critical value.

But as soon as the economist approaches the problems of the division of incomes in society in the light of this preliminary critical study, he can accompany his description and analysis of the existing forms of distribution with a discussion of their reactions upon the productive system. It will at once be plain that the object of distribution is twofold—to elicit the maximum production of wealth, and to afford the largest possible amount of satisfaction. Having posited these two ends to be served, he has next to discuss how far they conflict, or can be made to work together. It is evidently possible that they may conflict—if, for example, it is true that, in order to secure the maximum production, it is necessary to permit both huge accumulations of private wealth at one end of the social scale and dire poverty at the other.

This problem, however, takes on quite a different aspect if the economic problem of the accumulation of capital—that is, of saving for capital development—can be separated absolutely from that of the distribution of income. For the chief justification usually offered for large incomes is that they are the main source of saving, and therefore of the increase of wealth. The provision of new capital from sources quite apart from distributed incomes would remove this economic argument in favour of gross inequalities, and would leave only the secondary argument based on the necessity of high financial incentives in order to elicit the fullest efficiency. But this argument would lose most of its sting if incomes could be used only for spending and not for accumulation; for clearly, under such conditions, quite small inequalities of reward would be fully as effective in eliciting effort as large inequalities are now.

It would be, then, unnecessary to allow large scope for private profit, which is the chief incentive to production under the existing conditions. It would be unnecessary to pay interest to private persons in order to induce them to save. Wages would appear, not as costs of production to be kept down to a minimum, but as shares in the product to be maintained in due equilibrium with the quantity of goods and services available for consumption. There would still remain, of course, on the one hand, the problem of distributing the available supply of new capital among the industries and services asking for its use as a means of development; and interest might be retained as an instrument for rationing this capital. There would still be the problem of assessing the wages appropriate to different types of service, and of deciding the conditions of work. There would still be costs of production dependent on these charges, and prices for goods offered in the market which would be for the most part fixed on the basis of these costs. But it would be possible to sell some goods at less than cost where this was deemed necessary in order to prevent the disuse of productive resources—that is, where the threatened resources were of a kind that could not speedily be transferred to other uses. And, in relation to other countries, it would be possible to sell exports for what they would fetch, and to seek recoupment by fixing import prices at a level calculated to cover the cost of the exports for which they were, in effect, being taken in exchange.

All this, of course, assumes a regulated economy, based on

the public control and direction of the processes of capital accumulation. Such control seems to me to follow logically from the need to balance production and consumption in such a way as to secure a full use of all available productive resources. But this balance itself involves social regulation of prices as well as of production; for evidently the right amount of income to be distributed in order to balance the possible production depends on the level of the prices to be charged for the various products.

Accordingly the new Economic Theory for the twentieth century has to set out from the possible productivity of the economic system, has to devise means for applying a part of this productivity to the development of capital resources apart from the distribution of incomes, and has then to arrange for a sufficient distribution of incomes to absorb the product destined for consumption at the prevailing prices. These prices, in the case of any particular commodity, must be fixed at the same time as the quantity produced, and in relation to the total amount of consumers' income. A higher price for any particular product will usually mean a diminished consumption; and this will release more productive power for the making of other things to be sold at lower prices. Just as States now raise the prices of certain goods by taxation—alcoholic drinks, for example—and so diminish their consumption, the same end, or the opposite end of lowering other prices below cost, could be directly pursued under an economic system based on the central and co-ordinated control of production, prices and incomes. But it does not follow that there would be any widespread intervention to change the currents of consumers' demand; for most goods could continue to be sold at prices regulated in accordance with their costs of production.

Surely an Economic Theory devoted to the study and elucidation of the issues raised in the preceding pages would be vastly more useful, and far more closely related to realities, than much of what now passes current as the groundwork of Economics. If, indeed, the function of the economist were merely to describe the working of the existing system and to analyse its characteristics, without any attempt at criticism or any suggestion for its improvement, much of what I have said would be beside the mark. But, even so, a good deal would be relevant; for the disharmonies that exist are as much a part of the system as its harmonies, and must be included in it, even if they are to be left uncriticised. My discontent with the present shape of Economic Theory, as it is set out in the textbooks, arises partly from its failure to reveal these disharmonies, because it begins by assuming demand as a force independent of production, which it is not, and because it never relates its account of the factors in distribution to any coherent account of the working of the productive process. It fails and misleads, even in as far as its function is purely to describe.

But in fact Economics has never been content merely to describe what is, without implications about what is desirable, in an economic sense. The present shape of Economic Theory is based essentially on certain assumptions. Private property is assumed, and leads to the assumption of rent and interest and profits as necessary payments. Private accumulation of capital is assumed, and leads to the assumption that great inequalities of income are economically desirable. Private control of the productive process is assumed, and leads to the assumption that large incentives must be offered to the *entrepreneur*. Class differences are assumed; it is assumed that the economic function of the State is to defend these assumptions from attack; and, behind all else, there is still assumed a natural harmony which somehow causes the self-interest of each to coincide on the whole with the common interest of all.

I shall be told that the economist does not make these assumptions, that he is ready to discuss the economic effects of alternative ways of organisation, of Socialism or Co-operation as alternatives to private enterprise. It is true that he is ready to discuss these things; but he discusses them in terms of a theory shaped and designed to fit the conditions of Capitalism, and no others. I shall be told that in any case the economist's conclusions are economic and not ethical, in that his business is to point out what is desirable economically, and not in a moral sense. But the favourite demonstration of the economists, that all distribution is based on the rewarding of the various factors of production in accordance with their productivity, has undoubtedly a strong ethical aroma. Value is such a beautiful little word; and to say that, as matters stand, every factor of production is remunerated according to its value sounds as if everything must be for the best in the best of all possible worlds. To say that a man's remuneration depends on his productivity sounds much better than to say that he gets what other people are prepared, and find themselves compelled, to pay him, in order to secure his services. But in fact the first statement means no more than the second.

Moreover, in effect you cannot reward 'factors of production,' but only persons. Even if the 'productivity' of capital could really be compared with that of labour, it would not follow that the present owner of the capital had any claim to be rewarded in respect of it, or that it was economically desirable to let him go on owning it. But this is a question which the present structure of Economic Theory effectively covers up. It assumes the identity of capital and the capitalist, the landowner and his land, though they are in reality separable, and it is clearly a matter for discussion whether it is economically desirable to separate them or not.

As long as Economics is content to remain merely a study of prices it will never be able to escape from these assumptions; for in making the price relation its centre it evades the formulation of any real theory of production, or of any answer to the question how the fullest use of productive resources is to be ensured. And, on the side of distribution, the taking of price as the focus of discussion evades the necessity of relating effective demand to the real measure of satisfaction derived from consumption by consumers with incomes of different sizes. I know, of course, that the varying utility of a given unit of money to different purchasers is recognised; but the theory of the marginal utility of money comes in only as a sort of footnote to a general theory of value which begins by treating every money demand of equal amount as embodying the same amount of potential satisfaction. Unless this is assumed, the entire theory that free consumers' demand leads to the maximum of economic satisfaction clearly goes by the board.

Economics, if it is to answer the economic questions that are of the greatest importance to the modern world, must deal in terms of real goods as well as of their prices. But, as we have seen, the difficulty of this is that, whereas it is easy to measure different things against one another in terms of their prices, it seems impossible to find any other common quantitative standard. But this is no reason for confining ourselves to prices, if price turns out to be for many purposes a misleading standard, and if many of the vital questions we want to answer simply cannot be answered at all in terms of prices. I have suggested that 'amount of labour' theories of value, in economists from Ricardo to Marx, had at least the merit of attempting to measure real things in terms of the real amounts of economic resources used up in producing them. These theories thus at least attempted to measure value from a social standpoint; for the social point of view is essentially that of getting the greatest real production in return for effort, and not the largest surplus of profit over cost. Ricardo no doubt assumed that social value and market price would tend to coincide; but Marx did not make this mistake. He realised that the assumption that they would coincide arose from the deeper assumption of an underlying natural law embodied in the capitalist system.

The amount of labour theory, as Marx came to understand, could not be reconciled with facts on the basis of an assumed correspondence between prices and values. Orthodox economists realised this too, and discarded the theory as useless, seeking refuge in a study of the behaviour of prices, without any reference to underlying real costs or values. They kept the notion of an immanent economic harmony; but they transferred it directly to the working of the price system. It had, however, no relevance to this system, but only to the 'amount of labour' theory which they had discarded as useless.

But is the amount of labour theory, or something analogous to it, useless if we attempt to use it as a measure, not of prices, but of social costs? The real social cost, as distinct from the money cost to the *entrepreneur*, of any act of production consists of the sum of all the scarce productive resources used up in making it and delivering it to the consumer; and its net social value consists of its utility *minus* its social cost. But clearly we cannot, except in terms of money, actually do this sum in figures. We cannot add up, in figures, so many tons of coal, the use of so much land and fixed capital, so much manual and administrative labour, and get a total which can be simply compared with other totals of a similar composition. Nor can we measure in figures the different utilities of different goods unless we are prepared to use their prices as a means of measurement. We are all used to doing sums of this order in terms of the prices of the various factors involved. The question is whether we can conceive of social costs and social utilities without the support of the price system.

I should say that we do even now, in the sphere in which demand has become collective; for the State, in deciding to embark on some important public work, or in giving one such undertaking preference over another, is to some extent guided, not by their respective money costs in relation to any return that can be expressed in prices, but by weighing their social utility against the amount of the social resources their creation will use up. Into such a case price considerations enter largely, and they are of the first importance; but by no means all the considerations can be expressed in price form.

Still more is this bound to be the position where the State is in control of the major part of the economic system, and makes through its appropriate organs the main decisions about what is to be produced and what prices are to be charged. For under such conditions it is quite impossible to consider the problem of production simply in terms of money costs. Far more commonly, decisions about prices come after decisions about production, and are their results rather than their cause.

Thus, in a country such as the Soviet Union, it is obvious that the decision what shall be produced and what capital developments carried out with a view to the increase of production in the future is not made simply by weighing money costs of production against money prices of resulting satisfactions. The calculations of the Soviet Union under the Five Years Plan are doubtless made in terms of money, and express what is to be done in terms of the money cost of doing it. But the real basis of decision is in effect not mainly monetary. What the Soviet Union decides, when it makes its economic plans, is primarily to devote so much labour, so much land and material, so much of its available plant and transport, to producing coal, or steel, or building generating stations, or creating State farms; so much to making textile goods, boots and shoes, and other consumers' goods; so much to improving public utilities and social services, and so on. The decision is not made solely in terms of amounts of labour, or even of labour and other productive resources; but these are the main ingredients in it. 'Have we enough plant or skilled labour?' is a far more pertinent question in connection with some project of a Soviet planning organisation than 'Will it cost too much money?' Money cost is still a factor, I agree; but it has become a secondary factor.

The economist who has been brought up on the modern economic theories which take Capitalism for granted, and try to keep as far as possible within the orbit of the price system, is apt to find such a situation merely baffling, and even to deny that any economic answer is possible to problems stated in such terms. But clearly answers are possible, and I do not see how they can be regarded as non-economic. The conception of amounts of labour or other productive resources is just as economic as the conception of sums of money costs or prices, though the latter can be added and subtracted and the former do not admit of arithmetical summation. If Economics is to confine itself to price measurements, it is in danger of not being able to answer at all most of the economic questions which men will put to it in the next hundred years. For the more the world advances towards Socialism and undertakes the collective regulation of its economic life, the less will prices appear as objective data which can be made the basis of important economic decisions, and the more will they come to be controlled results of these decisions, which will have been made mainly on other grounds.

The consumer will no doubt continue to regulate his consumption mainly in accordance with price standards; for he will probably still get a money income, and have to keep within it. But even he may get more of his real income in the form of free services, or coupons of various sorts which will allow him to choose, say, between free seats at the theatre and a visit to a rest camp, or a trip abroad. Consumption, even so, will be regulated mainly by prices, as far as the consumer is concerned; but these prices will be more and more controlled prices, and not, even apparently, the results of any natural law, or interplay of supply and demand.

Production, on the other hand, will have ceased, over a wide field, to be mainly governed by price factors at all. It will be the result of collective decisions made in terms of the real productive resources available in relation to collective estimates of social need. Consumers' demand, in terms of prices, will doubtless remain as the most important single factor in the estimation of needs. But it will not be the only factor; and it will be itself influenced and conditioned by the existing levels of the controlled prices.

Present-day Economics is of almost no help in facing the economic problems of a community such as Soviet Russia, or even of the advance towards Socialism elsewhere. For it has shut itself up in the price system; and if you ask it questions of this sort, it either makes no answer, or answers in terms of an inappropriate series of postulates based on the price economy of the capitalist system. The Economics appropriate to a Socialist community has never been worked out; and this essay is but the merest adumbration of certain of the leading problems involved in working it out. What I am certain is that it will mean giving to Economic Theory a totally new shape, based far more on the study of real productive forces and of the right relationship between the productive and the distributive systems, and far less on prices, which will come to be regarded much less as data than as controlled expressions of the results of concrete decisions about the organisation of production and the distribution of real income.

# IX

# THE USE AND ABUSE OF ECONOMIC TERMS

MEN have now been trying for more than two hundred years to think accurately and consecutively about economic questions, and to arrange the results of their thinking in a systematic way. Economics, or Political Economy, has been for at least a century and a half a recognised study, if not a science. Now, it will be generally admitted that no science, and no study partaking of the character of science, can make steady progress, or build on sure foundations, unless it succeeds in defining clearly the essential terms and concepts of which it makes use. In the social studies, absolute precision in the use of terms may not be possible—that is one reason why they can hardly be sciences, in any full sense—but this does not alter the need for as much precision as the nature of the case will admit.

For in the social studies as much as in any others, unless we do define our terms with some approach to clarity we can hope neither to reason accurately nor to argue usefully one with another. We may not be able all to agree exactly what meaning can properly be attached to this or that particular term; but we should both try as hard as we can to find agreed definitions, and be at pains, where there is any risk of ambiguity, to be sure ourselves and make plain to our readers in what sense or senses we are using those words which occupy, as concepts, a vital place in our studies.

The difficulty of doing this, in the social studies and in Politics and Economics above all, arises from the fact that the concepts we employ and the words in which we express them are alike in everyday use by men and women who are not attempting to deal with political or economic questions in any systematic way. The facts and happenings which the economist or political theorist is attempting to analyse are, indeed, no more ordinary and everyday than the bodily happenings which concern the physician, or the motions of the stars. But healthy people do not have to think much about their bodies, or be at much pains to know how their mechanism works; and ordinary folk do little about the stars except gaze at them. Everyone, on the other hand, is practically and actively concerned in some degree with politics, and much more with the everyday matters which the economist sets out to discuss. Everyone buys and sells, and is brought so into constant contact with the price system. Most people work for a living, or share in the income of someone who works for a living. Most people either at some time hire labour at a wage or a salary, or are themselves hired. And most people, either individually or through some body with which they are connected, have direct experience of paying or receiving rent and interest, and of calculating profit or loss.

Prices, costs, wages, salaries, rent, interest, profits—all these and most of the other essential words and concepts which are the focal points of economic theory are familiar terms and concepts of the market-place and of the home. They are in every man's vocabulary; and they are in common and constant use. Accordingly, they are coloured words, possessing for everyone a large and variable associative content. Those who employ them in everyday conversation, or in business dealings, are usually clear enough for all practical purposes what they mean. The central core of meaning is in most cases not in doubt. But round it is a nebula of associations that varies widely from person to person and from group to group. A 'price' does not mean quite the same thing to a bookmaker and to a housewife. 'Cost' is not the same to the mind of buyer and seller, or to a housewife and an employer thinking of his 'cost accounts'. A stockbroker and a shareholder may use the term 'profit' in different connections and with a difference of meaning in relation to the same block of shares, because the one is thinking of a change in the stock market value and the other of the amount of dividend. Even wages do not mean the same thing to a coal-miner and a domestic servant who 'lives in', or rent to a farmer and the tenant of a council house. Interest is almost the only term both in common use and pivotal in economic theory that seems to have, for most people, pretty much the same meaning. And, in that case, the economist himself has to be excepted; for he is certainly apt to use the word in a sense very different from the ordinary.

The economist has to take these and many other terms as they come to him from the common parlance of everyday people. He has no choice about the matter; for the things he is setting out to discuss are the same things as these people are discussing every day of their lives. He is apt, however, to grumble that the terms, as they come to him bright and coloured with the associative content of everyday lives, lack precision, and to say that he can do nothing with them as they are. He must first clean and polish, rubbing away the coating of association until he gets down to the hard core of common meaning.

So far he is perfectly right; for, though the words will lose their brightness when the colour is rubbed away, the loss is from his standpoint gain, in that he is seeking to analyse rather than to create. He is not poet, to whom the associations of words are their wealth, but scientist, as nearly as may be from the nature of his subject; and the warmth and light of association defy scientific analysis. He is right, then, to do his best to strip bare the words he must use as the co-ordinating concepts of his study, though he must beware of forgetting that he can never strip them quite bare of associative content in his own mind. He is on the right lines, so far; but just at this point it is fatally easy for him to go wrong.

For the object of stripping his terms bare of their clothing of association should be to enable him to leave to them that essence of meaning that is the common factor of their everyday use. He should use them as meaning just that which they do mean to most ordinary people—the core of common, everyday meaning without the differences which arise from divergent experience. A stockbroker and a coalminer ought to be able to understand what, essentially and at bottom, a professional economist means by 'cost', or 'profit', or 'wages', fully as much as each of them ought to be able to understand what the other means. To that extent the economist ought to mean by the everyday terms he uses the same as the ordinary man. But all too often he does not; and he is under a ceaseless temptation, in his search for exactitude, to slip into meaning by the same word something fundamentally different.

This something different will be, of course, something far tidier and far more readily adaptable to the purposes of theoretical analysis than the plain man's idea of the words which he uses. And, accordingly, the economist will be able to play with his refined terms many intricate games of the most pleasing logical subtlety. But there will be most serious disadvantages as well. The first and most obvious is that a very difficult barrier will be erected in the way of the ordinary man's understanding of economic doctrines. For it will be impossible to adopt one terminology in elementary books designed for the general reader, and a quite different one in books intended to be read by specialists. The general reader, therefore, who does want to know something about Economics will find familiar words used in quite unfamiliar senses—even in senses which seem quite contrary to ordinary usage; and, unless he is very patient and clear-headed, he will be very liable to go empty away, and give up the entire study of economic problems as a bad job. He will be, moreover, exceedingly liable to misunderstand the economist's meaning, by taking in the sense he knows words which are meant quite differently. On this ground there is a strong case for keeping familiar words which must be used in Economic Theory as near as possible to the hard core of their everyday meanings.

Nor is this all; for the economist himself is a man as well, and accustomed to employing in everyday life the same terms as he uses for instruments of theory. He will be more than human if he does not show a tendency sometimes to slip from using a word in its refined, scientific sense into using it in its ordinary sense without being conscious of the change and its implications. When this happens, his own thought will become confused, and he will tangle up himself as well as his readers in an unnecessary dualism of meaning.

But is dualism unnecessary? I believe that it is, and, more than that, I believe that the attempt to create artificial senses for ordinary words has been responsible for some of the worst muddles into which even the most famous economists have fallen again and again. Where the economist wants to express an idea for which there is no word in ordinary thought, let him make a new word for the purpose, or take an existing word that is not likely to be misunderstood. But let him keep the familiar words of everyday economic parlance for the things they mean to ordinary men, and never, as far as in him lies, employ them in senses which involve a conscious divergence from customary usage.

The economist, when he does use a word out of its ordinary meaning, is usually doing one of two things. He is either narrowing it to something less than it means to ordinary people, or broadening it to something more. In either case, the results are apt to be unfortunate for Economic Theory, as well as misleading to the public. Let me try to illustrate what I have in mind, by reference to a few of the most common and fundamental economic terms.

The economist usually narrows the meaning of a current term for the purpose of making it more precise by eliminating from its significance what he holds to be impurities or complications that need separate analysis. Sometimes, in doing this, he prefixes to the current term some such word as 'pure' or 'economic', in order to indicate that he is using it in a special sense. 'Pure' or 'economic' rent, 'pure' interest, and 'pure' profit are examples of which everyone will think at once. But he seldom persists in using these prefixes quite consistently, whenever he is using the term in his special sense; and he is exceedingly apt to make analysis of the abstraction which he has created a substitute for analysis of the common term which he has discarded. Yet the purpose of Economics is not to construct a theoretical system —though that may be an essential part of its method—but to analyse the working of actual economic institutions. It is the impure reality, and not the purified abstraction, that has to be explained, if Economics is to be of practical use. Accordingly, while the economist may be fully justified in creating his 'pure' concept as an instrument of thought, he must always come back from it to the impure reality, and be convinced that the reality is more real than the abstraction, which derives all its importance from it.

Take the case of rent. The ordinary meaning of the term is, in general, clear enough. It means the sum paid for the hire of land or buildings, or both, or sometimes of business plant or certain other 'durable goods'. The economists, from West and Ricardo onwards, take this notion and abstract from it the notion of 'economic rent'. The theory of economic rent, worked out purely in relation to land, concentrates on an attempt to explain the differential character of the payments made for the use of land, in terms of differences in its fertility and situation. Certain lands are more productive than others: they yield larger crops. Therefore they command a larger rent, because the farmer who tills them will get more produce off a given acreage, and will have more surplus over and above his own keep and that of the labourers he employs. The amount of rent payable for land of any particular quality will depend on the total demand for agricultural produce in relation to the amount and qualities of land available. For enough land will have to be tilled to yield the total produce required; and this will involve the use of all the land that attains to a certain minimum standard of fertility. The 'marginal' land—the land it is barely worth while, but is just worth while, to till—will yield no rent; for it will produce only enough to maintain the farmer and the labourers working upon it, without any surplus. All land of superior qualities will produce more, and will therefore yield a differential rent corresponding to the degree of its superiority over the marginal land. The landlord will be able to extract all this surplus produce as rent, because it would otherwise pay farmers better to cultivate good land than bad; and they will accordingly compete in offering high enough rents for the better land to equalise their returns.

Economic rent is thus defined in the classical theory as payment made for the use of the original and indestructible powers of the soil, which are treated as consisting of the fertility of each parcel of land, and of its situation. It has, of course, been pointed out again and again that the original and indestructible powers of the soil can by no means be clearly distinguished from those qualities which it owes to the expenditure of capital upon it in clearance, drainage and manuring, or from the effects upon it of good or bad farming, and that situation, in the sense in which it confers an economic advantage, is by no means an original or indestructible quality, but arises from men's actions in settling cities, creating transport facilities, and the like. The qualities which are supposed to give rise to economic rent in the Ricardian sense cannot be isolated from other qualities belonging to a piece of land at any particular time; and it follows that the economic rent cannot in fact be distinguished either. It is never possible to say how much of the gross rent paid for a piece of land is economic rent, and how much is not.

This does not mean that the statement of the Ricardian law was not a great step forward in economic thinking. It certainly was. But the step forward consisted in the clear statement that rent is essentially a differential payment, and not in the attempt to isolate and distinguish economic rent as a separate category. For in fact the differential quality belongs to the whole rent in the popular sense of the term, and is not a peculiar property of 'economic rent' in any narrower sense. The rent that will be paid for anything that can be rented at all, except where non-economic considerations intervene, depends on the differential qualities of the thing rented, whether these qualities are original and indestructible, or destructible and acquired, and whether they are or are not the result of capital improvements. Ricardo's mind was blinded to this truth by his theory of the equal return upon capitals embarked in different employments, which caused him to believe that capital sunk in the land must be deemed to yield a profit at a standard general rate. This theory caused him to state his theory of rent in terms, not of rent as a whole, but of 'economic rent' as a narrower category, excluding the return on capital sunk in the land. He thus substituted a purely abstract and undiscoverable thing for the rent of everyday life, and proceeded to analyse his own concept instead of the real thing. There was some excuse for him in this, because the abstraction arose naturally out of his theory of profit. There is none for those who, having discarded his theory of profit, still cling obstinately to the unreal category of economic rent.

For economic analysis can be as readily, and far more productively, applied to the rent of everyday life. When a man rents a farm or a piece of urban land, with or without buildings upon it, he is not concerned to enquire how far what he is hiring is an original and indestructible work of nature, and how much a product of human labour and activity. What does concern him is the thing's power to yield him either satisfaction in use, or income if his purpose is to employ it as an instrument of production. The difference between the rents of shops in main and back streets is no more and no less the result of differential capacities to produce income than the difference between the rent of good and bad farming land; and two farms of equal revenue-producing qualities will tend to yield the same rents whether these qualities are due to natural causes or to the expenditure of capital on their improvement. The notion of 'economic rent' adds nothing to the notion of rent as it exists in ordinary parlance. Indeed, it only introduces a confusion, by suggesting that there are certain isolable and peculiar properties of land, in respect of which it follows a distinctive and peculiar economic law.

Or take the notion of interest. The plain man means by interest any payment that is made for the loan of money, in the sense of purchasing power. The economist takes this perfectly straightforward notion, and derives from it an abstract notion of his own, to which he gives the name of 'pure' interest. His object in this appears to be the simplification of the plain man's concept by eliminating from it the element in total interest which can be regarded as a payment for risk. The residue of 'pure' interest is then said to represent the rate at which the marginal savers of money discount the future—in other words, the intensity of their preference for present over future satisfactions.

But has this 'pure' interest any real existence, or even any value as a theoretical concept? It is, of course, true that rates of interest on borrowed money are influenced by the relation between the demands of borrowers and the supply of money available for lending, and that this supply depends on the willingness and ability of those who receive incomes to save.

It is true that willingness to save is affected by men's degree of preference for present over future satisfaction, and that, accordingly, changes in this preference are among the factors affecting interest rates. But the rate at which men discount the future is certainly not the only influence which affects the volume of saving—much less the quantity of money offered for lending, which is by no means the same thing as the amount saved. The distribution of incomes among the members of society is another factor of the greatest importance, and is in part quite distinct from any psychological discounting of the future; for much of the saving of the rich is automatic, out of surplus income, and is affected by the rates of interest obtainable, not directly, but only in as far as these rates make their total incomes greater or less.

A more fundamental point is that the element of risk cannot really be eliminated. The risks attached to the lending of money are of two kinds—those which depend on the status and solvency of the borrower, and therefore vary from loan to loan, and those which depend on the stability or instability of the value of money, or of the general economic system under which the contract to pay interest is made. Risks of the first type lead to differential interest rates for different borrowers, whereas risks of the second type lead to differentiation according to the period of time for which the loan is made. For, save at times of exceptional crisis, the second sort of risk is usually negligible in the cases of loans made only for a very short period.

It is, of course, recognised that there is no such thing as *the* rate of interest. There are many rates, varying with the period of time for which the loan is made, the purposes for which the money is to be used, and the status of the borrower. Interest rates are, in one sense, no less differential than rents. But, whereas in the case of rents the differentia lies in the quality of the thing hired, in the case of interest it lies in the position of the borrower and in the conditions attaching to the loan. Within a single monetary system, one piece of money, or one unit of money of account in the bank, is as good as another. The thing borrowed is not differential; but the interest paid upon it is.

If, then, pure interest has any existence at all, as a concept for analysis bearing some relation to conditions in the real world, it must be expressible, not as a rate, but rather as a series of rates for different classes of loans. For, even if the economist eliminates from his abstract conception of pure interest the differences in actual interest rates which arise from the differences between individual borrowers, in respect of the security of the money lent, he will be left still with the differences which arise from the varying periods for which loans can be made, and are bound up with the instability of money values and of the economic system within which the contract is made. There can, at most, be, not a rate of pure interest, but a graded scale of rates; and, so far from having eliminated risk from the conception of interest, the economist will have to admit that this graded scale is based largely on differences of risk.

It may be said that, none the less, the concept of pure interest is of value, because it does serve to isolate one class of risk from another, and because men's rate of discounting the future is, if not the only, at any rate the principal factor affecting the general levels of interest rates, apart from the particular differences arising out of the varying credit of debtors. But is this really so? Surely the plenty or scarcity of solvent and credit-worthy borrowers, or, in other words, the general degree of business confidence existing in a community, is also a powerful influence on interest rates, because it affects the willingness of those who have money to lend it at all, or to lend it to one large class of would-be borrowers as against another. There is no fixed relation between the interest rates charged for loans of different kinds, from day-to-day bank money to industrial overdrafts and from these to long-term debentures. The general condition of credit will react differently on the rates charged for loans of different sorts, quite apart from the differing creditworthiness of each individual borrower. Not only *the* rate of pure interest, but also any graded scale of rates of pure interest, based on the time element in various classes of loan, turns out to be an economists' abstraction which has no counterpart in the real world.

It is not, indeed, an abstraction which would do much harm, if analysis of it were not so often made a substitute for analysis of the real interest rates, with which the economist should be concerned. What we want to know about is not a hypothetical level of pure interest, but the causes of the varying interest rates which are actually paid. One element in determining these is doubtless the valuation of future in relation to present satisfaction in the minds of those with incomes out of which they can save. But this is only one element out of a number, and there has been an undue and unproductive concentration upon this one thing in the study of interest by academic economists.

Of profits I shall here say nothing, because I deal with the subject in a subsequent essay in this volume. I shall there attempt to show that the creation by certain economists of a concept of 'pure profit' has had far more unfortunate results than the attempt to isolate 'pure' interest from the impurities of actual interest payments. But, in this essay, I must now turn from instances of the narrowing of everyday economic terms, in the search for abstractions more amenable to theoretical analysis, to the opposite tendency to broaden the meaning of other terms, so as to include within them more than is included in non-professional speech and thought.

The most notable instance of this broadening is the use by certain economists, from Adam Smith onwards, of the word 'wages'. It is well enough understood in the everyday world what constitutes a wage. A wage is a contractual payment made by an employer for the hire of labour. It may indeed be a matter for practical dispute where wages end and salaries begin; but for our present purpose the distinction between wages and salaries does not matter. They are both essentially contractual payments for the hire of one or another form of labour.

But the economist, setting out from the observation of wages in this everyday sense, is struck by the fact that a wage is a payment for labour, but that not all labour is remunerated by what is ordinarily called a wage, or upon contractual terms. The independent worker (say the boot repairer working on his own) and the personal employer (say the master in a small workshop) also labour; but their remuneration is not commonly regarded as a wage. It differs, indeed, sharply from what is ordinarily called a wage in that it is not contractual, but consists of an uncertain revenue of surplus—excess of receipts over the costs of production. The economist, however, would like to find a word broad enough to cover all forms of payment for labour, or personal service; and sometimes he seizes ruthlessly on this word 'wages', and insists on using it in this inclusive sense. He begins to speak of 'wages of management', 'wages of superintendence', of a 'wage element' in business profits. As long as he remains consciously, in using such phrases, within the realm of metaphor, no great harm is done. But they are apt to grow upon him, and to be made the foundation of theories which seek to isolate a 'wage element' in other classes of income and to treat this 'wage element' and contractual wages in the ordinary sense under one head, as payments which rest on a common basis of personal service, and can therefore be subjected to a common analytic process.

As soon as he does this, one of two things happens. Either he ceases to have a theory of wages, in the sense in which the term is ordinarily used, and therefore fails to deal with the question he set out to answer, and ought to answer if Economics is to be of practical use. Or else he goes on formulating his theory of wages just as he would have done if he had continued to use the term in its everyday sense, and then imputes to the 'wage element' in other forms of income the same behaviour as he discovers in the actual wages paid under contract to employed persons. In the former case his theory of wages suffers, in the latter his theory of profits, and his analysis of the process of income distribution as a whole; for his enlarged wage category is no longer a real category of distribution at all.

It is easy enough to see why this happens. Just as the desire for tidiness causes the economist to narrow the meaning of some terms, so it causes him to widen the meaning of others. This particular widening, in the case of wages, is based on a desire, natural but unfortunate, for symmetry in the different aspects of economic theorising. The economist, in search of immanent harmonies in the economic order, wants the categories of production and of distribution to correspond. He begins—or rather his forerunners, the classical economists in this country, began—with a study of production. They found three factors of production—land, labour and capital—to which their successors added a fourth—business enterprise. To these three factors of production three—or four—classes of income receivers must, if possible, be found to correspond. Between land and landlord—rent receiver—the correspondence was easy to find, though, as we have seen, it was insisted that the landlord, *qua* landlord, received only 'economic' rent, and what he received on account of capital sunk in the land was regarded as properly profit rather than rent. To capital corresponded profit, and to labour wages. Interest was at this stage regarded as only a sub-form of the general category, profit. Then came the refinement which marked off the *entrepreneur* function for separate treatment, and recognised business enterprise as a distinct factor in production. A fourth category of distribution was therefore needed in order to preserve the balance; and this was provided by erecting interest into a distinct category corresponding to capital, and treating profit, as apart from interest, as the reward of enterprise, as apart from the provision of capital.

There were, however, in this revised definition of the categories of production and distribution all the sources of the utmost confusion of thought. Adam Smith thought of the capitalist *qua* provider of capital as receiving profit, which included interest, and of the same person *qua entrepreneur* as receiving a sort of wage. The categories of production and distribution corresponded to each other; but they did not correspond to the actual categories of the business world. For capital and labour were commonly united in the person of the *entrepreneur*; and his remuneration had to be regarded as partly wages and partly profit. But in fact he received only one form of remuneration, and there was no possible means of determining how much of it was due to his capital and how much to his labour; for his product was in fact a joint output of these two.

The trinitarian formula of production and distribution, in effect, purchased consistency at the cost of ignoring the actual forms of production and distribution in the business world. It led away from any analysis of the real forces determining the relative positions of the different economic classes in the productive system, or their relative shares in the product. But the attempt to introduce greater realism by adding a fourth category to both groups made confusion worse confounded. On the side of production, it cut the old category of labour into two, by separating the *entrepreneur* from the employee. That seemed sound enough; for the two did clearly hold quite different places in the productive system. But on the side of distribution no real correspondence could be found. Labour and wages balanced well enough; and so did land and rent, subject to the difficulty noted above. But the alleged correspondence between capital and interest on the one hand, and enterprise and profit on the other, was utterly unrealistic and absurd. For the difference between capital and enterprise is a difference between things and persons as factors of production, whereas the difference between interest and profit is the difference between money-lending on contractual terms and realisation of an uncertain surplus of receipts over costs. There is no evidence at all either that all capital earns interest, or that all profit goes to enterprise. Indeed, the evidence of the real world is manifestly against any such conclusion, unless we are to define both profits and interest in senses utterly remote from those which the terms ordinarily bear.

There is, in fact, no correspondence at all, under our present economic system, between the factors of production and the classes or groups of income receivers. The categories of production and distribution cannot be made to correspond; and any attempt to make them correspond is bound to result in either falsification of the facts, or barrenness. Labour, in the wide sense of personal service, may be remunerated either by a wage or in the form of profit. Capital may draw its dividend in the shape of a profit, or interest, or rent. And even land may be paid for in profit, where it is tilled by an occupying owner, or owned and not rented by the business firm whose factory, mine or shop stands upon it. It is, of course, possible so to define rent, wages, profits and interest as to treat them as the payment for land, labour, enterprise and capital, irrespective of the actual ways in which these factors of production are applied or the income from them distributed among the various claimants.

But the result will be a theory of distribution which bears no relation to the facts of the business world, and throws no light upon the real problems of the distribution of incomes in the world of today.

The term 'wages' ought therefore to be reserved exclusively for contractual payments made to employed persons; and any attempt to equate it to the remuneration of labour in all its forms should be resisted. There is doubtless in business profit an element which can properly be regarded as remuneration of labour—the labour of the *entrepreneur*. But this element is not in any real sense a wage; and it cannot be isolated. It is impossible to say, when a man applies both his capital and his labour to a single act of production, how much of his total return is to be attributed to each of these factors. All attempts to do this involve, in effect, the attribution of a fixed value to one of the two, and the treating of the residue as attributable to the other; and the fallacy is evident from the fact that either can be plausibly regarded as the residuary claimant. It is possible in theory to begin by isolating an element of labour, and attributing it to a quasi-wage, equivalent to what the *entrepreneur's* labour would be worth if he hired himself out as an employee. The residue is then regarded as remuneration of capital. Or it is possible to begin by isolating an element of interest on the *entrepreneur's* capital, equivalent to what it would earn if he lent it to someone else instead of using it himself. The residue is then regarded as the reward of enterprise.

It is possible to do either of these things in theory; but neither of them can be done in practice. For it cannot be determined either how much the *entrepreneur* could really get by hiring himself out as an employee, or on how much capital or at what rate his claim to interest ought to be calculated. Consequently, the theoretical division of his total remuneration into two separate elements leads nowhere, and throws no light at all on the forces which really affect the distribution of income in the business world.

The moral of this is that the economist, unless he is merely engaged in playing a pleasant game of mental acrostics, should always keep, in his use of everyday economic terms, as close as possible to the actual usage of the business world. He should neither narrow a term to mean something much less than the ordinary man means by it, nor widen it to cover much more. For his object is to study and interpret the actual conditions of production and distribution; and current usage is based upon these conditions. If the economist wants a term to describe something which has no everyday name, he can, of course, invent one; but he had better avoid taking a familiar term and making it mean something other than it ordinarily means. And, above all, if the economist invents an abstraction, by isolating some single element in a factor of production or in one of the categories of distribution, he must beware of substituting his analysis of the abstraction for an analysis of the real thing.

Nor is this all. He must beware as well of mixing up the two things—of slipping unconsciously from the abstraction to the real thing, and back again. This is most difficult to avoid if he uses for the abstraction a familiar name, such as wages, or profit, or rent, which is bound to have in his own mind, as well as in the minds of his readers, the colour and association of its concrete meanings in the everyday business world.

Of course, nothing that has been said in this essay is meant to suggest that the economist ought not to use the method of abstraction, provided that he keeps the distinction between the abstract and the concrete always clear in his own mind, and does not confuse the minds of his readers by employing familiar terms in unusual and misleading senses. Abstraction is, at certain points, a necessary, fertile and formative method of economic analysis. It is often necessary, for purposes of analysis, to break up a concrete phenomenon, or group of phenomena, into its constituent elements, to study one by one and abstractly the numerous forces playing upon a complex economic situation, and to find names for the abstractions thus used as the instruments of the analysis. Certainly Economics would have made much less advance towards precision than it has done if it had totally eschewed this method.

But it is none the less necessary to bear the dangers of the method always in mind. For the various forces which go to constitute a complex economic situation act, not independently upon that situation, but also on one another; and the final result of their action is not a mere sum of the particular causes, or even a mathematical resultant of their mutual interactions, but something in which causes and effects, and qualitative as well as quantitative forces, contribute to the result. For this reason, the favourite method of beginning abstractly with the supposition of a single force acting unimpeded and alone, and the adding in succession a series of other forces, as a means of approach by stages to the concrete reality, is apt to yield highly misleading results; for the essence of the real forces is that their operation is not successive, but simultaneous, and it may make all the difference which force is selected to begin with, and in what order the other forces are assumed as coming into play. There is no bridge of this sort from the abstract to the concrete; and it is usually best to attempt no such crossing. The 'pure' Economics of abstract analysis is invaluable to the economist as a training in methodology; but when he wants to throw light on a concrete economic situation he had better begin with that situation as it is, in all its complications, and seek to unravel it, than start with a simple abstract assumption far distant from the reality, and then try to approach concreteness by the successive addition of a series of further abstractions.

Nor, I think—to take another favourite trick of a good many economists—is it legitimate to take as the central point of economic study the assumption of a static society, to work out the fundamental terms and concepts in relation to such an abstract society, and then to treat the dynamic influences playing upon real societies as mere disturbances of an assumed underlying condition of static equilibrium. For human societies, at any rate in modern times, are not in their nature static. The 'disturbances' are fundamental to them; and any realistic analysis of their working must proceed upon dynamic assumptions. There is doubtless, in the economic world, a constant search for equilibrium—a proper and self-reproducing balance of forces. But this equilibrium itself is not static. It is the balance of a complex object moving with great velocity, and with constant readjustment of its parts.

This involves, in some degree, that the fundamental terms of economic theory cannot be static either. Rent, or profit, cannot mean just the same thing to a modern economist as it meant to Ricardo, or to a Frenchman as to an Indian, or even to an Englishman or an American. For even the capitalist system is not everywhere quite the same, even in its foundations; and the familiar economic terms are bound to be shaped, in both time and place, by changes and differences in the actual conditions which they are used to describe. The economist in search, above all, of scientific precision will doubtless find this dynamic and historical character of the economic process often a great nuisance. That is why theoretical economists and economic historians so seldom combine happily, or even seem able easily to understand each other's ideas. But the economist who wants above all to be realistic in his study of the economic workings of modern society will have to accept the limitations which this realistic approach involves; and he may reassure himself that his loss of abstract precision will be more than made up to him in other ways—by the broadening and enrichment of the subject-matter with which he will be able to deal, and by a closer and more fruitful contact with the minds of those who are not professional economists, but have to be practical economists, struggling with the tangled economic problems of the everyday world.

For Economics, in the world of today, is not merely everybody's business, in the sense that everyone has to practise it and make for himself economic judgments which may be good or bad, but also in the sense that an endeavour to understand it, in its wider public bearings, is nowadays an integral part of intelligent citizenship. Democracy, if it is to be made real, implies a democratic understanding of Economics; for Economics and politics can by no means be kept apart. The economist, then, has now a great mission of public education, to be reconciled with his duty of not pandering to the vulgar. He has to hold up the quality of his thought, while at the same time he has to simplify its expression and keep it near to ordinary usage. The most hopeful development in recent economic thinking, especially in the United States, is the advance which is being made towards more realistic methods of economic analysis.

Adam Smith had this broad, public conception of the place and method of economic studies to the full. The nineteenth century largely lost it; and it is the mission of economists in our own day to get it back, on a yet broader basis corresponding to the wider political and economic horizons of the modern world.

## X

## THE NATURE OF PROFIT

IT is, I think, a highly remarkable fact that nearly two centuries of consecutive economic theorising should have left economists still hesitant, ambiguous and at conflict in their uses of a term which every one of them is compelled, by the very nature of his subject-matter, constantly to employ. The economist takes his terms from the market-place; and he has often, in order to fit them for systematic use, to assign to them specialised meanings derived from popular usage, but importing into them at the same time an element of precise definition and of abstraction from the complex phenomena of daily life. Most of the terms of Economics offer some resistance to this treatment; and the economist can by no means rid them wholly of the wealth of association which belongs to them in ordinary speech. They come to him coloured and enriched by sentiment and usage, and no amount of purification in the wash-tub of abstract theory can purge their associations quite away. It has often been urged that it might be better, on this ground, for the economist, instead of taking and adapting to his purpose the warm and coloured terms of the market-place, to follow the example of many of the sciences, and to devise for himself new words that he could make all his own, and compel to mean precisely what he required. But the common verdict is strongly against this view; for Economics is of value as it serves to explain the phenomena of daily life, and any retreat by it into a realm of pure abstraction would deprive it of much of its value, and certainly of most of its appeal. There is thus an overwhelming case for the use of such ordinary terms as will serve to keep the economist always closely in touch with the real phenomena of the economic world; and, in fact, most of the terms adopted by him from ordinary speech have yielded reasonably well to his guardianship, and have submitted, with or without a special adjectival dress, to the importation of meanings precise enough for his purpose. The 'rent' I pay to my landlord, and the 'rent' of which I read in Marshall or Ricardo, different as they are, resemble each other enough for their underlying community to be easily recognised. The economist has, on occasion, to make the matter clear by calling the latter explicitly 'economic rent'; but more often the context makes his meaning plain without special invocation of the adjective. Similarly, the term 'interest' can be given a sense precise enough not to lead to much confusion, though here again he is compelled on occasion to speak of 'pure interest' or 'net interest' rather than of 'interest' *sans phrase*. 'Wages' is a good deal less precise; but perhaps its lack of precision as an economic term does not, in most discussions, greatly matter.

With 'profit', however, the situation is quite different. For in this case not only are economists still widely at variance about the meaning properly to be assigned to the term; but, even when they have framed definitions of it to their own satisfaction, they have still often much ado to remain faithful to them throughout their handling of the subject, and in some cases at least they appear to evade the difficulties only by failing to formulate any clear definition at all.

This is a serious matter, because the question of profit lies obviously at the very heart of economic analysis. The entire theory of distribution is based upon an attempt to study the payments or rewards meted out, under this, or any similar, economic system to the various factors of production, and to formulate the laws or tendencies regulating the sharing of these payments among the various claimants. To any such analysis, which includes profit at all, a clear conception of the nature of the profit return is evidently indispensable. Yet there is no question in Economics on which the different schools of thought still offer answers so divergent and, in many cases, so hesitant and elusive. To one writer, profit is a normal and fully justifiable incident of the economic process, while to another it is normal but wholly unjustifiable, as based on a monopolistic advantage; and to yet another it is justifiable, but exceptional, in that it depends either on a dynamic, as opposed to a static, economic situation, or on a special assumption of risks or uncertainties demanding an exceptional reward. There is no fixity in the senses which different economists assign to the term 'profit'; and there is no consistency in the arguments which they advance by way either of justification or of condemnation of the existence of profit as a distinct economic category.

These continuing ambiguities have their roots deep down in the history of economic thought. In this country, the term 'profit' or 'profits' begins its career, as a technical word of economic science, with Adam Smith. It appears in his writings chiefly as 'profits of stock', one of the three rewards to the three vital factors of production—land, labour and capital. The owner of land receives a rent, the owner of labour a wage, and the owner of capital, or stock, a profit. Adam Smith distinguishes between the so-called profit of the market-place and the stricter profit of economic theory, but only by eliminating from the latter an element which appears in many of its manifestations to varying extents. This excluded element consists of the 'wages' which are to be assigned to the *entrepreneur*, large or small, in return for the expenditure of his own time and trouble. This, in Adam Smith's view, is properly to be called, not 'profit', but wages; and profit remains as a residue after these wages of management or enterprise have been deducted from the gross return. Profit, in this sense, with the wages of management excluded, clearly includes what a modern economist would call 'interest'. But it does not consist solely of 'pure interest'; for Adam Smith suggests that twice the current rate of interest is normally regarded as constituting a 'fair profit'. Yet, though here Smith seems to differentiate clearly between profit and interest, elsewhere the difference is usually ignored. Profit and interest are treated, not as identical, but as obedient to a common law; and, in the general theory of distribution, interest, as a separate factor, receives no consideration at all. It appears, by implication, only as an element in profit; and 'profits of stock' are clearly understood as including interest on capital along with other elements, which are nowhere clearly defined.

Ricardo and James Mill carry matters no further. Indeed, both of them, considerably more than Adam Smith, use the term 'profit' without analysis or definition, purely as a term of the market-place, to which it is unnecessary for economic science to impute or assign a precise and consistent meaning. Ricardo divides the product of industry between rent, wages and profit without ever clearly explaining in what he supposes profit to consist, but leaves it evident that in it he includes the entire return on capital, and to be presumed that he includes also what Adam Smith had called the 'wages' of management. Ricardo's farmer seems to be remunerated wholly by a profit, whether his return comes from his own labour, or superintendence, or from the capital which he has sunk in the land. The landlord gets rent, the labourer wages, and the farmer profit; and between these three economic categories the entire produce of the land is divided. Possibly we are meant to regard landlord, labourer and farmer as economic abstractions rather than as individual persons, and, just as the landlord may farm his own land, and so draw, in effect, both a rent and a profit, so he may labour on the land, and so draw both a profit and a wage. But, even if this is the logical inference from Ricardo, it is certainly not stressed or explicitly stated; and in Ricardo's *Principles*, as in most of the early economists, far more stress is laid on the economic justification of profit than on the explanation of its nature.

Malthus, indeed, building on Adam Smith, goes a step further, and attempts a division of profit into two parts—a net profit, which appears to be the equivalent of interest in modern Economic Theory, and another element, which is defined as the return or reward received for industry, skill and business enterprise. Here is an attempt to distinguish between the return on capital, as such, and the special return received by the *entrepreneur* for his services to the work of production. McCulloch follows Malthus in this twofold division of the profit category, but makes the second element at once more explicit and more confusing by describing it as the return not only to the industry, skill, and enterprise of the *entrepreneur* (whose function had been already stressed in France by J. B. Say), but also for the assumption of non-insurable risks of business undertaking. He does not, however, attempt to distinguish the payment for risk from the payment for industry, skill and enterprise, but lumps these in together as the second factor in profit, making them a joint residue after interest on capital has been separately reckoned. The interest element remains, moreover, in both Malthus and McCulloch, a part, although a theoretically distinguishable part, of profit, and not an economic category separate from profit. And John Stuart Mill preserves this unity of profit as the total return to the capitalist, whether it be derived from his industry, skill or enterprise, from his capital, or from his assumption of risk. The elements in profit are separately catalogued; but at this stage in Economic Theory no attempt has yet been made to break up the profit category itself.

Thereafter, the paths diverge. Jevons and Marshall carry on the classical tradition of analysing the component elements in profit while preserving the unity of profit as the total gains of the capitalist *entrepreneur*, while, from Walker onwards, the Americans, and some European economists, attempt an actual dissolution of the compound 'profit' category into its component parts. Walker attempts to isolate the interest element, and arrives at a new conception of profit as consisting of the gains of the capitalist *entrepreneur* minus those elements which represent the interest on capital—his own or others—embarked in his business. Walker's successors push the process of dissolution still further, not merely isolating the 'wage', as well as the interest, element in profit, but attempting to divorce this element from it, and recognising the payment for risk as a separate 'cost' of the economic process present both in 'interest' and in 'profit', and therefore separable from them both, and finally erecting into a distinct economic category such gains as result from a preferential position of monopoly. The logical culmination of this process is found in the writings of Professor J. B. Clark, who, by successive abstractions from the profit category, has almost made profit disappear from the world of Economics, or rather has eliminated it totally from his abstract 'static' condition of that world, and permitted its survival only as a factor of change in the dynamic world of economic revolutions.

This 'dynamic' theory of profit is not without its rivals. In Great Britain, and to some extent in the United States as well, the narrowing of the profit category has pursued a different course. Profit has been represented as the return to, or reward for, the service of risk-taking. When it has been pointed out that 'risk' is not peculiar to profit-making enterprise, but besets every form of economic activity, two different replies are offered. One school of thought, restricting its view to the yields included in the term profit as it was widely used by the earlier economists, insists on a strict interpretation of the theory of interest, as including only a 'pure interest', which embraces no element of payment for risk, and classifies the entire return for risk-taking, both on borrowed money and on money directly ventured by its owner, under the category of profit; while another attempts to discriminate between different classes of risk, and represents those 'risks' whose incidence can be anticipated, and therefore guarded against by insurance, as giving rise only to an interest charge sufficient to cover the actuarial value of the risk, whereas those risks which are uncertain (and therefore insurable, if at all, only by the transference and not by the elimination of the risk) are represented as the source of profit (and also, of course, of loss) in the true sense of the term.

We have thus a number of different senses of the term 'profit', for all of which it would be possible to claim some respectable authority in the world of Economic Theory. It will be sufficient, for my purpose in this paper, to set out only the chief of these senses, neglecting minor variants, or even variants which, important in themselves, do not greatly affect the point of the present discussion.

1. 'Profit' includes the total gains of the capitalist, whether these are due to the employment of his own labour, or of 'capital' belonging to him or under his control, and whether these gains are due to the assumption of risks of any kind, insurable or uninsurable, to his possession of some sort of monopoly, or to any other cause.

2. 'Profit' includes these total gains, minus interest on capital employed in the business. This sounds simple; but in fact it admits of a number of different views. Thus, the 'interest'

excluded may be only interest on borrowed capital, or may include a computed interest on all capital sunk in the enterprise, whether borrowed or not. And the interest may be only pure interest, or may include a risk payment as well, at any rate in the case of borrowed capital.

3. 'Profit' includes total gains, not excepting interest, minus a 'wage' element, regarded as representing the reward due to the industry, skill and enterprise of the capitalist *entrepreneur*. This at once raises the difficult question of the basis on which this wage element is to be reckoned. Is it to be measured by the 'wage' which the *entrepreneur* could command as a salaried servant, or otherwise, in some other business, or by the addition which his activities may be estimated to make to the income-producing qualities of the business in which he is actually engaged? Or is there some other basis of reckoning?

4. 'Profit' excludes both 'interest' and 'wages', on one or another of the bases mentioned, and thus includes only payment for risk, except in so far as this has been included under interest or wages, and such other elements in the total gains of the capitalist as have not been included under one or another of these three heads. Profit, in this sense, becomes a term connoting primarily, but not necessarily to the exclusion of all other elements, a payment for some form of risk-taking.

5. 'Profit' excludes both 'interest' and 'wages', in one or another of the senses mentioned above, and also such risk payments as, by virtue of the predictability of the risks which they involve, are insurable in such a way as to eliminate the risk by spreading it, and can thus constitute a fixed and ascertainable charge upon costs of production. Profit, in this sense, becomes a term connoting primarily, but not necessarily exclusively, a payment for certain specific kinds of risk, which Professor Knight has attempted to distinguish from other risks by the term 'uncertainty'.

6. 'Profit' excludes both 'interest' and 'wages' and 'risk', both of an insurable and of an uninsurable kind—both sorts of risk being regarded as charges to be allowed for in the supply price of capital. Profit, in this sense, is commonly represented as the result of the dynamic character of the economic processes, and

regarded as non-existent in a 'static' economic world, in which every factor of production would receive its due payment, and nothing would remain as a profit 'residue', save in the special case of monopoly profit.

7. The seventh definition of 'profit' rests on a somewhat different basis. It represents 'profit' as essentially the return secured by the exercise of a certain kind of economic monopoly, based on the exclusive command of the means of production. On this view, monopoly profit appears not only as a peculiar phenomenon where competition between rival capitalist producers has been eliminated, or limited in its scope, but as a normal factor of capitalist production in general, arising from the monopoly, by a limited class or group, of the means of production, and the exclusion of those outside this class from an equal, or from any, chance of direct access to the means of production. This last is, of course, a variant of the Socialist or Marxian view, relating profit to the Marxian concept of 'surplus value'.

These seven views of the nature of profit admit, it will have been obvious as I have outlined them, of an almost infinite diversity of variations and combinations. Even if the seventh, or distinctively Socialist, group be for the moment omitted, there is room enough for diversity among economists of the various orthodox schools; and in fact hardly any two writers agree in the precise sense which they assign to the term. Writers of these schools vary, indeed, between two extremes. At the one extreme, they present their readers with a widely inclusive definition of profit, but do not attempt any precise definition of the nature of profit as such, or make any considerable use of the conception of profit as such in their writings; while, at the other, they attempt precise definition of profit by such a narrowing of the term as results, if not in the total disappearance of the profit category from the economic world, at all events in its survival as due only to exceptional causes or frictions in the working of the processes of production and exchange. The English school, on the whole, favours a wide interpretation of the term, unaccompanied by any attempt to assign to it a precise meaning, or to analyse carefully the place of profit in the system of production or distribution; while the American school has in the past favoured a narrow use of the term, and, in analysing carefully the nature of profits, so limited its meaning as to represent it as primarily the result of exceptional or unavoidable imperfections in the working out of economic laws.

To a very great extent, this ambiguity in the use of a vital economic term seems to me to result from the employment, at the outset, of a false analogy. We begin, in Adam Smith and in Ricardo, with a law of distribution which assigns to the three factors of production—landlord, labourer and capitalist *entrepreneur*—their respective shares in the product of the economic process. But it appears to be ignored in this analysis, and in many subsequent analyses founded upon it, that these three factors are not all rewarded in the same way. The landlord, in return for the land of which he is the lawful owner, and the labourer, in return for the labour power of which he is the lawful owner, receive contractual payments. Rent and wages are, in other words, actual payments made under contract to the possessors, recognised by law, of land and labour power. Profit, however, is never under any ordinary circumstances a contractual payment, or indeed a payment at all. No one, save in the highly exceptional case of a 'cost plus profit' contract, ever contracts to pay anyone else a definite amount of profit. The undertaker, in tendering for a particular contract, may estimate the price at which it will pay him to undertake the work by calculating his 'costs' and adding thereto a percentage of profit. But this calculation is his own private affair, and, if he gets the contract, his estimates may not be borne out in the actual execution of the work. He tenders, save in the exceptional case noted above, at a fixed price; and the person or body which accepts his tender agrees to pay him, not a stipulated profit, but a stipulated price, out of which have to come all his expenses of carrying through the work. His profit, if it exists, thus appears, not as a contractual payment, but as the residue of a contractual payment, after his outgoings in the execution of his contract have been duly met.

I am not, of course, suggesting that there is any element of novelty in this conception of profits as a residue—a difference between outgoings and receipts. Such a conception is implicit in all the definitions of profit that were mentioned above, and is involved in the very idea of profit. What I am suggesting is that this conception of profit as a residue sharply marks it off from the other factors in the distributive process with which it is usually equated, and that the failure to make due allowance for this difference is the main cause of the failure of successive generations of economists to formulate a satisfactory theory of profit. They agree in treating profit as a residue—though, if I were concerned with historical analysis of the theories of profit, I should have to admit certain reservations and qualifications of this statement[1]—and these differences consist mainly in their more or less determined attempts to reduce the amount of this residue by the abstraction from it of certain alleged 'quasi-contractual' elements. But, while treating profits as a residue, they fail to pay sufficient regard to the fact that this residuary character marks it off sharply from the other forms of payment with which they are comparing or equating it. Accordingly, they treat it as a quasi-contractual element in the normal expenses of production, and thus attempt to eliminate its essentially residual character by representing it as a payment whose amount is fixed, no less than that of directly contractual payments, by the inexorable operations of an economic law.

In modern economic writings, this alleged law is commonly formulated as a law of substitution at the marginal point of indifference. The complementary factors of production—land, labour and capital—are employed in such combinations as tend to the creation of the maximum amount of utility, and the employment of each factor is thus pushed to the point at which each yields, in respect of the final or marginal dose, a marginal return. The remuneration accorded to each factor thus depends upon its marginal utility, or its marginal productivity, which is the same thing; for, if this were not so, the principle of substitu-

---

[1] *I.e.*, where the theoretical treatment of profits appears to be based on treating it as equivalent to interest, and having a tendency to equality of returns between different employments. Thus, the residual charcater of profit disappears in the Ricardian analysis, which makes the landlord the sole esiduary legatee of the productive process.

tion would ensure such rearrangement of the productive forces as would restore the lost equilibrium of the marginal doses.

Now, this theory, which is evidently not devoid of truth, is clearly conceived in terms of contractual payments. The *entrepreneur* is conceived as hiring, in return for fixed contractual payments, so much land, so much labour, and so much capital, and as varying his effective demand for each of these factors of production in such a way as to make the remuneration paid for each depend on its marginal productivity. It is pertinent to observe that, even in these cases, it is upon the anticipated, and not upon the actual, productivity of the various factors that the marginal demand of the *entrepreneur* is based, and that loss or gain may result from fortunate or unfortunate errors of anticipation on his part. He cannot *know* the marginal productivity: he can, in the real world, only anticipate what he thinks it is likely to be. But, apart from this point, to which I shall return later, we have, so far, a picture of the *entrepreneur*, not risking his own or anyone else's resources in production, but simply hiring the services of land, labour and capital in return for certain contractual payments fixed by the interaction of his and other *entrepreneurs'* demands and of the valuations placed on these services by their legal possessors.

In practice, of course, the *entrepreneur's* contract cannot be absolute. He may contract to pay so much for land, so much for labour, and so much for the capital which he hires; but unless he has large personal resources which he is not venturing in the enterprise for which he is hiring the resources of others, all those who place resources at his disposal must involve themslves in some degree of risk—risk that the *entrepreneur* may not keep his contract. Debentures and loans vary greatly in effective security: landlords have been known not to get their rents; and labourers have both failed to secure the wages due to them for work done, and been flung out of a job before the contracted period of their service has expired. Risk attends the hiring out of any of the factors of production to the *entrepreneur*; and, to some extent, the price charged for the hiring contains an allowance for the risks involved, or at least for the risks anticipated when the contract is made.

My main point, however, is that so far we are wholly in the realm of contract—albeit of contracts involving risk. The promised rewards to land, labour and capital are so far purely contractual payments, consisting of rent (though not of pure 'economic' rent), of wages (though of wages including, perhaps, a risk element based on the uncertainty of continuous employment), and of, not profit, but interest, involving a contractual return to capital varying with the anticipated risk attaching to the loan. But the *entrepreneur* who, by promising these contractual payments, has possessed himself of the vital factors of production, is not working for a contractual return which he will be able to retain as his own reward of enterprise. Two cases here present themselves. In the commoner, the *entrepreneur* is uncertain of the prices which the goods produced with the aid of the land, labour and capital under his control will actually command—in other words, he is contracting to make certain fixed payments in anticipation of an unfixed return. In the less common case, where he has taken on a contract to deliver certain goods at a fixed price—for example, a house or group of houses—he is still uncertain of the total costs in which their production will involve him; for he has not been able to reduce all the payments which he has to make to a contractual form or to a fixed amount. He does not know precisely how much material he will have to use, how much labour it will take to complete his contract, how long he will have to pay interest on the capital which he has borrowed for the purpose. His reward is therefore uncertain, even if he is working wholly with land, labour and capital borrowed on contractual terms and on a piece of work for which a contractual price has been fixed in advance. He is a risk-taker, even if his risk is taken wholly with resources, apart from his own time and trouble, that are provided by others, and involve their sharing in some degree in the risks which he has assumed with their help.

In such a case as this, the contract is in due course executed. The price is paid for the completed work. The costs of the hired land, labour and capital add up to a certain amount. The *entrepreneur* has either enough to pay all these costs, with or without something over for himself, or he has not. If he has not, those who have provided him with the resources will have, according to the precise terms of the contract, varying claims upon any personal resources he may possess, apart from the actual price paid him for the work. If these resources are ample to meet every contingency, the suppliers of the resources need have incurred no risk, and may accordingly have supplied land, labour and capital to the *entrepreneur* on terms involving no insurance against risk. If he has no adequate resources, the risks of those who have supplied him may, or may not, have been adequately covered by the prices which they have charged him for the required accommodation. The risk essential to the contract must fall on someone; but it may fall, according to circumstances, in different ways—upon the *entrepreneur* himself, if he has resources which are not risked in the contract; upon those who have supplied him with the resources for its execution, and may have exacted from him a premium for the assumption of the risk; or, if he has himself insured against loss on the contract, or if any of his creditors have similarly insured, upon those who have provided the necessary insurance.

In the case of an *entrepreneur* working wholly with borrowed resources, apart from his own trouble and toil of superintendence (and even without these, if he has delegated the entire work to salaried deputies), the profit upon the transaction, if there is any profit, seems on the face of it to consist of the net gains of the *entrepreneur* after all his costs, including the cost of borrowed resources and any necessary insurances, have been met. We appear to have here a plain case of pure profit; and the plausible view seems to be that which represents this profit as the reward for the assumption by the *entrepreneur* of a certain kind of risk—namely, the uncertainty attaching to the economic outcome of the undertaking. But even this is not so clear as it sounds; for the actual risk assumed by the *entrepreneur* clearly depends on the extent of the resources which he possesses, apart from his own toil and trouble expended upon the contract. If he has no other resources, he must shift the risk, because he is not in a position to bear it himself. And he will probably have to pay for this shifting of the risk in higher interest, perhaps higher rent, and possibly higher wages to those whom he employs. He may, it is true, not have to meet all these charges; for he may succeed in hiring labour, or even some other factor of production, without payment of the appropriate charge for risk. But this will represent the acquisition of a productive factor at less than its true value, under the assumed conditions, and can only be the result of some friction, or maladjustment, of the economic order which gives him an exceptional advantage.

Now, the assumption of most schools of orthodox economists, as I understand it, is that the operation of the law of substitution will result, subject to the inevitable frictions of the economic system, in reducing the normal gains of the *entrepreneur*, under the conditions here assumed, to a remuneration equivalent to the marginal utility, or productivity, of the toil and trouble in which he involves himself by the assumption of the contract in question. His profit, unless he enjoys any exceptional position of monopoly or luck, will be normally of the nature of a wage—a wage appropriate to the industry, skill and enterprise which he applies to the work of production. And this appropriate wage will be determined, like other wages, by the marginal productivity of the particular qualities of industry, skill and enterprise of which the *entrepreneur* happens to be possessed. This beneficent result will be secured by the operation of the competitive principle; and, even under conditions of combination, the same result will largely obtain, because combination seldom assumes the form of absolute monopoly, but usually, as in cartels, involves some sort of internal sharing of rewards externally determined between the members of a limited group.

This view seems to me to rest upon a mistaken analogy. It is true that the lenders of available resources—land, labour and capital—by competing one with another, determine within each group, and to some extent between groups, their respective rewards by a competition which results in the employment of each according to its marginal productivity, in the sense of its money value to the hirer. But to the extent to which this is true—and it is by no means wholly true—of contractual payments, is it true of the work and remuneration of the *entrepreneur* himself? It approaches most nearly to truth in the case which we have so far examined, in which the *entrepreneur* is working wholly with hired resources, at any rate apart from his own toil and trouble. But even in this case, the ability of the *entrepreneur* to command the services of the various factors of production differs, and the price which he must pay for these services varies, according to the security which he is able to offer that the terms of his contract will be observed. The rich *entrepreneur* has an advantage over the poor *entrepreneur*, in that he can effectively assume or risk obligations which the other is not in a position to assume. His costs of production are affected by this, and accordingly his prospects of profit are affected, quite apart from the degree of industry, skill and enterprise which he applies to the carrying through of the contract. Even under these conditions, then, his 'profit' cannot be reduced purely to 'wages of management'.

The situation becomes far more complicated when we turn to consider either of the two forms of risk-taking productive enterprise which are most common in the modern business world. In the first of these the *entrepreneur*, while he may be operating in part with borrowed, or hired, resources, is also in part applying resources of his own to the enterprise upon which he has embarked. In the second, the capital owner, instead of lending his resources to an *entrepreneur* in return for a contractual payment, invests them in the share capital of a joint stock concern, and so becomes himself a joint undertaker, though he assumes no part in the actual conduct of the business in which his resources are embarked. (The reader will please note that I am using the terms '*entrepreneur*' and 'undertaker' for convenience in different senses. By '*entrepreneur*' I mean an actual organiser of business enterprise, whether he operates wholly or partly with his own capital or not, whereas by an 'undertaker' I mean someone who invests his money directly as a shareholder, and not by way of loan, in a business enterprise, whether he assumes any share in its organisation or management or not.)

In either of these cases, the whole or a part of the resources embarked in the enterprise takes a form both legally and economically different from that which we have been considering hitherto. Physically, the form of the enterprise may be precisely the same. The same goods may be made, or services rendered, with practically the same expenditure of energy, physical, material and mental. But, economically, the form of the enterprise is altered. For it no longer owes certain fixed contractual returns as payments for the use of all the factors of production embarked in it. In as far as it is operated with capital belonging either to the *entrepreneur* or to a body of shareholding joint undertakers, this capital ceases to exercise any contractual claim upon the business (for a man cannot enter into a contract with himself) and becomes a claim which is essentially residual in character. The business has to meet out of its assets (or out of the whole assets of the undertakers where it has not assumed a joint stock form, with limited liability) all the contractual claims upon it. What is left after this has been done belongs to the *entrepreneur* or to the joint undertakers, and constitutes, from the accounting standpoint, his or their 'profit'.

A part of the question before us is whether this balance-sheet use of the term 'profit' is to be recognised as economically valid. It is, of course, obvious that, if we do use the term in this sense, businesses carried on with equal resources and equal efficiency and under precisely the same physical conditions, but with differing economic compositions of the capital (and, I may add, also of the human effort) applied to them, will yield different amounts of profit. For the contractual return to the hired resources will figure not as a profit but as a cost, whereas the non-contractual return to the *entrepreneurs*' or undertakers' resources will figure as a profit and not as a cost. This is sometimes used as an argument against employing the term 'profit' in this sense, on the ground that businesses carried on with equal efficiency under identical physical conditions ought to yield equal profits. But why should they? Such an answer begs the question. They must indeed generate equal amounts of value and of 'surplus value', if we choose to employ that term; but unless their economic, as well as their physical, composition is the same, they need not distribute these amounts of value, or surplus value, in the same way.

The desire to represent all equal amounts of capital (and all equal amounts of labour) as having a tendency to generate an equal economic return, and the desire to link this tendency up with a general law of distribution in accordance with the principle of marginal productivity, lie at the root of the attempt to give to the term 'profit', and also, as we shall see, to the terms 'interest' and 'wages', a sense which will impute to it a constant relation to the amount of capital or effort for which it is the economic return. But the inevitable result of this method of argument, pushed to its logical conclusion by certain American writers, is, if not the total disappearance of the profit category from the economic world, at any rate its survival only as a result of friction which hampers the perfectly smooth working of economic laws. The profit which survives is the result of artificial monopoly, which hampers the working of the law of marginal productivity, or of the uncertainty (or unpredictable risk) which is involved in the changing character of the economic world, or of sheer luck. In a world perfectly competitive and endowed with perfect foreknowledge of the future—not necessarily a static world, but a world of foreseeable change—all profit, in this sense, would disappear.

To the implications of the terms 'monopoly' and 'competition', as they have been used above, it will be necessary to return. Here, however, our concern is with the process by which profit, a thing so clearly seen and sought by the common man, is made by the economist to perform this remarkable vanishing trick. This process is based essentially on a refinement of the classification of incomes begun by Adam Smith, and carried further by Malthus and McCulloch in England, by Walker in America, and by many other writers. Adam Smith, as we have seen, drew a distinction between profit, in the sense attached to the term by the man in the street, and profit in the economic sense. The latter was to exclude wages of management, the remuneration of the time and trouble of the *entrepreneur*; and economic profit was thus regarded as 'profit of stock', the remuneration attaching specifically to the capital rather than to the service performed. Capital, or stock, became on this view the residual claimant to the product of industry, and the returns to the different stocks were equalised by the process of competition.

In drawing this distinction, Adam Smith clearly gave both 'wages' and 'profit' new senses differing widely from their ordinary meanings. A wage became the reward attached to any form of service, no matter how it was rendered, and a profit that of any form of stock, no matter how it was applied to production. Adam Smith's immediate successors did not follow his lead, but preferred to treat profit in a sense more nearly corresponding to current usage, as the total return to the *entrepreneur*, whether it came to him as the reward for applying capital or personal effort. This involved, we may note, also a corresponding redefinition of 'wages', so as to exclude the remuneration of the *entrepreneur's* own labour. But, while restoring the term 'profit' to a more ordinary sense, Malthus and McCulloch set on foot a new process of definition, by attempting to divide profit internally into certain component parts.

Since then, as we have seen, one economist after another has followed up these two lines of argument. On the one hand, there has been the body of opinion which has attempted, by the exclusion of successive elements from the popular idea of profit, to reduce the concept to a residue so small as to be comparatively unimportant; and, on the other, there has been the attempt, while leaving the term inclusive, to distinguish one from another the separate elements which it is held to contain.

By far the most important aspect of both these attempts lies in their treatment of profit in relation to interest. One school treats profit as merely a residue after interest has been deducted on all the capital employed, no matter what the manner of its employment may be, while the other finds in profit an interest element which is capable of being separately distinguished.

A expends £1,000 of his own capital in a productive process under his own control, and receives with its aid £1,100 by selling the product—a profit of 10 per cent on the capital employed. B expends £1,000 of capital borrowed at 5 per cent, and sells his product for £1,100 a year later, thus realising a net £50 for himself after paying interest. Is £50 of A's profit to be regarded as interest, which he would have had to pay if he had borrowed the £1,000 instead of owning it? If so, his profit is 5 per cent and not 10 per cent. But B's profit cannot possibly be regarded as 5 per cent, for he did not sink £1,000 in getting it. A's and B's returns cannot be compared in terms of percentages. If, indeed, the whole creative power were attributed to the capital itself, we could say that the two sums of £1,000 *used by* A and B had each returned a yield of £100, consisting in the one case of 10 per cent profit and in the other of 5 per cent interest and 5 per cent profit on the sum so used. But this would imply that the yield was wholly due to the money, and not at all to the use made of it by A and B.

The instance here taken is not, however, normal in type. For when A and B set out to use the capital in their hands, whether it be their own or borrowed, they can as a rule only use it either by relending it at interest to someone else, to whom the problem of using it will thus present itself in the same form, or by changing it from £1,000 into something quite different. A uses his to buy machines, to hire a factory, and to pay for labour and material which he requires for the production of certain goods. B uses his in order to buy a piece of land or some shares in a company, in the hope either of receiving a rent or dividends, or of being able to sell these again for more than he paid for them. As soon as either A or B uses his £1,000 in any of these ways, what he is using ceases to be £1,000, and becomes the things he has bought with the money. These things cost him £1,000, and may have been worth just this amount when he bought them. But there is no reason to suppose that they will continue to be worth just £1,000 even for a minute after he has bought them. They may be worth more or less, according as he has bought wisely or foolishly, luckily or unluckily, and according to the use he makes of them after he has bought them. The £1,000 expended on their purchase no longer exists—at any rate as his. As a mass of free purchasing power, possessing a definite monetary magnitude, it has either simply ceased to be, by conversion into the things he has used it to produce, or it has passed into someone else's hands, if he has used it, not for fresh production, but to buy something already in being.

This is, of course, commonplace enough. But note the consequence. If A's £1,000, although it has been thus transformed into something else, is to be said to yield him an interest, or if the profit he makes by the use of what he has bought with it is to be said to contain an interest element, how is this interest or this element to be calculated? There is no reason for calculating it as interest on £1,000; for the £1,000 is no longer in his possession. A will no doubt for some time go on remembering that the sum which he originally expended was £1,000, and will tend to think of his return as so much per cent on £1,000. But how long will he go on doing this? Will his £1,000 retain for ever a purely fictitious existence as £1,000, merely for the purpose of having his interest, or the interest element in his profit, calculated upon it, irrespective of what happens to the value of money or to the value of the things into which the £1,000 has been transformed? If someone's great-grandfather invested £1,000 in buying spinning machinery in 1790, is this £1,000 still at work, as £1,000, tending to return interest at a standard rate, and must this interest be deducted before we can find out how much profit the great-grandson is really making today, or be at least distinguished as a separate element in the great-grandson's profit? Any such contention is the merest nonsense; and yet it is implicit in the attempt either to treat all capital as returning an interest which must be deducted before the amount of profit can be ascertained, or to distinguish a separate interest element in profit. For we cannot distinguish the interest or the interest element unless we know on what we are to calculate it; and, if we discard the magnitude of the original investment, what are we to put in its place?

There is, indeed, one heroic way out of this difficulty which some people have attempted to adopt. The amount of capital on which the interest, or interest element, ought to be calculated can be found, they say, by valuing the current assets of the concern in which the capital has been sunk. If it is worth £100,000 (say at its current Stock Exchange value), then there is £100,000 of interest-bearing capital in it, and interest on this sum must be deducted before arriving at the profit. If this is done, no profits will usually remain. For the current capital value is nothing other than the capitalisation of the expected future profits of the concern. The argument is thus clearly circular. It consists simply in re-expressing the amount of profit

## X. THE NATURE OF PROFIT

as a rate per cent of the current capital value, and then calling it interest.

A very similar problem to that which we are now discussing arises in connection with the classical theory of economic rent. Capital sunk in the land is supposed to yield an interest, which must be distinguished from the economic rent. But it has no such tendency. Capital sunk in the land is amalgamated with the land, and the future rent is paid for the improved land as a whole, according to its anticipated revenue-yielding qualities, and not in part for the land as it was (but is no longer) and in part for the improvement effected by means of the capital. The economic rent and the interest cannot be distinguished. There is one rent only, and this is based on the differential income-yielding capacity of the land as it is, improvements and all.

The position in respect of capital is precisely the same. Marshall, of course, recognised this when he described the economic returns derived from the productive use of durable goods as being of the nature of 'quasi-rents'. A's capital, once sunk in his business and converted into commodities, loses its character as money capital and its power to yield any sort of interest, and becomes a value proportionate to the income-generating capacity of the business as it stands. Its value, some would say, is measured thereafter by the discounted marginal productivity of the goods which it has become. And this applies not only to durable goods, or fixed capital, but also to circulating capital, as long as it remains in the form of commodities and not of money. The circulating capital is merely nearer to the money form: the difference between its status and that of the fixed capital is one of degree, and not of kind.

The point of my argument is that the return which the *entrepreneur* or undertaker, in the sense given to these words in this paper, derives from his capital is one and indivisible, and can be neither separated nor analysed into distinct component parts. Nor, it follows, can the return which the *entrepreneur* derives from his own capital embarked in his business be distinguished from the return which he gets from his toil and trouble in managing that business. He gets, for his composite service of personal labour and capital outlay, a single return;

and this return is properly to be described, in economic science as well as in ordinary language, as profit. The attempt to exclude from this profit a separate element of 'wages of management', or to isolate such an element within it, breaks down no less completely than the attempt to separate or isolate an element of interest. And the same difficulties would be fatal to any attempt to pick out and delimit a separate return or element arising as 'payment for risk'.

The profit category, I am contending, is one and indivisible, and properly coincides with the use of the term in ordinary speech. A's profit—remember that in our example A is using entirely his own capital—is the difference between his takings and his outgoings—that, and neither more nor less than that.

What, then, of B's profit? B, in our example, was operating wholly with borrowed capital on which he contracted to pay interest at a fixed rate. He made a surplus of £100 over his costs, apart from the interest on the borrowed money, and had £50 left after paying this interest. His profit is £50, in precisely the same sense as A's profit was £100, though they have been using precisely the same amounts of capital and using them with the same efficiency to produce the same quantities of goods, which they have then sold at the same prices. Their profits differ because their costs differ. B's profit is solely the result of his own toil, trouble and enterprise and of the risks attaching to the application of his personal service to this particular form of production; whereas A's profit is the result of an application of his own capital as well. It is tempting to say that £50 of A's return ought to be regarded, not as profit, but as interest on his capital; but it is quite untrue. For, if A and B now resume operations for another year, and again produce identical commodities under identical conditions of production (apart from the composition of their respective capitals), but this time both have to sell their products for £1,080, what are we to say? B has still to pay £50 in interest, leaving him only £30 profit. A has £80. Are we now to regard £50 of A's return as interest and only £30 as profit, assuming that the entire loss due to worse trading conditions is at the expense of his personal toil, trouble and enterprise, and none at the expense of the value of the

## THE NATURE OF PROFIT

durable instruments of production, etc., into which he has converted his capital? There is plainly no warrant for such a view; and if A now seeks to sell his durable goods and get his money back, he will soon discover that their market value has been affected by the decline in the current expectation of profit from their use.

It is, of course, true that, if the decline in A's and B's profits is not peculiar to their trade, but part of a general decline in business profits over a wide field, this lessened expectation of profit will be likely to react on the rate of interest at which new money can be borrowed for business enterprise. Thus, if B is operating with money borrowed only for a short term, he may be able to replace his old borrowings at 5 per cent with new borrowings, at 4 per cent, and so raise his profit from £30 to £40, while A's profit remains at £80 as before. The rates of interest charged for business loans and the current expectations of profit from the embarking of resources in production are closely linked up together. For, in ordinary business transactions, money is only borrowed because the borrower hopes to be able to use the loan, either by itself or in conjunction with resources of his own, and perhaps with his own toil and trouble, in such a way as to realise a profit for himself after paying the interest. The existence of profit is not the sole reason for the existence of interest; for there are other forms of borrowing besides ordinary business loans. But, in ordinary industrial operations, the expectation of profit is the source of the demand for loans. The levels of profit and interest are thus intimately connected; but it does not at all follow either that all profit contains an interest element, or that all capital, however applied, earns interest, or can have an appropriate interest imputed to it.

This view of the nature of profit, and of the relation of profit to interest, squares both with the practice of business accounting and with the view of the ordinary man. It is undoubtedly the best usage of the term 'profit' for the economist to adopt. The only ground on which objection can be taken to it is based on the assumption that equal capitals applied to production with equal efficiency ought to tend to yield equal profits. But why should they, unless they are applied in the same way? It is not the use of capital, but its use in a particular and distinctive way, that gives rise to profit.

What, then, is this distinctive way? If I have money which I design to use as capital, I have a choice of methods open to me. I can apply my money by lending it out to someone else in return for a promise, or contract, to pay interest at a fixed rate. Or I can apply it myself, or in association with others and their capitals, directly to production for an uncertain and non-contractual return. The first of these uses of capital does not bring in a profit to its owner; the second does—or, of course, a loss, if the enterprise fails. This distinction is perfectly clear and precise; and there is no valid reason for the economist to wish to go behind it.

If, however, the economist does want a term to describe the return on all forms of capital, whether it be lent or invested, and whether it consist of a sum of money or a supply of durable goods, he will need to find some term other than profit for this purpose. Marx, treating land as a form of capital, comes near to such a term in his use of the word 'surplus value', which is not profit, but the common fund out of which rent, interest and profit are drawn. But Marx complicates his use of the term 'surplus value' by entangling himself in the fruitless distinction between productive and unproductive labour, which causes him to say in the end that clerks' and warehousemen's wages, as well as rent, interest and profits, have to be paid out of surplus value. Moreover, Marx's surplus value must obviously include not only the whole return on capital in all its forms, but also the return to the *entrepreneurs* for their own expenditure of toil, trouble and business enterprise; for they are certainly not remunerated for these, in Marx's terminology, by means of wages. Surplus value does cover the whole return on capital in all its forms, including land; but it includes other elements as well.

Nor can this be avoided. For, as we have seen, there is no possible means of distinguishing or separating the parts of the *entrepreneur's* return which come to him as payment for his toil and trouble from the earnings of the capital which he has embarked in his business. For this reason the conception of a return upon all capital, however used, is not a fruitful conception for the purposes of economic analysis. It does not represent a real, or practically isolable or measurable category.

But this does not mean that the conception of 'surplus value' is unimportant. Its importance, however, lies in the distinction which it draws, not between payments for capital and payments for labour, but between contractual wage incomes on the one hand and all other incomes, 'earned' or 'unearned', on the other. It is a vital concept for the study of the underlying conditions of the wage contract; but it throws no light on the nature or delimitation of profit, or interest, or rent as distinct categories of distribution.

Profit, then, in a monetary economy, can be simply defined as the surplus which arises from selling a product for more than the total cost of producing it—any interest on borrowed resources used in the production being reckoned as part of the cost. If this view is accepted, it follows that all profit, and not merely one particular element in profit, partakes equally, if at all, of the nature of what Alfred Marshall called a 'quasi-rent'; for it is all a return derived from the differential income-producing capacity of a body of resources applied to production. It is not possible, as Marshall seemed sometimes to suppose it was, to pick out that element in profit which can be attributed to the productivity of a 'durable good', such as a factory or a machine, and isolate this, as a quasi-rent, from the profit due to the productivity of the enterprise of the factory's owner. But it is correct to regard the entire net return accruing from the owner's use of his durable goods as a differential return of the same nature as the return derived by an occupying owner from the joint application of his land and labour.

Quasi-rent is, however, an exceedingly bad name for such a return. For rent, like interest or wages, is essentially a contractual payment, whereas profit is not. All Marshall means is that different 'durable goods', such as factories, have, equally with different parcels of land, differential capacities for producing income, and are therefore equally capable of giving rise to rent. This is, of course, perfectly true; and a factory will yield a rent if its owner lets it to someone else instead of using it himself. But, if he does use it himself, it no more yields him a 'quasi-rent' than a parcel of land yields rent to an occupying owner. For the part of the return arising from the use of the land or factory cannot be quantitatively marked off from the part which arises from the other factors which contribute to the total net product.

It is therefore misleading to regard profit, or any part of profit, as a quasi-rent. The truth is that rent and profits, and to a great extent wages also, are returns which accrue to the owners of things, including personal qualities, which possess a differential capacity to generate income. The importance of Marshall's 'quasi-rent' lies only in the recognition that the possession of this differential capacity is by no means peculiar to land. Interest is alone among the classical participants in the distribution of income in not being a differential payment in this sense, because, within a single monetary system, one unit of money is as good as another.

This brings me to my final point. If rent, profit and wages are alike differential payments, and interest mainly depends upon the expectation of profit, it seems plausible to conclude that, in the present economic system, each factor of production is rewarded in accordance with its productivity; for in what else than this does the capacity to yield income consist? It is relevant to point out that this way of arguing is really tautological; for if productivity=capacity to yield income, clearly each factor in production will get an income that accords with its productivity. The statement means absolutely nothing.

As we have seen, however, certain economists have attempted to define profit as the result of economic monopoly, which would tend to disappear under perfectly free conditions of competition. In doing this, they have narrowed the meaning of the term profit so as to confine it to an exceptional type of gain, and have eliminated from it in turn the element of interest on capital, the element of payment for risk-taking, the element of payment for business enterprise and the time and trouble of the *entrepreneur*, and every element which could in theory be refined away by analogy with some other kind of payment. I have insisted in this essay that these exclusions are illegitimate, and that the profit category must be retained as an inclusive whole. But is this wide definition of the term in any way inconsistent with the recognition that it is based on monopoly, in a wider sense of the word monopoly than most economists have been willing to admit? This wider monopoly is, indeed, related, not to profit specifically, but rather to what Marx called 'surplus value', to the sum of values accruing to the recipients of rent, interest and profits. And it is true enough that there are monopolistic elements in the return to certain classes of wage- and salary-earners as well, wherever these depend either on naturally scarce personal qualities or on acquired skill depending on expensive education or training. There is obviously a monopoly element in many professional incomes under conditions which throw the differential costs of education on the parents, and so make the higher forms of education, despite the growth of scholarships and allowances for maintenance, still largely a class prerogative.

But the entire return which Marx called 'surplus value' depends on monopoly in a somewhat different sense. For the power to bring together the necessary factors of production is itself a monopolistic power, from which the great mass of the population in all advanced industrial countries is excluded. This is not to say that the peasant, who does possess this power in some degree, is better off than the industrial worker. Manifestly, he is not; and neither Marx nor any other economist has ever suggested that he is. Nor is the independent worker, who works on his own materials, necessarily better off than the wage-earner, or as well off. For not all monopolies are equally advantageous; and the benefits of monopoly in the modern world accrue chiefly to the owners of large-scale business.

## XI

## THE ABOLITION OF THE WAGE SYSTEM

THE demand for the abolition of the wage system has been long familiar in Labour and Socialist propaganda. What does the demand mean? Some Socialists, notably the Fabians, have dismissed it as futile, on the ground that, in their view, wages constitute a form of payment with which no social system can possible dispense. It will always be necessary, they tell us, to pay a man so much an hour, or a day, or a week, or a month, as the remuneration of his labour; and they enquire what advantage there can possibly be in discarding the term wages, which is sanctioned by use and wont, merely in order to replace it by some other term with the same meaning.

If this were all the advocates of the abolition of the wage system meant, the Fabians would be incontestably right. But this is very far from the truth. What is demanded is not simply a change of name, but a change of status—the establishment of a new set of relations and a new estimation of human rights. A wage, as the word is understood in Socialist and Trade Union circles, is not merely a daily or weekly payment for work done, but a payment made on certain definite terms. In the eyes of those who seek the abolition of the wage system, these terms are degrading and inconsistent with the recognition of elementary human rights.

What, then, is a wage? It is, in effect, a reward for work done, calculated either in accordance with the time spent by the wage-earner in the employer's service (time-work payment), or in accordance with the amount produced under the employer's orders (payment by results). But observe the accompanying conditions. In the first place the wage, being a reward for work done, is only paid, with certain very rare exceptions, when the workman is able to find an employer ready to employ him.

## CHAP. XI. ABOLITION OF WAGE SYSTEM 259

When the workman is unemployed he receives no wage, though he may under modern conditions receive a smaller payment under some public scheme of unemployment insurance or relief. And, even when he is technically in employment, he can be temporarily suspended or deprived of work for part of the week, or even in some trades for part of the day, or be placed on systematic short time, because his employer is unable or unwilling to use his services for the whole week, or to pay him a full week's wage for a full week's work. Certain favoured groups of workers have indeed succeeded in getting what is called a 'guaranteed week'; in other words, they are assured of a full week's wages for any week in which they are actually in employment at all. But this is exceptional; and there are numerous classes of workers who have not been able to secure even a 'guaranteed day'. Moreover, even these more favoured workers can be discharged either without notice, or at a day's, a week's, or a fortnight's notice. Among manual workers, as long a period of notice as a month is indeed a rarity. Once discharged, they have no further claim to a wage, until they are able to find a new employer to engage them.

What are the conditions which enable them to find an employer or to get regular work and wages when they are in employment? Except in the public services and in the case of workers engaged for the direct utility of their labour to the employer, such as domestic servants, the indispensable condition is that the employer should consider it economically worth while to employ them; and this normally means that he must have an expectation of making a profit by means of their labour. It is true that, with an eye to the future, an employer may sometimes keep men at work, even when he looks for no immediate profit as a result; but, in the last resort, he must always be guided by the prospect of profit. For otherwise he will be driven to close his works when his resources are at an end. He cannot afford to go on employing workers at a loss. It is the expectation of profit on the employer's part that, under the existing system, determines and conditions the employment of labour, and, consequently, the payment of wages to the workers.

This is, of course, no more than a simple statement of the

positive conditions of present-day industry. But I have to insist on what follows from these conditions. Under this system, the worker lives in a state of constant insecurity. The fact that the world and his fellow-workers have need of the products of his hands is no guarantee at all that he will find work; for the only demand that the system recognises is economic and not human demand. The loss of work by the workman has the effect of diminishing at once both the total volume of purchasing power and the amount of goods offered for sale. It is sheer loss both for him and for society. But a situation in which the amount of purchasing power distributed as wages depends on production, while the amount of production, in its turn, depends on the purchasing power available, is treated as a law of nature; and the continuous insecurity in which almost the whole of the working class lives is regarded equally as an indispensable condition of business enterprise.

This continuous insecurity is in fact a characteristic feature of the wage system. It is unavoidable, as long as production is allowed to depend solely on the individual employer's or business's hope of profit. Some optimists have proposed to get rid of the insecurity of the wage system without disturbing any of its other characteristics. Each industry, it is suggested, ought to maintain its own unemployed, or, in other words, to give to all the workers in its service the guarantee of the uninterrupted receipt of a standard wage. As an alternative, it has sometimes been proposed that the State should guarantee every worker, instead of an insurance payment well below the normal wage, full maintenance at his regular standard, raising the necessary funds either by a special levy on all industries or by general taxation. I do not say that such steps are impossible; but it is surely clear that either involves a complete recasting of the industrial system, and its reconstruction on a basis which would no longer make the earning of a profit the determining cause of production and employment. For full maintenance by each industry of the whole body of workers attached to it would, in bad times, mean heavy loss, which would have to be met from some source other than the current takings of the industry; while the State, if it undertook to maintain all the workers at full wages, would obviously have to find means of setting them to work, even if the product of their labour was worth less than the full cost of production, including their maintenance. It is not easy to abolish one characteristic of the wage system without oversetting the system itself.

In any case, the insecurity in which the wage-earner lives is not the only, or even the principal, defect of the wage system. In return for a wage, the workman sells his labour-power to the employer. Aided by the strength of his Trade Union or appealing to industrial legislation, he may succeed in making this sale subject to certain conditions. But no Trade Union has yet succeeded in establishing control over the purposes to which the labour-power of its members is applied. In fact, any attempt on its part to do this would certainly be denounced as an unwarrantable interference, and a dangerous onslaught on the rights of management and control vested in the heads of the business. The workman may be called upon to make things—armaments, for example—which would be, in his opinion, much better not made at all; but he will be told that it is none of his business to beat swords into ploughshares. Or, again, he may be compelled to manufacture luxury goods, even when he knows that there is, in his branch of production, a scarcity of vital necessaries. The mason is not asked whether he prefers to build palaces for millionaires or cottages for workmen. All that is determined, not by considerations of human need, but by the employer's expectation of profit. The workman is employed only on condition that he makes what the employer bids him make, without regard to the social utility or uselessness of the work imposed upon him, and without concern for the greater or less urgency of different human wants.

But, it will be asked, why should the building operative or the engineer demand, or why should they be granted, the right of choosing what work they will do? This surely is a matter for the consumer. So it is. But I am none the less disposed to insist on the fact that, under the present system, the consumer is no more consulted than the mason or the engineer. The consumer is you and I; he is everybody; but we have no other means of influencing the course of production than by influencing the employer's expectation of profit; and even this is strictly limited by our capacity to pay. It would doubtless be reasonable to demand that the workman should recognise and subject himself to the demands of production, if these were determined by the community as a whole, on a basis of its needs. But there is no reason why he should willingly submit to the control of productive effort if this is based on the employer's expectation of profit, this expectation being based, in turn, on a wrong distribution of purchasing power.

It is, however, a fact that the workman does not submit voluntarily, and does not give of his best under the present system. Over a great part of the industrial field, the wage-earners in general see no reason for giving more by way of labour than their personal interests absolutely require. They will produce enough to avoid the danger of being sacked: they can, in some cases, be stimulated by the offer of material inducements in the shape of payments by results; but on the whole the pace of production is indubitably slowed down by the worker's full awareness that his labour, instead of being applied to the satisfaction of social wants, is used only as a source of private profit. On this account he sees no reason for doing more than a minimum amount of work; and this cannot be attributed to him as a fault, for it arises inevitably out of the conditions of production. If these conditions are taken for granted, it can even be said that the question of reasonableness is not regarded as arising in his case; for production pursues ends which bear no relations to social needs which he would be ready to recognise.

In the third place, not only does production lack all social incentive, but also the worker has no responsibility, and no sense of responsibility, for production. His Trade Union may be able, by means of a collective agreement, to impose on the employer restrictions as to the manner in which he may use the worker's labour-power. It may be able to regulate rates of wages, hours of labour, overtime, and even to some extent factory discipline and the organisation of work. It remains none the less true that the authority of the Trade Union is limited by its economic power, and all that it can do is to impose restrictions designed to safeguard its members' interests. The employer or his representative gives the orders; the employer assumes and keeps the responsibility for production, and jealously excludes the workers from all share in the control of the business, except under conditions which imply submission to his point of view, as in some Works Committees and similar bodies exerting an illusory share in the functions of management.

Under these conditions, it would be ridiculous to expect the workers to feel any sense of responsibility for production. For responsibility is the correlative of power, and implies the right to make decisions. If it is asked how far this right is conceded to the workers in the year 1932, it is only necessary to refer in reply to the recent discussions in the engineering industry, in the course of which the employers have shown a lively opposition to any interference whatever by the workers in workshop questions as essential to their welfare as the 'manning of machines', on the ground that this would be an encroachment on 'managerial functions' and a departure from the proper functions of Trade Unionism.

In short, the wage system involves for the workman an utterly inferior status. The wage-earner's situation is one of entire insecurity, in which he is unable to look confidently even a month ahead, unless he is in a specially privileged position. It is not easy for a man to retain his manhood intact under these conditions. Threatened by such a danger, it is hard for him either to stand up for his rights, or to profess just and courageous ideas. His situation is degraded and degrading; he is the social inferior of all those whose security for the morrow is greater than his own. Nothing so holds back the working-class movement, or thwarts and represses the personality of the working class, as the incessant dread of unemployment. Besides, the wage system denies the worker all sense of either social direction in, or personal responsibility for, his work. In order to drive him to produce, it appeals, not to his professional honour or his desire to serve the community in accordance with his powers, but to his fears, his needs, and his economic cupidity. It drives him to labour harder because his wife and children must have bread, by offering him a few shillings extra as a piece-work bonus, and then takes these shillings away from him, by cutting the piece-work rate, when, reacting to this inducement, he has consented to increase his output.

I maintain that a system which rests on these motives is unjust and inhuman. And I maintain no less firmly that it is inefficient. It not merely ignores, it is flatly in opposition to, the most powerful force that can be enlisted on the side of human progress—the sense of free and well-directed service. For a man to give of his best, three conditions need to be fulfilled; and all these three the wage system flatly denies. In the first place, men ought to be able to count on security, not absolute, but reasonably adequate, for themselves and their families, and ought to possess the assurance that their incomes depend, not only on some individual's zest for profit, but on the community's power to provide its members with the means of living, and of living well. In the second place, men ought to have the assured sense that their labour is serving a useful purpose, not merely from the standpoint of an individual or corporate profit-maker, but from that of society and its members. In the third place, they ought to have the consciousness that they are responsible for the manner, good or bad, in which they render the service which is in their trust, and that they are charged by the community each with his own task as his particular contribution to the common task, which cannot be effectively performed unless everyone does his part with a will.

The abolition of the wage system implies, then, three things—first, the establishment for all workers of as much security as society is capable of affording, or, in other words, a guaranteed right to income in return for a continuous will to work; secondly, the determination of the course of production by the community as a whole, in due relation to human needs, and not with the quest for the greatest possible private profit; and thirdly, collective and individual responsibility, implying for the workers the individual and collective power to regulate their service under autonomous conditions, subject only to their fulfilment of the demands of society for production. These three things make up the legitimate aspiration of the working class; and this aspiration will become a positive demand to the extent to which the working class can gain confidence in itself, despite the depressing conditions of its present status. The day when this demand has been satisfied will witness a great increase in the responsiveness and efficiency of labour; and it will also bring with it a great improvement in sheer human quality, as new possibilities of self-expression open before them in art and science and in life itself. Society can neither be in health nor get the best from its members as long as it refuses to most of them any effective security or responsibility. But security and responsibility cannot be gained without a radical change of the social system; and it depends largely on the attitude of the possessing classes whether this change comes peacefully or by a cataclysm which involves a wasteful destruction of existing values as a means to the creation of the new.

# PART III
SOCIALISATION

## XII

## PUBLIC AND SEMI-PUBLIC CONCERNS

IN the Liberal Yellow Book, published under the title of *Britain's Industrial Future*, there is an interesting chapter bearing the name of 'The Public Concern'. The authors begin this chapter with a round assertion that, in the light of the modern developments of business enterprise and public control, the old controversies between Socialists and anti-Socialists over the question of 'nationalisation' are to a great extent obsolete. They go on to describe in detail the extent and growth of public or semi-public concerns engaged in the actual administration of industries and services, and, without proposing definitely that the scope of this sort of management should be for the present widened, evidently see in it a means of bridging the gulf between capitalist and Socialist ideas about the control of industry. The list which they present is indeed formidable; and, when it appeared, doubtless many people were surprised to see how far State control and operation of industries and services had in fact already advanced. The Yellow Book went on to suggest changes in the methods of administering many of these socialised, or half-socialised, enterprises, in order to make them more efficient and flexible in their working. The authors evidently desired to make publicly administered services adopt methods more nearly like those of privately owned industry, to place them under forms of business management immune from political intervention, and in this way to reconcile the apparently conflicting standpoints of Collectivism and Individualism. I shall be attempting in this paper to restate the case from a somewhat different point of view.

The argument most commonly adduced against State participation in the actual conduct of industry is that State action in this sphere is most often inefficient and inelastic, and that the machinery of State—embodied in the typical Civil Service departments—is unsuitable to the practical control of industrial operations. Judgments that State trading enterprise is habitually inefficient seem to be for the most part *a priori*, and to be highly uncertain and ambiguous in the standards of comparison which they adopt. Is it with the best or the worst, or the norm or the average, of private business that State enterprises are being compared? No one seems to know, or at any rate to make the basis of the comparison clear. It is at least not proven that State enterprises such as the Post Office, even where they are run on Civil Service lines, are inefficient in comparison with the great bulk of private industry.

Nevertheless, most people nowadays, including the majority of Socialists, do appear to hold that the direct conduct of industries through Civil Service departments is not the best method of industrial organisation, even where the case for State intervention to control an industry or service has been sufficiently made out. Socialists have for a long time been veering towards the idea that publicly administered forms of enterprise ought to be conducted through some sort of *ad hoc* trading body, with accounts clearly separated from the national Budget, and with methods of administration conferring a wider discretion than can easily be reconciled either with the Civil Service tradition or with the present forms of parliamentary control through a responsible Minister. Consequently, there is an insistence, among Socialists, on the working out of alternative forms of public control and administration; and many who are not in any sense Socialists recognise the inevitability of public ownership and control over a wide field, and are seeking, from an opposite point of view, to devise methods of administration that seem to them consistent with their hostility to Socialism as they understand it.

Let us begin with an example illustrating each of these attitudes. Mr. Herbert Morrison, as Minister of Transport, recently published the outline of a scheme for the complete co-ordination of the traffic control of Greater London. Under this scheme, which Mr. Morrison confidently proclaimed as based on the most up-to-date kind of Socialism, the privately owned London traffic combine was to be amalgamated with the publicly owned tramway systems of the L.C.C. and other bodies into a unified service under public control. This service was to be administered, however, not by the L.C.C. or any other Local Authority, but by a special *ad hoc* authority—a commission of business experts and representatives of the interests concerned, operating under powers conferred by a special Act of Parliament, and subject to State control in such matters as charges and payments to those who had capital invested in any of the amalgamated businesses. There was to be set up a public authority, armed with large powers and authorised to conduct the entire passenger transport services of Greater London as a publicly controlled monopoly, under powers to be conferred directly by Act of Parliament. But this concern was to be in form a business body, and not an elected authority directly responsible either to the general body of the metropolitan electorate, or to any special body of electors constituted for the purpose.

Or take, on the other side, recent Conservative criticisms of the Post Office. Lord Wolmer and other critics, including Liberals as well as Conservatives, want to take the management of the Post Office out of the hands of Civil Servants, and entrust it—or at least the telephone service—to some sort of Statutory Corporation run on business lines, on the model of what Signor Mussolini has already done in Italy. Some Socialists at once waxed very indignant over Lord Wolmer's proposal; but on the face of the matter it appeared to resemble closely what another Socialist, Mr. Morrison, was proposing to do in the case of London traffic.

Nor need we remain wholly in the realm of projects. The most important industry in Great Britain that is undergoing a thorough process of 'rationalisation' is the industry of electricity supply. The Act reconstituting the industry was passed by a Conservative Government. Yet, in effect, it nationalised completely one great, and key, section of the electrical industry, the bulk transmission and wholesaling of electrical power, in addition to establishing an extensive system of control over both the production, or generation, and the retail distribution. This

Conservative Act has at least half-nationalised the electricity industry; but it has done this, not by placing its conduct in the hands of a Civil Service department or under the traditional forms of parliamentary control, but by establishing, in the Electricity Commissioners and the Central Electricity Board, new public authorities wielding a very large measure of the public power in relation to the services which they control. It is safe to say that if the Electricity Acts had been brought forward by any Socialist Government, they would have been heavily condemned by Conservatives as involving a destruction of private enterprise and a long step towards Socialism. But, as matters stand, we have the startling paradox that the most Socialistic piece of legislation passed since the war has been enacted, with very little opposition in any quarter, by a Conservative Government.

This rise of what are coming to be called 'Semi-public Concerns' is one of the most important features of the post-war economic system. There is, of course, in one sense nothing novel about them; for bodies operating under some sort of public authority, and with some degree of public participation and control, existed long before the war, both in other countries and in Great Britain. There were railways, as in Belgium, owned by the State and operated by private companies under licence; there was the well-known German instance of State participation, on behalf of State-owned mines, in the Rhenish-Westphalian Coal Syndicate; and there were, in Great Britain, mixed bodies controlling vital services, such as the Port of London Authority established a few years before the war. But we had not learnt, in pre-war days, to think of the Semi-public Concern as a distinct form of economic organisation, capable of being applied over a wide field as an alternative alike to private enterprise and to direct management by the State or by municipal bodies.

Of late years, however, this alternative form of economic organisation has emerged more and more clearly, albeit in many different forms. We have, in this country, the outstanding examples of the Joint Electricity Authorities and the Central Electricity Board in one field, and of the British Broadcasting

Corporation in another. Russia, where a vast experiment in State Socialism is in progress, has organised her industries under the control of a whole series of 'trusts', each endowed with a wide autonomy under the Soviet Republic and its central economic organs. Germany has experimented in 'mixed' enterprises, based on a coalition of public and private capitals and public and private representatives on boards of directors; and the British State has followed up its earlier holding of Suez Canal shares by investing in the British Dyestuffs Corporation and the Anglo-Persian Oil Company. Even such a concern as the Imperial Cables and Communications Company illustrates the difficulty, in these days, of drawing a clear line between public and private enterprise; and such bodies as the Public Utility Societies, which take a growingly important part in the work of State-aided housing abroad, and to a less extent in this country, while they may be in form purely private ventures, are so linked up with the State by borrowings and grants as to be, in effect, semi-public in the real nature of their operations and policy.

Of course, we can see now, as we look back, that the system of private enterprise has never been wholly private. In mercantilist days, the great regulated and joint stock companies, from the Merchant Adventurers to the East India Company, were in large measure agents of the State, as well as bodies of private traders pursuing their own interests. And before the East India Company, supreme exponent of latter-day Mercantilism, had been finally shorn of its trading privileges and functions, the rise of new forms of joint stock enterprise was compelling the State to adopt new methods of regulation and control. Turnpike Trusts were, in effect, regulated joint stock companies; and canal companies, railway companies, gas companies and other public utility concerns followed, with necessary variations, the model laid down for the Turnpike Trusts. Needing compulsory powers, which they could get only by Act of Parliament, they had to accept in return, even in the heyday of *laisser faire*, at least some small measure of public control. This was, in the mid-nineteenth century, as small as the State, dominated by the ideas of the Manchester School, could make it; but it was never wholly absent. It is impossible for even the most rigid individualist to endow private bodies with public powers without exacting at least some control in return.

Control tended, moreover, to become more extensive as the century advanced. We can watch the State, intervening at first as little as possible in the affairs of the railways, and endeavouring to regard them as purely private concerns, driven nevertheless to exert a growing control over their operations, by regulating charges for goods and passengers alike, and at length, in 1921, extending a reluctant and partial control even over the payment of wages. We can see the State, compelled to extend special powers to gas companies and electricity supply companies, exacting in return either a regulation of charges or a statutory restriction of the dividends to be distributed. We can watch the evolution of statutory Port Authorities, with varying degrees of private and municipal control, up to the new model of the Port of London Authority shortly before the war.

My point here is simply this—private enterprise has never been wholly private in any of those fields in which business can be carried on only by bodies armed with special powers to invade private rights. A railway must have compulsory powers to acquire land, and a gas company to tear up the streets. The ordinary powers of the Companies Acts are inadequate for their purposes, because they convey no authority to invade private rights. Such powers can be conferred only by statute. Accordingly we have had, ever since the joint stock structure became the normal form of large-scale business organisation, two kinds of companies—ordinary companies under the Companies Acts, and parliamentary companies, deriving their special powers from private Acts of Parliament, and subject, as a *quid pro quo*, to at least some measure of public control.

I might, of course, instance here that supreme mystery, the Bank of England, with its peculiarly Athanasian relations with the Government and the Treasury—a private concern whose affairs are so interwoven with affairs of State that its Governor seems sometimes as if he governed Great Britain, and no man can really tell how far the Treasury controls the Bank, or the Bank the Treasury. But perhaps it is best for my present purpose to leave such high and confusing mysteries alone, and to tread in this paper on less hallowed ground, after a whispering, with all due reverence, of the holy name.

In general, then, a company, or body, acquires something of a public character as soon as it requires and acquires special public powers of interference with private rights, and accepts in return for these powers some measure of public control over its working. But the great mass of public service concerns which are in this position still remain essentially and mainly private affairs. Their capital is privately owned, and they work, under regulations imposed by the State, for private profit. The State in some measure controls them; but it does so from the outside, and without positive participation in their conduct. The words 'Semi-public Concern' imply something more than this. But how much more?

Some form and degree, shall we say, of positive public participation in their conduct? Thus, the Port of London Authority and the Joint Electricity Authorities, where they exist consist in part of direct nominees of public bodies, such as municipalities. The B.B.C. and the Central Electricity Board are governed by persons directly nominated by the Government. The position of these two differs, in that the B.B.C. has no privately owned capital invested in it, whereas the Central Electricity Board operates with privately owned loan capital which may be publicly guaranteed. If the Minister of Transport realises his project of a public traffic combine for Greater London, we shall have another concern similar in structure to the Electricity Board—a body using privately owned capital, but operating under the control of directors nominated by the State through the appropriate Minister of the Crown.

It is necessary, at this point, to draw a distinction between three types of concern, any of which may be called 'semi-public' in a certain sense. The B.B.C. may serve as an instance of the first type. In it there is no question of making a profit, or, at present, even of earning interest on borrowed capital. It operates with an income drawn from licences collected under public authority, and is governed by persons who are appointed directly and exclusively by the State. How the B.B.C. succeeds, under these conditions, in financing its schemes of capital development, except to the extent to which it can meet capital expenditure out of income, I do not pretend to know. My point is that in form the B.B.C. is a purely public body, in which private enterprise makes no appearance at all, but that it is managed, not directly by the State, but by an independent body of governors whom the State appoints, and then leaves free to administer the business in their own way, or at least subject only to the most general and informal control by the Government in matters of high policy. It is, indeed, possible to question the Postmaster-General, who answers for the B.B.C. in Parliament, or the Prime Minister, about its affairs; but the Member of Parliament who attempts this commonly gets very little satisfaction. Nine times out of ten, he is simply told that the matter he wants to raise lies entirely within the discretion of the B.B.C. itself, and has nothing to do with the Government. This is not quite true; for doubtless the Government can interfere if it wishes. But normally it does not wish to interfere: it greatly prefers to shift the responsibility to the governors whom it has appointed.

In finance, it is true, Government control is more real and effective. For the B.B.C. gets only the revenue which the Government allows it to have. The proportions of the licence fees collected by the State which are to go to the B.B.C. and to the Exchequer are determined by the Government; and this limits the B.B.C.'s power either to provide expensive services or to embark on heavy capital commitments. But even in matters of finance there is no detailed control of expenditure—no Treasury control such as exists over other public services. The B.B.C. has to keep within its permitted revenues; but within those limits it is practically free to spend its resources how it likes. We have, then, in the B.B.C. a service which is completely under public ownership and financed entirely by funds collected under State authority, but hardly at all under Government or parliamentary control in respect of the services it provides, or its success or ill-success in satisfying public demand.

The B.B.C. is, indeed, a highly irresponsible body; for it is largely free from the checks of private, as well as from the controls of public, enterprise.

The second type of concern which it seems desirable for us to study is best illustrated in the example of the Central Electricity Board. In this case the governing body consists, like that of the B.B.C., wholly of public nominees, appointed for a term of years, and left free within the powers granted by Parliament to administer the service in their own way. There is here even less State control over executive policy than in the case of the B.B.C.; and the State, if it wishes to influence the policy of the Board—say, by speeding up works with the object of providing employment—has to negotiate with it almost as it would with a privately owned industrial enterprise. But, whereas the B.B.C. has no capital, and draws its revenue from licences, the Central Electricity Board finances its operations, which involve large capital expenditure, by way of loans; and the money is provided by, and remains in the ownership of, private investors. These investors, however, get only a fixed rate of interest, and have no control over the actions of the Board. They are merely functionless bondholders, whose service is confined to the lending of capital. There are no shareholders; and the question of participation in control by those who supply the capital therefore does not arise. It is possible for the enterprise to take this form, without the State incurring a dangerous liability for guaranteed interest, because the nature of the undertaking is such that it seems likely to be able to earn a steady dividend without serious risk merely by adjusting its charges. Of course, bad management, or major changes in the structure of industry in general, might cause it to fail in this. But the danger is not regarded as serious. Defects of management are not likely to do more than cause the public to pay more than it need for electricity, and therefore use less. The point is not likely to be reached, at any rate in the near future, at which not even by raising charges can the service meet its interest obligations. But obviously this is so because the service of electricity supply is in a special position. In most industries and services there is a real risk of conditions arising in which interest on all the capital employed cannot be provided out of the revenue of the undertaking.

The third type of semi-public undertaking is found where control is actually shared between public and private representatives, so that the State, or some lesser public authority, has gone definitely into partnership with a body of private shareholders. This is the position in the German 'mixed' concerns, and, in this country, in the Port of London Authority and in the Joint Electricity Authorities which exist in certain areas. There may be some provision whereby dividends are limited or fixed in a body of this sort; but, unlike the other two, it may set out to work for a variable profit, and not merely to earn a fixed interest on borrowed money.

It would be possible to instance a fourth type—the leasing of a publicly owned enterprise to a private company to administer, as in the case of the Belgian railways, or the German railways under the Young Plan. But there is, as far as I am aware, no example of this type at present in Great Britain, though some critics of the Post Office have urged of late that the telephone service, at any rate, should be handed over to a statutory company to administer on these lines.

What do these developments signify? A recognition, I think, on the one hand that the conduct of many vital services can be no longer left to the unregulated control of private enterprise, and on the other that the existing mechanism of the modern State is unsuited to the conduct, or even to the detailed regulation, of industrial and public service undertakings. There is on the one hand a desire, and even a necessity, to bring certain vital services under co-ordinated public control, and on the other an unwillingness to do this under what may be called, for short, Civil Service conditions. There is, further, in certain fields a desire to co-ordinate private enterprise without altogether superseding it; and the most obvious way of doing this may be the creation of co-ordinating bodies in which the representatives both of the public and of the private undertakers who are left in the field take part.

There is, moreover, another factor. The assumption of the nineteenth-century economists was that, if capital was left free to flow where it chose, it would, in its pursuit of maximum profit, flow naturally into the channels of maximum public utility. Today, hardly anyone would maintain this view without serious qualification. It has been found indispensable, in certain instances, to guide the flow of capital and credit by special inducements offered by public bodies—guarantees of interest or principal under the Trade Facilities Act, inducements offered by municipal bodies in respect of rates to industrial enterprises to settle in a particular locality, even direct State provision of capital and State investment in private undertakings, such as the British Dyestuffs Corporation and the Anglo-Persian Oil Company. There have been, moreover, projects, not fathered exclusively by Socialists, for the better direction of the process of investment through a National Investment Board, and for a revival of the method of State guarantees in the provision of capital for the reorganisation of the depressed trades, such as cotton and steel. The Bankers' Industrial Development Company represents an attempt in this field to escape from the necessity of direct State action by making the banks in some measure agents of the State; and the Bank of England has a somewhat similar auxiliary of its own.

All these and all similar proposals raise the question whether public money can be voted, public credit pledged, or the investing classes be given public inducements to interest themselves in a particular type of enterprise, without the necessity for some public participation in the control of the businesses in question. If the State is to provide capital or guarantees, or subsidies or inducements, must it not be in a position to control the way in which the money is spent, and the policy of the businesses which are to spend it? At the least, must it not be able to assure itself that its help is being used to the best public advantage?

It might be urged that the State could get the necessary minimum of control merely by the exercise of its powers as creditor or guarantor, and without any direct participation in the conduct of the business. But it may fairly be doubted whether this method is likely to be effective. The co-ordination of electricity supply could not have been brought about save by a

State body strong enough to stand up to the interests of power companies, private supply companies, and municipalities, and to organise the national grid system with the aid of wide compulsory powers. Nor will the problem of a co-ordinated gas service, recommended in the Reports of the National Fuel and Power Committee, ever be effectively handled except along somewhat similar lines. It is true that, in the case of coal, an experiment has been made in the regulation of output and prices by statutory bodies representing the industry itself, without direct participation by the State; but the success of this experiment is very doubtful, and the policy of entrusting compulsory powers to non-responsible bodies is, to say the least, open to serious objection. Similar ideas underlie the Agricultural Marketing Act recently passed by Parliament; but, personally, I doubt the success of either experiment.

Even less is to be hoped for from attempts by the State to persuade industries to reorganise themselves without the use of compulsory powers. Little progress has been made towards national reorganisation in the case of either iron and steel or cotton, despite an infinite outpouring of words and persuasions. It seems to be clear that reorganisation in these cases will call for two things—the exercise of wide compulsory powers, and the creation of a public, or semi-public, body authorised to exercise them.

Of the existing semi-public concerns in Great Britain, the most important and instructive is the Central Electricity Board; and it is worth while to look somewhat more closely at the plan which it embodies. The service of electricity supply, like most industries, embraces three main functions—production, wholesale distribution, and retail distribution to the consumer. Retailing is done by municipal and private local stations throughout the country. Most of these stations have in the past also generated their own electricity, so that the wholesaler has been absent as a separate concern. But there have been also, in some parts of the country, power companies selling power both to big industrial consumers direct, and also to retail distributing stations—publicly and privately owned. The new scheme is based upon the rationalisation of production under varying forms of ownership, and on the socialisation, under the direct control of the Central Electricity Board, of the entire business of wholesale supply. Of the existing producers of electricity, a great many are put out of action as producers, and generation is concentrated in a limited number of selected stations, built or to be built, in order to lower costs by concentration upon the most efficient units—public or private. All power so generated is then bought at wholesale prices by the Central Electricity Board, and sold by it to the retailers, public or private—that is, the private or municipal distributing stations, many of the old generating stations being retained as distributors after the loss of their productive function. The State, acting through the Electricity Commissioners, who are responsible for selecting stations and drawing up the schemes for main line transmission over the whole country, thus undertakes to organise the rationalisation of the service, and to eliminate the less efficient productive units; and the State again, acting through the Central Electricity Board as a business body, controls producers and distributors alike by the possession of a monopoly at the wholesale stage of bulk transmission of electrical current. Only the middle stage—wholesaling—is completely socialised; but this enables the other stages also to be controlled.

It is not unlikely that this form of organisation will serve to some extent as a model for schemes of socialisation in other industries and services. For it may be that in some other industries as well the key point for the State to occupy is the direct conduct, not of productive operations, but rather of wholesale marketing. May not a vital part of the solution of the coal problem, for example, be found in creating a unified State coal marketing organisation, as well as a body of Commissioners empowered to close collieries and to bring about compulsory amalgamations? Admittedly, the coal problem is far harder than that of electricity. But may we not have been mistaken in endeavouring to tackle it at first too exclusively at the producing end, and latterly, when we have transferred our attention to other aspects, in attempting merely to regulate output and prices rather than co-ordinate methods of sale?

Similarly, in the case of the cotton trade, may not the way to the recovery of such foreign markets as we can reasonably hope to get back lie through the creation of a unified marketing organisation to supersede the countless private merchants who are now trying to make a living by competition in a dwindling market? The creation of a unified producing organisation in Lancashire is, for the present, too ambitious a project; but unified merchanting, combined with compulsory powers of amalgamation, might well equip the State with a powerful instrument for reorganisation similar to that which has been achieved in the case of electricity supply. I am not suggesting that all industries and services can be tackled in the same way, but only that here is a fruitful field for further experiments.

This proposal brings us face to face with a vital point of policy. When the State resorts to attempts to rationalise industry by public co-ordination and control of the processes of marketing, should it seek to work through the persons now engaged in the operations concerned by means of representative bodies of some sort? Or should the new unifying and controlling agencies consist, like the Central Electricity Board, of full-time public servants free from all responsibility to the firms engaged in the industry? I feel no doubt that, in most cases, the second method—which has been so far very successful in the case of electricity—is the right one. Representative bodies will be too much at the mercy of the conflicting claims of vested interests, and too conservative in outlook, to bring about the radical changes that are needed. Single-mindedness is essential to the successful conduct of any big economic enterprise; and it is very difficult for a body which represents different vested interests to be single-minded. Doubtless, the State will be wise often to pick, for the key posts of socialised enterprise, men with wide experience of private business. But the personal transference of loyalty ought to be complete; and it will not be if those responsible for conducting a service on behalf of the State still continue their connection with private business.

It has been the purpose of this paper to discuss the emergence, in recent years, of new forms of large-scale business enterprise that are as unlike the Collectivism to which many Socialists used to look forward as they are unlike the ordinary capitalist joint stock concern. On the one hand collectivists have been compelled to realise the sheer impossibility of any effective Parliamentary control over a large mass of nationally owned and publicly administered industries and services, and also the unsuitability of Civil Service methods, and above all of Treasury control, to the work of industrial management. It is understood, too, that Budgets will be plunged into hopeless confusion if trading and spending services are lumped together, and that a rule which confiscates all surpluses to the Exchequer may work out very unfortunately if it is applied to a developing service under public control. There is consequently among Socialists a ready recognition that new forms of administration for socialised services will have to be devised and made the subject of experiment; and to this extent the 'functionalist' case advanced by the Guild Socialists has been incorporated with the general body of Socialist doctrine. Socialists still insist that there can be no ultimate independence of the socialised business unit from control by the representatives of the community; for the various services have to be co-ordinated as instruments of a common policy, and this policy has to be directed in accordance with the public good. Final control of high policy by Government and Parliament must therefore be preserved; but it is widely agreed both that the appointed directors of socialised services must be given a very considerable autonomy and freedom from interference, and that parliamentary control is an ill-devised method for the oversight of any save the broadest and most far-reaching questions.

On the other side, Anti-Socialists have been compelled by the mere logic of events to admit the need for a considerable enlargement of the province of State action, as well as for unification of services in which competitive methods are now clearly wasteful and inefficient. Their tendency, naturally enough, is to endeavour to bring about unification, where the need for it is plain, with the minimum of public intervention, and when public bodies such as the Central Electricity Board have to be set up, to leave them, after defining their powers, almost completely immune from political interference with their administrative methods and policies. They want public control to assume as far as possible the shape and behaviour of private business, and the semi-public or public concern to look as like the private joint stock company as it can.

There is thus plenty of ground for difference left between Socialists and Anti-Socialists in working out the application of any particular scheme, even where it is agreed that unification under some measure of public control has to be carried into effect. But it is no longer easy to say, in such cases, precisely where, from the standpoint of economic structure, Socialism begins or Anti-Socialism ends. They run into each other at the edges; and the difficulty of drawing a sharp line is likely to grow greater with further changes in the technological basis of industry. Already in Germany the later developments of the cartel system, and of State control over it, have caused a significant blurring of the outlines of Socialist and capitalist economic policy.

This does not mean in the least that the differences between Socialists and Anti-Socialists are disappearing, or even growing less. But it does mean that they are assuming new forms, and that the superficial issues are tending to change. The battle is no longer, even in the field of industrial policy, between unrestricted and unorganised private enterprise on the one hand and the nationalisation of a number of separate industries and services on the other. It has taken a far wider range; for Socialists are now standing not so much for nationalisation as for a planned economy based on the co-ordinated public ownership and control of the entire range of vital industries and services, whereas Anti-Socialists, admitting the need for unification and some measure of public control in particular cases, are concerned to prevent just that political intervention which is for the Socialist the necessary instrument of a planned economy working in the public interest. There is a certain field of economic structure within which the circles of Capitalism and Socialism show some tendency to overlap. But the centres of the two rival systems remain as far as ever apart.

## XIII

## THE ESSENTIALS OF SOCIALISATION

THERE was a time when the contrast between Socialism and private enterprise seemed plain and striking. Under private enterprise, the means of production were owned by individuals who, by reason of their recognised ownership, were able to levy toll of rent, interest and profits upon the community as a whole. Under Socialism, the means of production would be collectively owned and administered; and the toll of rent, interest and profits would cease, the entire product of labour being appropriated to the uses of the entire community. It was all beautifully simple: and in the propaganda of Socialism it was only necessary to point the contrast in order to make out a magnificent ethical case.

Of course, nothing has happened to impair the fundamental justice of the familiar picture. It remains true that, under Socialism, the means of production (or at least all that matter from the general standpoint) will be collectively owned, and that the levy of tribute by a possessing class will have ceased. But, valid though the contrast is, it does not help Socialists greatly when they are facing the day-to-day problems of a gradual transition from Capitalism to Socialism, or trying to insinuate wedges of Socialism into the prevailing capitalist system. Some Socialists say that the difficulty arises only because this is to attempt the impossible, and Capitalism and Socialism (on the instalment plan) cannot live together. Gradualist Socialism, they tell us, is an illusion; it must be all or nothing. For such Socialists, the *constructive* work of Socialism can begin only after a revolution which has thoroughly and once and for all dispossessed the capitalist class. They may be right, in the sense that Socialism will never be fully achieved by constitutional means alone. Indeed, I think they are. But it does not follow that Socialists are exempt, in the present, from the need to insinuate bits of Socialism into the economic system; for he who whistles today for the English Revolution is assuredly wasting his breath. For the time being, it is the business of Socialists to get as far on towards Socialism as they can by constitutional methods.

As soon, however, as this limitation on immediate policy is accepted the difficulties begin to appear. They were not serious when Socialists were merely agitating, without hope of immediate success. But now that we are getting used to the idea of Socialistic, if not Socialist Governments, believers in Socialism have to work out a positive policy for these Governments to apply; and almost the first problem that confronts them is the preparation of plans for the socialisation of some at least of the vital industries and services of the country.

The old idea of socialisation, on which most of the earlier propaganda of Collectivism in this country was based, had at least the merit of simplicity. An industry—say, railway transport—was to be acquired for the community by buying out the shareholders, who were to receive some form of compensation assessed on an equitable basis, and were thereupon to lose all connection with the industry. The State, owning the railways, was then to provide for their future management by putting a Minister of the Crown at their head, and conducting them, as the Post Office is now conducted, under Civil Service control. There were, it is true, disputes even in those days about compensation. Some people wished to buy the shareholders out for cash, raising the necessary funds by an addition to the National Debt. Some wished to give Government debt in exchange for the shares, without any cash passing. Others preferred a system of terminable annuities, charged upon the national revenue; while yet others repudiated the principle of compensation altogether. It is curious to remember that in those days the Fabian Society was still ranged, according to its basis, against compensation, and proposed to expropriate the shareholders subject only to 'compassionate allowances' designed to meet cases of hardship.

There was, in those earlier days of Socialist propaganda, far more talk about the basis of compensation than about the forms and methods of future management and control. This latter question, indeed, was hardly discussed at all in Great Britain until the two or three years before the war, when the doctrines of Syndicalism, Industrial Unionism, and Guild Socialism were beginning to make headway. But then this problem came rapidly to the front. Syndicalists and Industrial Unionists, hostile to State action in all its forms, attacked alike State ownership and State control, urging that both ought to be vested in working-class bodies. The railwaymen and the miners were to manage their industries as trustees for the community. There was to be no State ownership, because under the new conditions there would be no such thing as ownership at all, in relation to the means of production. The Guild Socialists for their part wanted public ownership; but they agreed with the Syndicalists in repudiating State control. They wanted the management of each industry to be entrusted to a self-governing National Guild, so organised as to represent the various grades of workers by hand and brain who were necessary to its conduct. A number of Trade Unions, including the miners, the railwaymen, and the Post Office workers, worked out for themselves schemes of socialisation which were clearly Guild Socialist in tendency.

I have no space in this paper for any full discussion either of these schemes or of the numerous projects of socialisation and workers' control which have been brought forward in recent years.[1] I must come at once to the most recent of all these schemes—Mr. Herbert Morrison's Bill for the unification of London passenger transport. At once we find ourselves in a different world from that of pre-war nationalisation with direct State management, and hardly less far away from the Guild Socialistic plans of the 'reconstruction' period after the war. We are far nearer to the conception which underlay the Conservative Electricity Act of 1926, with some admixture of ideas from the Coalition Railways Act of 1921. Indeed, it is not easy to say, on the face of the matter, whether Mr. Morrison is

[1] An outline of the more important schemes is, however, added as an Appendix.

proposing to socialise London transport or to reconstruct it, as the railways were reconstructed in 1921, under private ownership and control.

For Mr. Morrison's Bill does not propose that the State should buy out the existing shareholders of the combine. Instead, a new inclusive corporation is to be created; and the shareholders are to be given stock in this body in place of their present holdings. Power is taken to buy out the smaller privately owned companies either for cash or for stock; and the properties of the municipal bodies concerned are to be acquired for a consideration payable, not in cash down, but either in annual instalments or by an issue of stock. Moreover, the dividends payable by the undertaking are not to be fixed in the form of an annual interest charge, but are left at the discretion of the Board, subject to Treasury sanction, and are apparently to depend on profits, and to vary between 5 and 6 per cent according to the profits earned by the combined undertaking. The earning of 5 per cent profit is apparently to be a first charge, in the sense that fares, which will be subject to public control, will be fixed at a level designed to yield this rate; but the variable dividend is to give the shareholders a further return if the undertaking is so managed as to increase efficiency and bring down costs. These provisions recall certain sections of the Railways Act of 1921.

An anomalous provision, not included in the Bill, but apparently forming part of the agreement between the Ministry and the combine, gives the stockholders power to appoint a receiver if their 5 per cent dividend is not paid. It is not clear what the powers of such a receiver would be, or how the provision is justified by the Ministry.

The directorate of the new body, as the Bill now stands, is to be appointed by the Minister of Transport, without provision for the representation of any interest or group. This proposal has already raised protests from three distinct quarters. The London County Council is demanding direct representation of municipal interests; the Trade Unions are demanding representation of the workers; and certain shareholding interests are demanding continued representation of the shareholders.

# XIII. ESSENTIALS OF SOCIALISATION

Now, Mr. Morrison's Bill at once raises, in decisive form, the question which this paper sets out to discuss. Was the Labour Government proposing to socialise London transport, or to hand it over to monopolistic private enterprise? Both views have been advanced with some show of reason; and it is none too easy to decide between them.

Let us, then, set out, as clearly as we can, the main questions that arise.

If we can answer these questions, we shall be in a fair way both to defining the essentials of socialisation, and to deciding in what light to regard Mr. Morrison's Bill.

*1. Is socialisation compatible with the continued existence of a body of share- or stock-holders, with claims to interest or dividend upon the undertaking?*

In any scheme of socialisation, if compensation is paid at all, some claim must be created. But this claim may be either against the assets or earnings of the undertaking, or against the State. It may seem to make very little difference which form the claim takes. It used to be urged that a claim valid against the State would be more secure than a claim against any particular undertaking, and that accordingly the State could acquire an industry more cheaply by issuing Government debt than by any other method. But there are now objections to direct State borrowing because of the great increase in the size of the National Debt and the necessity for frequent conversion operations, which have depressed State credit. The State is therefore reluctant to borrow in order to pay compensation in cash; and it is urged that this can be avoided if share- and bond-holders in any undertaking that is taken over are allowed to retain their shares or bonds, or issue new shares or bonds in exchange. The continuance of private shareholding seems, however, to imply the continuance of private ownership, and is objected to by Socialists on that ground. This objection applies less to redeemable bonds than to perpetual shares; for it is possible to urge that the bonds should be gradually paid off, until the entire undertaking is publicly owned. Moreover, the continuance of shareholding would be more likely to lead to a demand that the holders should share in control than a continuance of bonds. I conclude, then, provisionally that private shareholding is not compatible with socialisation.

2. *Does it make any difference whether such a claim, if it exists, takes the form of a claim to a fixed rate of interest or to a variable dividend?*

Socialists used to argue in favour of fixed interest rates, in order that the public might get the advantage of the State's superior borrowing power and appropriate all profit above a low fixed rate of interest. But, of late years, the danger to industry of increasing fixed interest charges, which form part of the cost of production, has become more and more evident. This does not matter greatly where an industry or service is of such a sort as to be able to rely on earning a regular surplus irrespective of trade fluctuations, though even in such a case, if the general level of prices falls, the effect may be to make an unnecessary present to the *rentiers* (and *vice versa* if prices rise). But it matters far more in any industry which is liable to fluctuating trade conditions, or open to outside competition. Thus, it may not matter much in the case of a London traffic monopoly; but it would matter greatly in the case of railways, or coal, or steel. There is, accordingly, a *prima facie* case for making the return to the providers of the capital required, even for a socialised undertaking, vary with the fluctuations in its earning capacity. But this, it may be said, involves giving the providers of capital the status of shareholders rather than bondholders; for herein lies the essential difference between them. This is true, according to capitalist ideas; but there is no reason why we should accept these ideas. The State could give to the private providers of capital bonds secured, cumulatively or not, solely against the net earnings of the undertaking—*i.e.*, a sort of income debenture without power of foreclosure, analogous in some respects to existing types of income debentures and in others to preference shares, but without even nominal rights of ownership. This is virtually the position of preference shareholders in many private undertakings today.

I conclude, provisionally, that the form of compensation

should be an exchange of existing shares for income bonds secured only against the net earnings of the socialised undertaking, and bearing a limited, but not a fixed, rate of dividend rather than a fixed rate of interest.

3. *Does it make any difference whether the claim, fixed or not in amount, is valid only against the net earnings of the undertaking, or is guaranteed in whole or in part by the State?*

If the return on capital is to be made only out of the net earnings of the undertaking, it is to be presumed that the commission managing the industry will be instructed so to conduct it as to secure a reasonable dividend, and that any powers of price control exercised by the State will be employed with this idea in mind, as under the Railways Act of 1921, the various Electricity Acts applying to private undertakings, the Gas Acts, and so on. In other words, the socialised undertaking will be allowed and instructed to charge prices sufficient to pay what is regarded as a reasonable return on capital, provided that the trade will bear such prices. Such a method would preclude running the socialised service at a loss, or at less than the 'reasonable return', except with the aid of a direct State subsidy, as long as a profit could be made by raising prices. But it would exempt the State from guaranteeing dividends or interest on capital embarked in an undertaking which could not earn a reasonable return even by raising its prices. In other words, it would leave the owners of the capital to bear losses due to a real depreciation in the earning value of the undertaking. It would also avoid burdening either the State or the undertaking with heavy fixed charges. It will be objected that it would leave the providers of the capital to risk their money without having any control over its use. But this is already their position in large joint stock undertakings; and they would have, even from the capitalist point of view, no real grievance if the price-fixing authority were definitely instructed to permit prices sufficient to yield a reasonable return, as long as this could be done.

My conclusion is that, ordinarily, claims should be valid only against the net earnings of the undertaking, but that this should not preclude the State, in order to encourage new investment, from guaranteeing a fixed or minimum return upon such investment for a limited period of years. This has, of course, been done in certain cases—*e.g.*, for the London Tube Railways under the Trade Facilities Act. It is a matter for discussion whether the claims should be cumulative or not. I am inclined to think that they should not.

4. *If share- or stock-holders continue to exist, is it consistent with socialisation to give them any share in the control of the undertaking, or any representation on the directorate?*

This question has already been answered inferentially under section 1. The answer is 'No'.

5. *Is it consistent with socialisation that the directors should be appointed for a period of years, and be irremovable during that period, or ought the State, or other appointing body, to have a continuous right of recall?*

It is assumed that, in any case, directors will be removable for misconduct. The question is whether they are, or are not, to be removable on grounds of policy. This raises several difficult questions. It is bound up, in the first place, with the question of political control. How far are the directing bodies of socialised undertakings to be autonomous, or under Government control? I hold strongly that they must be ultimately under the orders of the Government in matters of policy, however little it may be desirable for the Government to interfere with their day-to-day management of the undertaking. This is best secured by giving them a large measure of autonomy, but leaving them removable at any time at the Government's pleasure. This is proposed in the London Passenger Transport Bill, whereas the Central Electricity Board's members are irremovable during their period of office.

But another question is also involved. If, and in as far as, members of the directing body are nominees of groups or interests other than the State, how far are they to be removable by these groups or interests? Representation is apt to become unreal if the representative becomes a full-time salaried servant of the State, and is not subject to recall by those whom he is supposed to represent, save at the end of a period of years. One remedy would be to make the period of appointment of such members short; but this might mean that they would carry less weight, and be less effective, than State nominees serving for longer periods. Power of a represented body to recall its representative at any moment would be liable to abuse. I am inclined to suggest that (*a*) State representatives should be appointed for three years, subject to recall at any time; (*b*) representatives of outside bodies should be appointed by the State on the nomination of such bodies for three years, subject to recall at any time by the State, but not by the nominating body. This rule might, of course, be varied in particular cases. I am only laying it down as a broad generalisation.

6. *Ought consumers to be represented on the directing body? Or ought local authorities to be represented on any other ground than as representing the consumers?*

The case for consumers' representation is that the policy of socialised undertakings deeply affects their interests. It is, however, doubtful if direct representation of consumers on the *managing* body is the right way of protecting these interests. There is far more to be said for providing (as in the Labour schemes of 1919 and 1925 for the coal industry) something in the nature of a Consumers' Advisory Council, on which various interests can be represented, and for giving this body, subject to the final decision of the Government, a power to object to the policy of the managing body. The London Traffic Advisory Committee has powers of this order conferred upon it in the London Passenger Transport Bill. Clearly, consumers' interests ought to be represented in some form. We can best, however, return to this question at a later stage.

In the case of localised undertakings, there is evidently a case for the representation in some form of the local authority or authorities concerned. In as far as the local authority claims to represent the consumers, what has just been said applies to its claim. But the situation may appear different where an undertaking previously conducted by a local authority is being taken over by a Statutory Board or Commission (as in the case of the L.C.C. trams). In such a case, the local authority is really in the same position as the body of shareholders in a private undertaking that is socialised; and I do not see why it should be represented on that ground. There may, however, be a special case for representation of the local authority on the Statutory Board where, as in the instance of a Local Port Commission or Authority, there is need for close collaboration in the conduct of related services by the two bodies.

I conclude, then, that in general consumers should be represented, not on the Managing Board, but in some other way, and that the question of local authority representation must be settled, not on general principles, but in each particular case.

7. *Ought the workers engaged in the undertaking to be represented, as a matter of principle, on the directing body, or given any statutory share in its control? If so, what form should their representation take?*

I do not propose to argue over again the case for workers' control, in the sense of participation by workers' representatives in the control of socialised industry. I propose to assume that such control ought to exist, and to discuss what form it ought to take. If, as I think, the Board or Commission actually managing an industry must be kept small, in order to work efficiently, and must consist largely of persons chosen on account of their technical qualifications and managerial abilities, it follows that there can be no room for any considerable number of persons chosen simply as representing the workers engaged in the industry. There may be room for one or two, but not more. Moreover, the managing body must be full-time; and it is doubtful how far a man chosen originally as representing the workers can continue to represent them if he becomes a salaried servant of the State or the enterprise, and is not subject to recall at any time by those whom he is supposed to represent. I conclude, therefore, that real representation of the workers on the managing body is impracticable in any full sense. This should not prevent Labour men from being appointed to the managing body when they have the right qualities; but men so appointed should not be regarded as satisfying the working-class demand for representation, which must be provided for in some other way.

I think the solution lies in the German system of the so-called 'double directorate'. The German joint stock company has two executive organs, a *Vorstand*, or Managing Board, and an *Aufsichtsrat* (or Council of Control): the former consists usually of full-time managing directors, and the latter of part-time representatives of interests and groups concerned in the conduct of the undertaking. I should favour the adoption of this form of organisation for socialised enterprises in this country. There should be, first, a Board or Commission, consisting of full-time officers, and chosen on grounds of technical or managerial competence, and not as representatives of any interest; and, secondly, a part-time Council of Control, composed mainly of representatives of the groups concerned. On this Council, the workers should have a substantial representation, and there should also sit on it representatives of related industries and services with which close co-ordination is desirable, of local authorities where they are closely concerned, and of consumers, while at least one member should have the specific function of representing the Government as the holder of a watching brief. There should, of course, be no representation of shareholders. The Council, I think, should meet often enough to exert a real influence on policy, and the reports of the Managing Board should require its approval. There should, however, be a limited right for the Managing Board to appeal to the responsible Minister in case of differences between it and the Council over certain defined questions. There should be, further, in many industries, Regional Councils, related to the regional management; but it is doubtful if these ought, in most cases, to have more than advisory functions. The precise structure necessary can evidently be settled only in relation to each particular industry or service. A structure appropriate to railways might be largely unsuitable for building or coal-mining.

Workers' and other representatives on the Council could be either appointed for quite short periods or be subject to recall at any time. They would receive not a full-time salary, but only fees for work done, and would thus be able to preserve their really representative position. Workers' representatives should, I think, be chosen by the Trade Unions chiefly concerned in the industry.

This section is not intended to be a complete treatment of the question of workers' control. It does not touch at all on control locally, or in each particular works or workshop. It relates only to the form of the controlling agencies for the socialised industry as a whole, and should be read strictly in this light.

8. *Should the State reserve to itself the right to appoint some or all of the directing body, and, if so, what principles should it follow in making its appointments?*

This question has largely been answered already. I think all appointments either to the Managing Board or to the Council of Control should be made by the State. But in the former case the State would appoint absolutely, subject only to such consultation with outside interests as it might deem desirable, whereas in the latter it would be appointing largely on the basis of nominations made by other bodies (as it does now in the case of workers' and employers' representatives on the I.L.O., and in many other instances). In the case of the Managing Board, the chief consideration should be to get the best possible technical and managerial ability combined with real belief in socialisation. It is obviously wrong to appoint a Board that disbelieves in its job, however good its technical and managerial qualifications may otherwise be. Stress should be laid on the need for appointing a reasonable proportion of men with first-class technical knowledge, and for having some members with special ability and sympathy in the handling of personnel.

In the case of the Council of Control, the State should accept the nominations of the bodies entitled to representation, while reserving the right to dismiss a representative and call for a fresh nomination. In certain cases, where there is no one body plainly entitled to nominate, and the bodies concerned cannot agree, the State may have to choose between the nominations sent in; and in certain other cases an unorganised interest may have to be represented by direct State appointment. But as far as possible, nominating bodies should be chosen, and left free to make nominations which the State would accept without question.

I am disposed to prefer appointments for a specified period to appointments for life or for an indefinite tenure, subject to the provisions for recall outlined in an earlier section.

9. *How, and in what forms, should new capital be raised for the development of the industry or undertaking?*

There appear to be three possibilities: (1) Direct provision by the State, or by some special body, such as a National Investment Board, acting as an organ of the State; (2) raising of capital by the industry or undertaking itself, backed by a State guarantee; (3) raising of capital by the industry or undertaking itself, without State guarantee. There appears to be no sufficient reason for ruling out any of these methods. Their relative advantages depend on the circumstances of each case. Thus, method (3) would probably be unworkable in the case of depressed industries, or wherever there was not enough confidence on the part of the investing public to get the capital taken up. Moreover, it would become increasingly difficult if, as seems probable, the supply of funds available for investment in the hands of the public were to fall off. It has already been suggested that, where method (2) is employed, the State guarantee of dividends should be given only for a limited number of years. On the whole, method (1) seems likely to become of increasing importance in the course of the transition to Socialism. I do not, however, propose to discuss here how a National Investment Board would work. That is a subject large enough for separate treatment.

The above conclusions relate only to cases in which capital has to be raised from outside the industry. It is anticipated that normal capital developments will in the main be financed from reserves accumulated by socialised undertakings out of surplus income, just as many joint stock concerns are accustomed to finance normal developments out of reserves. It is therefore suggested that socialised undertakings should be free to build up reasonable reserve funds, and that their surpluses should not be automatically appropriated by the Exchequer. This, of course, would not preclude the taxation of such surpluses, either at the standard rate of income tax, or at any other rate that might be fixed, or the lending of surpluses in the hands of one socialised undertaking to another, with the consent of the State (*e.g.*, through the National Investment Board).

This method of financing development out of reserves seems to me an integral part of any real system of socialisation, in which presumably the final aim is the complete elimination of the private investor from the sphere of socialised industries and services.

10. *Should the undertaking aim at rendering service at cost price, or at making a profit (over and above any capital charges)? If the latter, how should the profit be disposed of?*

The chief reason why Socialists have usually been opposed to socialised services being run at a profit is (*a*) that this tends to depress wages and salaries in the service, and (*b*) that, incomes being unequal and socialised services usually catering largely for poor people, the profit will be made largely at poor people's expense. Both these contentions are true; but neither would apply under a system based on economic equality. As we approach such a system, by far the easiest way of financing capital development will be for State services to be run at a profit, and for surplus funds to be used as capital in the ways described in the previous section. In other words, the community will distribute in wages and salaries only the amounts it means people to be free to spend, and not also the sums it wants them to invest; and funds for investment will be provided directly out of the product of industry before incomes are distributed to individuals. It is even worth while to make an approach to this system in the case of any industry which we may now decide to socialise. A reasonable wage should, of course, be fixed for the employees; and no surplus should be deemed to exist until the wage-charge has been fully met. But over and above this there is no reason why sums should go to the employees. The claim of the consumer to reduced charges is strong, in the case of consumers' services, while great inequalities of income continue to exist; but this is not a valid argument in the case of industries making producers' goods, providing services, or producing luxuries. On the whole, there is a strong case for extending the sphere within which socialised undertakings are to be allowed to charge enough to have a surplus.

The question of the disposal of this surplus has been answered in the previous section. Any surplus should go (*a*) to building up reasonable reserves in order to finance developments, or (*b*) in loans to other socialised undertakings—subject in both cases to such taxation as the State may decide to exact. The point is that surpluses should normally be retained by the socialised industry, and should not pass automatically to the Exchequer.

We have now attempted to answer all the questions raised at an earlier stage. How far have we succeeded, in the process, in defining the essentials of socialisation? We have suggested that it is not compatible with the continuance of private shareholding, at least in any form which will give the shareholder any sort of control over the socialised undertaking. But we have urged that this does not preclude the existence of stock bearing not a fixed, but a variable dividend, as long as this dividend is subject to a maximum, and is secured only against the earnings of the undertaking.

In relation to the form of control, it has been suggested that the difficulties can best be met by the creation of two distinct bodies—a full-time Managing Board or Commission on a non-representative basis, composed mainly of technical and managerial experts; and a part-time Council of Control, consisting of representatives from interested groups and parties, and including a strong representation of the workers engaged in the service.

Further, it has been urged that these directing bodies must be appointed by, and subject to recall by, the State, and must not be accorded powers which will make them independent of the Government in matters of policy. This last point, however, is so important as to deserve some further argument.

Socialists presumably stand for a co-ordinated control of the economic life of the nation in the interests of all. This involves that the various industries and services must be subject, in matters of high policy as distinct from day-to-day management, to a common authority. This authority may be either the State itself, or a supreme economic organ created by the State (*e.g.*, a representative National Economic Council or Economic Parliament). But it is simply inconsistent with socialisation to set up a directing body for a single industry or service, and to make that body independent both of other industries and services and of the central Government of the country. Unless and until a separate Economic Parliament or Council is created, each socialised service must be managed and directed by a body subject to Parliament and the Government, however wide its autonomy in day-to-day matters of management may be made. This, it has been suggested, can best be done by making all members of such bodies subject to recall at any time by the Minister responsible for them to Parliament.

This, however, is no reason why the directing bodies should not be given very wide autonomous powers, provided that their members are subject to recall, and that disputes on matters of principle between the Managing Board and the Council of Control can be referred to the Minister for decision. Indeed, it is obviously expedient, subject to the power of removal, to leave the directing bodies the fullest freedom in the execution of policy, while reserving to the Government the power to initiate or approve the policy itself. It would not be difficult in most cases to draw the line between matters which the directing bodies might do on their own responsibility, and matters requiring the Minister's sanction. Broadly, the distinction is that between laying down a policy, and taking the expert measures needed to give effect to it.

This paper has been written in the belief that we ought to be as precise as possible in trying to clear our minds about the essentials of socialisation, and in drawing a line between the types of scheme we are prepared to accept as measures of socialisation and those we are not. According to the principles here laid down, the creation of the Central Electricity Board was, I think, an act of socialisation, though by no means satis-

XIII. ESSENTIALS OF SOCIALISATION 301

factory in all respects. The creation of the Imperial Cables and Communications Company was definitely not an act of socialisation. On Mr. Morrison's London Passenger Transport Bill final judgment must be deferred until it has emerged from the ordeal of a Joint Committee of both Houses of Parliament, with a clear Conservative majority.[1]

A NOTE ON POST-WAR SOCIALISATION SCHEMES.

The scheme for nationalisation of the coal-mines which the Miners' Federation laid before the Sankey Coal Commission in 1919 provided for the future management of the industry (after State purchase at a fair price) by a full-time Mining Council. Half of the seats on this body were to be reserved for the Miners' Federation; the other half were to be filled by persons nominated by the State so as to represent the other groups and grades connected with the industry—technicians, managerial grades, and experts in related industries and services. This Council was to enjoy a wide autonomy in the conduct of the industry, so that the cry was at once raised that the miners were syndicalists who proposed to abrogate the sovereignty of Parliament, and to hand over the community of consumers to the mercy of a producers' monopoly.

The railwaymen's scheme was less elaborate, and proposed a less radical form of workers' control. But the influence of the ideas which it and similar plans embodied can be plainly seen in the original proposals brought forward by Sir Eric Geddes for the regrouping of the railways in 1920. This scheme provided for the inclusion on the directorate of the new grouped railways of representatives both of the manual and of the managerial grades. In the event, this proposal was not adopted. The railway companies opposed it strongly; and the Trade Unions gave it away in favour of the provisions, embodied in the Railways Act of 1921, for special tribunals for wage regulation and for a system of Whitley Councils throughout the

[1] Shortly after this was written the Labour Government fell, and Mr. Morrison's Bill was shelved. We have now to wait and see what a new Government, of 'national' composition, will do about it.

railway service. The new railway directorates were constituted, like the old, of shareholders' representatives. But the Railways Act of 1921 was a scheme, not of socialisation, but merely of compulsory amalgamation under private ownership; and accordingly the working-class demand for representation was far less strongly pressed than it would have been if the railways had been taken over by the State.

It is, however, interesting to note that, even at this stage, one Trade Union, the Railway Clerks' Association, was pressing for a scheme of railway nationalisation along rather different lines. The railway clerks wanted the State, having acquired the railways, to entrust their management to a small body of full-time Commissioners, to be appointed by the Government for a term of years. Among these Commissioners were to be representatives of Labour; but on appointment they were to become salaried Civil Servants, in no way subject to recall by those by whom they had been chosen as representatives. This proposal differed radically from the miners' scheme, which contemplated that the Mining Council would consist largely of persons chosen by, and responsible to, the Miners' Federation. But the railway clerks agreed with the Miners' Federation in wanting a scheme under which the governing Council or Commission, however composed, would possess a wide measure of autonomy, and not be subject to the detailed control of a Minister, or of Parliament, or to the customary forms of 'Treasury control' as it applies to such departments as the Post Office.

In the period of depression after 1921, plans of socialisation, and the entire propaganda of workers' control, fell into the background, hardly to emerge again until the renewed struggle in the coal industry in 1925 and 1926. Then the Labour Party and the Miners' Federation appeared before the Samuel Coal Commission with a new and agreed plan of socialisation. This plan, covering other forms of power and the transport services in addition to coal-mining, proposed the creation of a Power and Transport Commission, appointed by the State on a non-representative basis, to take over the co-ordinating control of the entire group of services which it was proposed to socialise. The

Commission was to consist of full-time persons, and was to have wide autonomous powers. Under its general direction were to be the managing bodies for the separate industries and services, such as coal-mines, railways, electricity. The plans for these bodies were not worked out in detail; but as far as the mines were concerned, the representative Council proposed by the miners in 1919 was to be retained, with slight changes (see Appendix), subject to the co-ordinating control of the non-representative Commission. We have, then, at this point, in the minds of advocates of socialisation, a mingling of the two ideas. Moreover, the Labour schemes of 1919 and 1925 both made provision also for an advisory Coal Consumers' Council, on a representative basis, with powers to bring pressure on the body charged with the actual management of the industry. The consumers, however, were not, as such, to be represented upon the managing body.

After this project the next stage was reached with the Conservative Electricity Act of 1926. This, it will be remembered, set up the Central Electricity Board, and made it responsible for the management of the new 'grid' system of main-line power transmission. The members of the Board were nominated by the State as salaried officers; but neither they nor their employees rank as Civil Servants, or even as employees of the State. The Board, moreover, raises its capital for itself, on fixed interest-bearing terms which may be backed by a State guarantee. It has thus its own body of stockholders; but these stockholders have no voice or vote in the conduct of the undertaking. The Central Electricity Board is definitely a creature of the State, and subject, in the final resort, to State control through the Minister of Transport. But it is not a form of State enterprise in the form in which these words used to be understood; and it has a body of private stockholders, and is intended to raise future capital by a direct appeal to the public.

## APPENDIX.

*(Extracted from certain schemes and Acts bearing on the Socialisation of Industry.)*

1. NATIONALISATION OF MINES AND MINERALS BILL.

Fabian Society Tract, 1913. Provides for acquisition by the State and direct management by the Minister of Mines and a staff appointed by him and under his control.

2. A BILL TO NATIONALISE THE MINES AND MINERALS OF THE UNITED KINGDOM.

M.F.G.B. 1919 (presented to the Sankey Commission). Provides for acquisition by the State and for the appointment of a Mining Council of a President and twenty members, of whom ten are to be appointed by His Majesty and ten by the M.F.G.B. Appointment for five years. Members to devote whole time. A Minister of Mines and a Parliamentary Secretary to be appointed and to be responsible to Parliament for the affairs of the Mining Council. District Mining Councils to be appointed (half nominated by Mining Council and half by M.F.G.B.). A Fuel Consumers' Council to be appointed by the Crown as an advisory body.

3. REPORT BY LORD SANKEY, 1919.

Mines to be acquired by the State and a Minister of Mines appointed. The Minister to be advised by a National Mining Council and a Standing Committee appointed by it. The National Mining Council to consist of representatives from District Mining Councils, equally representing miners, consumers, and persons of commercial and technical knowledge. Councils not full time.

4. REPORT BY LABOUR REPRESENTATIVES ON SANKEY COMMISSION, 1919.

Agrees with Sankey Report, subject to larger Labour representation on lines of 2 above.

5. REPORT BY SIR ARTHUR DUCKHAM (SANKEY COMMISSION), 1919.

Proposes creation in each area of a District Coal Board, as a statutory company, amalgamating all existing collieries. Proposes Board of Directors of not less than seven for each Board; two of these to be appointed by the workers, one by the agents, managers and under-managers, and the rest by the shareholders. One Government representative, a mining engineer, to attend, but not vote.

6. EVIDENCE OF MINERS' FEDERATION TO SAMUEL COMMISSION, 1925.

A Power and Transport Commission to be appointed (replacing Electricity Commission), to consist of six full-time experts representing expert knowledge of coal, electricity, gas, transport, commercial questions, plus a Chairman. The President of the Board of Trade to answer for the Commission in Parliament. The Commission to regulate both private and public power and transport undertakings.

A National Coal and Power Production Council to be appointed, consisting of an equal number of executive and administrative officials and of miners and by-product workers (say, twelve in all), elected by their respective organisations, plus, say, two representatives of the Power and Transport Commission, together with the chief officers of the Central Coal Administration and the Chief Inspector of Mines in an advisory capacity. The Secretary of Mines to preside over the Council, which should meet at least fortnightly and be responsible for the conduct of the industry. Provincial Councils to serve under the Council, consisting of a Chairman and Vice-Chairman appointed by the National Council, with six representatives of the workers and six of the technical and administrative staffs, with the chief area officers and the District Inspector of Mines in an advisory capacity. A Consumers' Council, representing employers and workers in coal-using industries, local authorities, Co-operative Societies, etc., to be appointed as an advisory body.

7. GEDDES' PROPOSALS FOR RAILWAY REORGANISATION, 1920.

Proposes six railway groups, with directorates composed of (*a*) representatives of the shareholders in a majority, and (*b*) representatives of employees, of whom one-third might be leading officials co-opted by the rest of the Board, and two-thirds members elected by and from the workers on the railway.

8. DRAFT BILL OF RAILWAY CLERKS' ASSOCIATION AND ASSOCIATED LOCOMOTIVE ENGINEERS AND FIREMEN, 1921.

Proposes acquisition by the State, and management by seven Commissioners, under the Minister responsible to Parliament. Of the first Commissioners, the Chairman and two others to be appointed by the Minister, one by the Treasury and three by the Government on the nomination of the railway Trade Unions. Commissioners to be full time and perpetual, subject to removal by the Crown.

9. ELECTRICITY SUPPLY ACT, 1926.

A Chairman and seven other members to be appointed by the Minister of Transport after consultation with such representatives or bodies representative of the following interests as the Minister thinks fit—*i.e.*, land, government, electricity, commerce, industry, transport, agriculture and labour. Board not necessarily full time, but salaried, and to hold office for from five to ten years as the Minister may decide before appointment.

10. LONDON PASSENGER TRANSPORT BILL, 1931.

Board to consist of a Chairman and four other members appointed by the Minister of Transport after consultation with the Treasury. The members to be persons of wide experience and capacity in industry, commerce or finance, or in the conduct of public affairs. Members to hold office for not more than seven years, as the Minister may determine.

## XIV

## THE METHOD OF SOCIAL LEGISLATION

WHEN Lord Hewart and other critics protest against the growth of the virtual law-making powers of the modern 'bureaucracy', it is easy enough for them to make out a clear case, to the extent of showing that these powers have, of late years, been increasing very fast indeed. Their troubles begin when they are asked to suggest a remedy for a situation which everyone agrees to be in some measure unsatisfactory and the product far less of deliberate intention than of sheer force of circumstances which no way has yet been found to control.

The nature of these compelling circumstances is clear enough. In the modern world, legislation has become much more pervasive and much more complicated than it used to be. These characteristics arise directly out of the conditions of modern life, and especially of the modern economic system. A hundred years ago, Great Britain had indeed a complicated system of Customs and Excise, which Sydenham and others, following Huskisson, were labouring hard to simplify; but, apart from this, the body of legislation dealing with social and economic matters was very small, and the administrative equipment behind it slender indeed. There were Factory Acts on the statute book even then; but there was no factory code, and no inspectors had yet been appointed. The whole mass of legislation providing for enclosures was carried through without the supervision of any central department. The Poor Law, on the eve of reform, was still in the hands of a host of local bodies, operating without any central control; and while such measures as the Acts of Settlement involved endless administrative complications, these questions were left to be fought out in the courts without the central Government taking a hand. Only with the establishment of the new Poor Law Commission in

1834 did the now copious stream of orders and regulations begin to flow out from a central department of State, as it had flowed at an earlier period under Elizabeth and the earlier Stuarts from the Council or the Court of Star Chamber.

Social and industrial legislation, which alone I shall attempt to discuss at all in this paper, are above all responsible for the growth of administrative activity. And, although the stream of orders and regulations began first to flow from a body —the Poor Law Board—which made no financial contribution to the cost of the services which it supervised, it will hardly be contested that the later swelling of the stream depended largely on the development of 'grants-in-aid'—in the broad sense of contributions paid by the Exchequer in aid of services whose detailed administration was entrusted to local bodies. The State, paying in part the piper, claimed a say in calling the tune. Indeed, it could hardly avoid doing this; for money applied by Parliament was voted for specified purposes and subject to conditions, and it was indispensable both to see that these conditions were observed, and to secure equality of treatment, according to prescribed principles, between area and area. Nor could this long remain simply a question of equal treatment of one area with another; for as soon as money was paid out by the State for the benefit of individuals, as under the Education Acts, or to-day under various forms of social insurance and provision, it became essential to ensure equal treatment between individual and individual. Thus, the more the system of grants-in-aid was extended, the more the stream of orders and regulations was swollen.

Apart from this, the growth of legislative intervention in industry made uniformity of enforcement a more and more important matter. The earlier Acts relating to factories and mines were very laxly administered; but even if they had been fully put in force their prescriptions were relatively few and simple, and did not, as a rule, greatly affect the employer in his conduct of industry. But, as legislative intervention became more stringent and far-reaching, it came to matter more to secure uniformity of enforcement; for, if the law were enforced against Mr. A. and not against his competitor, Mr. B., was there not manifest unfairness? Moreover, the more stringently a law is to be enforced, the greater becomes the need to adapt it to all the special circumstances of each case. A few general provisions relating to factories and workshops generally may do well enough for a beginning; but the modern factory code has to provide separately for each type of factory or workshop, and for all the various incidents that may arise in establishments of each type.

It is, however, manifestly impossible to do all this directly by legislation. Modern Acts of Parliament are, indeed, often very long, and swollen out by elaborate schedules which lay down conditions for their working. But the longest Acts very often give rise to still longer orders and regulations, which proceed from the Government departments entrusted with their administration. Anyone who becomes a subscriber to the published series of statutory rules and orders learns a good deal in the first month about the complexity of modern methods of administration. And, even so, he receives only a fraction of the snowstorm of circulars that falls out of Whitehall upon the lesser administrators of the modern State system.

Even if it were possible, it would be clearly undesirable further to enlarge the verbiage of Acts of Parliament by causing them to embody directly the rules and regulations which are at present 'made by the Minister' after an Act has become law. This would not only make almost impossible the getting of the required Acts through a House of Commons grossly overburdened already, but also give to the regulations themselves a most undesirable amount of inflexibility; for Parliament would be far too busy making them to spare time for their amendment if it made them wrong. There is, indeed, a great deal to be said for the view that we put too much detail into our Acts of Parliament now, and that Parliament would be wiser to content itself with prescribing by law only the general principles, and to leave the details to be filled in by some less cumbrous and time-absorbing method. We have no regular analogy in this country—save under a few very special Acts, such as the Emergency Powers Act—to the presidential decree of other countries. But often, when Parliament has fallen sadly behind its programme of work, and measures of vital importance are held up purely for lack of time, one is sorely tempted to wish that we had, in this country, some method of making law less difficult to set in motion and admitting of easier correction than the orthodox procedure of the Houses of Parliament.

Take as instance of our present difficulties the parliamentary history of the unemployment insurance system. How much valuable parliamentary time has been absorbed of late years in tinkering with that troublesome measure, which no party proposes to rescind, but all eagerly wish to bend this way or that. I think we have tried to put far too much detail into the Unemployment Insurance Acts—far too much, or far too little. We have tried to determine strictly by Act of Parliament who has, and who has not, an individual claim to benefit; and we have tried to do this by means of a uniform measure which ignores all differences between one industry or class of workers and another. The result is inevitably unsatisfactory. It gives the Civil Service a rigid set of rules to administer, without so framing those rules as to meet the difficulties of each particular class of case. It is clearly out of the question, on grounds of both desirability and practicability, to amplify the Acts so as to include the variants called for by each separate industry. It would, therefore, in my judgment, be far better to put less into the Act, and to leave in the hands of some body other than Parliament a fairly wide discretion to frame regulations dealing with particular classes of insured workers, either by industries, when that seemed best, or by types of unemployment, such as short time, or seasonal or casual work.

But as soon as this is suggested an obvious difficulty arises. In whose hands is this power, at present either wielded directly by Parliament or not wielded at all, to be placed? It is out of the question to entrust it to the Minister and his advisers of the Civil Service; for the common cry is that they have too much power already. Certainly neither Parliament itself, nor that section of public opinion which is most vocal, would tolerate any proposal to transfer more of the legislative power into the hands of the Civil Service. Nor, I presume, would Civil Servants themselves desire it; for it would expose them to additional unpopularity, and make them in effect arbiters of public policy in an obviously undesirable degree. The power might, indeed, be nominally that of the Minister, and the responsibility that of the Cabinet. But both Ministers and Cabinets have too much on hand already to be capable of taking on more; and, rightly, public opinion would regard any step of the kind proposed as a further stage towards government by the permanent officials.

What, then, are we to suggest? Suggestions, in order to be useful, must be particular, and not general. For there is evidently no one body to which could be entrusted the task of filling out the details of all the various measures enacted by Parliament for the regulation of social and industrial conditions. At all events, let us stick for the moment to the particular case. I should like to see the Unemployment Insurance Acts themselves much less detailed and more flexible, and the power of making regulations under them entrusted, as it is in Germany, to some sort of Statutory Commission set up under the authority of Parliament. This Commission would doubtless be nominated by the Minister of Labour for a period of years; and its orders and regulations might be made operative only with his sanction, as are the orders of a Trade Board today. But the actual legislative process, within the general framework constructed by Parliament, would then become a matter, neither for Parliament itself nor for a Civil Service department, but for a representative Commission analogous to a Trade Board, but exercising power, within its reference, over a much wider field.

It could be further laid down, if it were thought desirable, that all regulations of importance should, in addition to receiving the approval of the appropriate Minister, be laid on the table of the House of Commons, and become operative only if no resolution hostile to them were carried by the House. This would mean in practice that on most occasions the drafts would go through *sub silentio*, but that it would be possible at any time to challenge a debate in Parliament if an important question of principle arose. The power to make regulations would, of course, be confined within the limits laid down in the Act of Parliament itself, and any regulations made in excess of these powers would be *ultra vires* and unenforceable—a matter upon which the ordinary Courts would preserve an undiminished power to pronounce. But, within the general prescriptions of the Act, regulation-making—which is, let us agree, a subordinate kind of legislation—would become the function of a special body, constituted for that purpose and for general supervision of the administration of the Act.

This proposal has, I know, its difficulties. It makes the Minister the spokesman in the House of Commons of a policy over which he has a right of veto, but which he does not positively originate or control. It makes the actual Civil Servants who have to administer the Act take their orders partly from the Minister and partly from the Board or Commission, or rather wholly from a Minister acting in part as the mouthpiece of the Board. But neither of these difficulties seems to me to be, in practice, very serious. The first is not serious as long as the Minister possesses the right of veto, nor the second as long as the regulations of the Board reach the Civil Servant transmuted into orders approved by the Minister. Similar conditions have applied, and have worked quite well, in more than one field.

Of course, a great deal depends on the amount of moral authority behind the Statutory Commission. If this were simply a board of ordinary Civil Servants, as much objection would be taken to its possession of regulation-making power as to the exercise of the same power directly by a department. The change would be hardly more than of name. It would be indispensable, therefore, to equip the Board with some degree of representative authority external to the department, in order that its recommendations and orders might carry sufficient weight.

In the particular case of unemployment insurance, this would clearly involve a Commission broadly representative of the Trade Unions and employers' associations chiefly concerned with the working of the system. The representatives of these interests might be chosen in any of a number of ways; and to them might be added persons chosen by the Minister to represent the public interest—a leading accountant and an economist, maybe, among them. But these are details into which it is unnecessary to go

## XIV. SOCIAL LEGISLATION 313

at the present stage. The general nature of the proposal is plain enough not to admit of doubt.

What would be its advantages? Five seem to me to be of outstanding importance. First, it would be possible to make the system far more flexible, to adapt it more exactly to different groups of cases, and to prevent abuses from growing up within it owing to the attempt to apply a common rule to many widely varying conditions. Secondly, it would be possible to rectify mistakes, and to adapt the system to changing needs and circumstances, without undesirable expenditure of valuable parliamentary time. Not nearly so many amending Acts would be needed as have been needed in recent years. Thirdly, the representatives of employers and employed, who have now no responsibility for the fair or efficient working of the system, would have a responsibility, and would be enlisted to help in making it work with the minimum of friction or abuse. Fourthly, it would be possible to consider desirable amendments less in an atmosphere of party controversy. And fifthly, the permanent officials would be relieved of an unpleasant and unpopular responsibility imposed upon them by the inadequacies of the existing statutes.

As against these very great advantages I can see no really serious disadvantages of any kind. Doubtless, those who wish to make party capital out of the unemployment insurance scheme, on either side, would be baulked of many of their opportunities. But is that a disadvantage? Doubtless, Parliament would have handed over to a subordinate body what is virtually a part of the law-making power. But is that a disadvantage for a Parliament which has so many laws to make that it is in increasing danger of making none of them well? It is a familiar criticism of some heads of great enterprises that they do not know when to delegate authority, and attempt to keep far too much in their own hands. The same may be true of a Parliament, which, as its work increases, must find means of getting some of the subordinate functions off its hands, in order to concentrate its attention on those which cannot be delegated.

I have taken this particular instance of the Unemployment Insurance Acts because it seems to offer an excellent chance for an experiment that might be acceptable to many people who would reject out of hand any proposal of a more ambitious sort. Everyone admits that the unemployment insurance scheme has got into a mess, from which it ought to be rescued. I venture to suggest that the trouble arises largely from both legislating for, and seeking to administer, the scheme in a wrong and inappropriate way—from attempting to frame an Act of Parliament covering all the cases with a series of inflexible general rules, and from placing outside all share in administering the Act the classes of persons on whose behaviour and attitude towards it its success or failure mainly depends.

We may now return from the particular to more general considerations. Such a Statutory Commission as I have proposed for unemployment insurance differs *toto cœlo* from such Advisory Committees as form part of the regular furniture of most Government departments. These Advisory Committees are generally well thought of neither by the Civil Servants who have to deal with them nor by the unfortunate persons who spend their time sitting upon them. There are exceptions; but they are generally failures, or at least not much more than window-dressing. The reason is, I think, fairly clear. These Advisory Committees have no positive work to do. Their function is purely critical, and not constructive. The Civil Servant, who has the job to do, does not usually welcome their interference with his doing of it. Their meetings are too intermittent, and their attention too perfunctory, for them to get any grasp of the work on its administrative side. They are, moreover, often consulted only when it suits the Minister and his advisers within the department to consult them, and shoved aside, or left in the dark, whenever it does not suit. Even so, there are good and useful Advisory Committees, especially those which deal with scientific matters and have a strictly limited reference which prevents them from dissipating their energies. But most Advisory Committees—even most Advisory Councils—with a wide or undefined reference are futile. At most, they provide for occasional meetings between leading Civil Servants and persons outside the service whom it is useful for them to meet.

The Statutory Commission, even if its decisions need ratification by the Minister before they can become operative, stands on quite a different footing, because it has a definite job to do—a definite task of administration placed in its hands. It demands, of course, correspondingly more from its members; but it also gets more, because its members feel their giving to be more worth while. If we are serious in wishing to enlist the help of outside bodies in the work of government and administration, they are likely to get and give far more by being represented on Statutory Commissions than through any number of Advisory Committees or Councils with far wider and higher-sounding terms of reference.

All this, however, deals with only one aspect of the problem, albeit considerably the most important. In any process of government under statute, it is necessary to consider first the drafting of the statute, secondly its passing into law, and thirdly its administration. If we are to get good laws that will work well it is of vital importance that full attention shall be given to the first of these stages. As Parliament will certainly be very short of time, and is in any case neither an expert body nor one whose atmosphere conduces to good draftsmanship, it is essential to get a draft statute into the best possible shape before ever it is introduced into Parliament. Now, drafting is at present mainly a departmental matter, subject to the endorsement by the Cabinet of the drafts prepared in the departments. At present, it is very common for a Bill to receive its first reading in the House before anyone knows what it is going to contain. It is then sprung upon Parliament and the public, as a measure to which the Government is already committed, before there has been any opportunity at all for public discussion of its merits.

Of course, this does not always happen. Mr. Neville Chamberlain, for example, circulated a memorandum containing the main proposals of his Local Government Bill, and invited full discussion upon these proposals, long before the Bill itself was introduced, or the Government committed definitely to it. And often a Bill, even if its main proposals are not published beforehand, has been discussed in advance with certain of the interests directly concerned, and perhaps agreements reached which are subsequently embodied in certain of its clauses. Again, the outlines of the Bill have sometimes been discussed in advance with one of those Advisory Councils or Committees of which I have spoken slightingly above.

Of all these courses, that adopted in the case of the Local Government Bill is by far the best. As far as possible, all proposals for new social legislation ought to be plainly formulated, and published abroad for general information, well before it is intended to introduce the Bills embodying them. This ought to be done in such a way as to make it clear that the Government is in no way committed to the details, and is prepared to hear all criticisms and objections before proceeding to formulate its Bill in a definite and committal form. If only this were more often done, much waste of parliamentary time could be avoided; measures could be introduced into Parliament in better shape; and the public would be better informed about the pros and cons of Government policy. I do not suggest that this course can be followed in all cases, but only that wise statesmen will seek to follow it whenever they can.

This, however, pushes the matter back a stage further. Before the proposals are formulated and published, as well as at the stage between this publication and the actual introduction of a Bill, there will be need for some amount of consultation with outside bodies. Sometimes the process begins with a Royal Commission or Departmental Committee, which formulates proposals that are then discussed both in the departments and in Government circles and, perhaps, with outside interests. I should like to see such commissions and committees more definitely instructed than is now the case to draw up positively the heads for any legislation they might think desirable, and empowered not only to take evidence from outside interests before formulating any proposals, but also to consult with such interests on any proposals which they might formulate, before presenting their report to the appropriate Minister.

Again, I do not suggest that this method of close consultation with outside interests before a Bill is even drafted can be universally applied. There will be some questions on which a Cabinet is determined to bring forward its own legislation, whatever the interests concerned may say, and to present its proposals in a finished form before the interests are given a chance of saying anything at all. But there are many more measures which could be improved, without sacrifice of anything regarded by the Cabinet as vital, by consulting as fully as possible at the earliest moment, and so reducing to a minimum the subsequent struggles in the committee stage.

Then again, when a Bill has got into draft, it is often the best course to allow a reasonably long interval before the committee stage begins, in order that the interests concerned may have every opportunity of raising points of substance, and having them met where they can be met, without the need for prolonged discussion in Parliament. The aim of any sensible Government will usually be to get its Bills through Parliament in the shortest time and with the least possible friction; and it will therefore be eager to conciliate critics whose points can be met without sacrifice of principle at the earliest possible stage.

The less of detail a Bill contains, the less usually will there be for the interests to lay hold on in it for purposes of amendment in Committee. But, as matters stand today, this does not necessarily mean that the Bill will have a smoother passage; for criticism may fasten on sins of omission as well as sins of commission. The reluctance of certain religious interests to let the School Attendance Bill go forward until the question of the non-provided schools had been settled was an obvious instance of this; for the fact that the Bill contained no reference to this question by no means disarmed the critics. It will often be necessary for a Minister, before producing his Bill or while it is before Parliament, to engage in negotiations with outside interests on matters with which the Bill does not directly deal. Assurances on this or that point will be demanded; and it will by no means be always possible for the Minister to take a high hand.

These matters may be of two kinds—matters which will involve subsequent legislation, or at least subsequent endorsement by Parliament, and matters which are intended to be dealt with by regulation, usually at the discretion of the Minister. Matters of the first class are obviously Cabinet questions; and their treatment cannot be affected by any change in the procedure of legislation such as I have been discussing in this paper. But in relation to matters of the second class, the position of the Minister and the Government in resisting undue pressure by any particular interest would, I think, be greatly strengthened if the regulation-making power ceased to be a departmental matter, and became a function of some sort of representative Statutory Board or Commission. For it would be clearly useless to badger the Minister for pledges which he would be no longer in a position to give. An aggrieved interest might still, of course, urge its supporters to vote against the Bill; but something of its present power to bluff would be taken away.

I have so far suggested certain changes in our methods of legislation and administration—and certain readjustments of the uncertain boundaries between these two—without questioning at all the present structure of the law-making machine. I am, however, like most other people who want to get things done, profoundly dissatisfied with the present working of the parliamentary system. The conditions of modern society have crowded both upon Parliament and—what is no less important—upon the Cabinet far more work than either can be expected to perform with even tolerable efficiency. A change in the form of legislation, applied to the social reform measures which are so expensive in parliamentary time, might do a little to relieve the pressure by transferring a good deal of detail from the Bills to regulations made under them; but it would not enable Parliament to get through its business in a reasonably satisfactory way. I am making the proposal far less with a view to removing parliamentary congestion than to making it possible to provide a more flexible basis for administration and to amend what is amiss more readily in spite of the congestion of Parliament.

For any remedy for the major difficulties of the modern legislative process far more drastic measures will be needed—measures which I have no intention of discussing in this paper. We may be compelled, as Mrs. Webb has suggested, to have two Parliaments or assemblies, working side by side, with distinct spheres of action, one body dealing entirely with social and economic matters, and the other with political and international questions. We may have to assimilate our procedure in dealing with social questions far more nearly to the procedure of Local Government, and to break away, in this field, from the parliamentary tradition. We shall certainly have to devise means of relieving the Cabinet from the pressure of a mass of routine business, in order to liberate it for thinking out a policy on matters of fundamental importance. But all these problems raise far wider issues than I want to discuss at present. I have contented myself with putting forward, very tentatively, certain secondary suggestions that might be no less tentatively applied. It will, perhaps, be convenient if I summarise them here in order to facilitate discussion.

(1) Wherever possible, we should put less detail into our laws, and aim at providing only a general framework, to be built upon by regulations capable of amendment without passing a new Act.

(2) Wherever possible, the power to make the necessary regulations should not be left to the Minister and his department, but entrusted to a statutory body, broadly representative of the interests concerned, and of the public generally. Regulations so made should require the sanction of the Minister, and should lie upon the table of the House of Commons, before becoming operative.

(3) Wherever possible, before a Bill is presented to Parliament on any matter involving administrative complications, heads of proposals should be drawn up and circulated in advance, and published; and consultations should take place between the department and the interests concerned.

(4) Wherever possible, after a Bill has been introduced, time enough should be allowed to elapse between its publication and the beginning of the committee stage to allow further consultations to take place.

(5) Advisory Committees are usually of little value, except in relation to scientific matters, unless they have fairly narrow terms of reference, a perfectly definite job to

do, and at least some measure of responsibility for administration (even if this responsibility is subject to the Minister's veto). In fact, an ounce of Statutory Commission is worth a ton of Advisory Committee.

(6) Royal Commissions and Departmental Committees should be encouraged to formulate actual heads of proposals for legislation, and to discuss these with outside interests before presenting their Reports.

It will be observed that I have said nothing of the often-mooted proposal to set up a representative National Industrial Council, or some similar body, under Government auspices. I do not, in fact, believe that such a body could be made to work successfully. It would have to be advisory, or at any rate this is the form in which the proposal has so far been put forward. It would have to have wide, and somewhat indefinite, terms of reference. And I do not well see how it could be given a clear and definite job to do. I am not saying decisively that the time for the creation of a representative National Industrial Council will never come, though I am very doubtful if it will. But I am sure that the right line of advance for the immediate future lies in the creation not of one high-sounding body of this type, with a far-flung reference and a purpose and status by no means well defined, but rather in a plurality of less ambitious experiments in particular spheres. And I should like to see a beginning made with the entrusting of the administrative regulation-making power over unemployment insurance to a special Statutory Commission.

## XV

## WHY I AM A SOCIALIST

I SUPPOSE that, for all Socialists, Socialism serves, in some part at least, as a guide to the whole of life. It is not merely a matter of political or economic policy, or a source of guidance in economic or political conduct, but at the same time a way of living in harmony with oneself, as well as with others. In my case, I know this is so. I could not be less a Socialist even if I were sure that all the practical policies of all the Socialist Parties in the world were demonstrably wrong. For to disagree with all these policies—unpleasant and upsetting as it would be—could not, I think, shake the basis of my Socialist conviction. That conviction goes deeper than any practical economic or political policy can possibly go: indeed, all such policies are but fallible means to the attainment of the end which is the true idea of Socialism in my mind.

This idea of Socialism is not a system, though there are certain features which any system that is to attempt to represent it must somehow embody. It is rather a way of living in relation to others, without which, at least as an ideal, I should find it impossible to live at peace within myself. It is not easy to sum up, or to express apart from the material integument of practical policy in which it must be clothed; but this paper is an attempt, honest if not wholly successful, to lay it bare, and to say wherein, for me, being a Socialist truly consists, and what part Socialism plays in the conception of my inner life.

Let me say at the outset that, like most people, I am often conscious of living out of harmony with this inner ideal. I blame myself—and yet I do not wholly blame myself—for that. It is partly my fault; but it is also in part a matter of environment. For this Socialist ideal essentially involves living in and with the world, and not apart from it; and this implies, in large measure, an acceptance of the environment. The Socialist cannot afford to make too wide a cross—as Samuel Butler would have said—with the habits of living of those with whom he comes in contact. His ideal is, through and through, an ideal of sociality; and he cannot, on the plea that his idea of sociality is not yet received by the world, withdraw from the world into an isolation of his own. By doing that he would be denying his ideal even more completely than by living after the world's way.

This, of course, is no entire *apologia*. Quite apart from that cause, I fall short of what I set out to be in many other ways. Socialism, like any decent creed, may be a means of making a man behave better than he would without it; but it is no guarantee of good behaviour. Socialists have no more pre-eminence in personal virtue than in the moral abandon with which anti-Socialists used to be prone to credit them.

For my present purpose, however, the question of personal adequacy is beside the point. I am seeking to define my conception of the Socialist ideal, and not my capacity for living in accord with it. And I have got thus far—that the Socialist ideal is essentially an ideal of sociality, that it involves a conception of life as lived with and among other men, and that this living with others is a fundamental part of the inner life of Socialism.

William Morris stated a part of this aspect of the Socialist ideal when he wrote in his *Dream of John Ball* that 'fellowship is heaven, and lack of fellowship is hell'. And there is, in the statement of the creed attributed to the hedge-preacher of the Middle Ages, this further element that seems to me vital to the Socialist idea. The Socialist kingdom is of this world, and of no other, not in the sense that it is a purely material kingdom, but in the sense that its ideal value is to be realised here, on the earth that we know and among men like-minded and like-bodied with ourselves, and in no other-worldly or after existence, different in character and opportunity from the world we know.

About immortality, the Socialist may hold what view he pleases. For my part, I have never desired individual immortality or been able to conceive it as in any way possible. I want to survive in and through my work, and in and through my successors in this world; but in no other way that is peculiar to me. My individuality, the self that underlies my actions and reactions, appears to me to be something essentially transient, something that is bound to wear out, and that I want to wear out in doing something worth while. I, as an individual, do not want to survive death; and I am sure I shall not survive it.

But, while this view is fundamental to me, I have to recognise that it is not part of the common stock of Socialism. What is essential to the Socialist idea is that, whether a Socialist believes, or does not believe, in some sort of personal or individual immortality, he should believe that his business in this world is to realise in this world as much as he can of his ideal. An otherworldly Socialism is inconceivable; and the Socialist ideal seems to me to be inconsistent with any that regards this world as merely a place of tribulation and of purgation for a better life to come.

Fellowship, then, is the first principle of this deeper life of Socialism. And fellowship involves, above all else, treating men as ends and not as means. 'Each to count as one and none as more than one' is, for many purposes, an admirable political and social maxim; but it is far too quantitative to be more than a very imperfect way of expressing the ideal. For fellowship does not count heads; or, if it does, it counts everyone as more than one—in fact, as infinite.

Perhaps I can put my point more clearly in another way. Socialists, in practical affairs, seek to achieve a higher standard of social justice than prevails in the world today, or has ever prevailed in it as yet. But social justice is not of the essence of Socialism. For justice seems to imply a meting out to each of something quantitative and limited, whereas Socialism itself implies a real living in and for one another. A mother is not content to be just to her child; nor can a Socialist be content to seek justice for the human race. Fellowship involves social justice as a practical, political and economic conception; but it also involves much more. Men can be just to their enemies; but fellowship cannot live with enmity.

That this idea of fellowship jars continually with one's daily ways of living is evident enough. It is simply impossible, in the ordinary affairs of the world, to transcend social habits that are in direct contradiction of it. Differences of wealth are always marring fellowship, and, within what we call a single 'community', differences of social class interfere with it even more. I do not mean that fellowship cannot overstep these differences. Clearly it can, as it can overstep differences of nationality, of colour, of religion, and of everything else that divides man from man. But a wall is none the less an obstacle because you can get over it with a ladder; and all these differences are formidable obstacles in the way of fellowship. Personally, I am most conscious of the obstacles that arise from social and economic inequality, because I am most often brought up against them. Though I may say, and really believe, that 'a man's a man for a' that', I cannot, in fact, get away from the obstacle that Society has made one a pundit and another a hewer of wood and a drawer of water, and has given to them different upbringings supposed to accord with their different stations in life. With some men I have community of culture, education, ways of speech and social behaviour; and with others I have not. Whatever my social views and ideals may be, that is a present fact from which there is no escape, and of which I cannot help taking account.

Practically, what I want most of all is to make these differences vanish in a fuller and more rounded life for the whole human race. I want this for all the world; but, rightly or wrongly, I want it more, and feel a greater responsibility for bringing it about, in the part of the world in which I live. I do not feel Nationalism, in this sense, to be at all inconsistent with Socialism, or with that Internationalism which all true Socialism evidently involves. That there are dangers in this selective fellowship with those of a limited and particular society I am well aware; but there is also danger that a sentiment too diffused may be too difficult to relate to the practice of life. My fellowship with my neighbour should be the means of fostering and not of subduing my fellowship with those who dwell further away.

This impulse of fellowship which is at the bottom of my idea of Socialism is, I want to make it plain, a very different thing from any sort of altruistic sentiment in my mind. If the thesis be egoism and the antithesis altruism, then the synthesis, I should say, is Socialism. For to me, as a Socialist, Society is not something outside myself, but something of which I am a part, so that my well-being and that of Society are inextricably intertwined. I do not mean that I cannot enjoy personal happiness, or a high degree of well-being, even in a society that seems to me largely unhappy and diseased. I can, and do; but I think I could not enjoy these things unless I were, in some measure, also trying to realise my ideal of a social happiness and a social well-being common to me and to my fellow-men, and unless I believed that there was in the world already, and had always been, a sufficient foundation of community to serve as a starting-point for the fuller achievement of these things. It is a part of Socialism, I believe, to regard Society not as an artificial construction made by men against nature for mutual protection through some social contract, but as fundamentally and inherently natural to man.

This sense of Society as natural carries with it a denial of the opposition so often supposed to exist between regulation and liberty. It is no paradox for the Socialist that liberty does not consist simply in being let alone, but can be fully realised only within the framework of a common life. In one sense, indeed, all Socialists are Anarchists in their ideal; for they regard coercion as an evil, and the presence of coercion in the organisation of Society as a sign of its essential imperfection. But coercion and regulation are two very different things. The world is already full of rules and customs that most people observe without coercion or consciousness of duress. They can break these rules if they will; but usually they do not want to break them. The Socialist ideal seems to me to involve the substitution of the rule of consent for the rule of coercion. Perfect consent I do not expect ever to be realised; but it remains the ideal. And it is a possible ideal because the fundamental fact of man's sociality is there to build upon. There is a consciousness of consent; and in a healthy and well-ordered Society, the area of this consciousness will tend steadily to grow.

It will grow easily, however, only in proportion as the obstacles to sociality are removed, and removed in the right way. I have said that the thing nearest my heart is the removal of those differences, largely the product of economic inequality, which within a single community shut me out from full fellowship with my fellow-men. But it matters *how* these differences are removed. It is possible to conceive of their disappearance through the destruction of the higher culture of the Society in which they exist. Even if this happened, I have faith enough to believe that a Society thus cut down to the roots would in process of time build up for itself a new culture that might be better and more universal than the old; but this way of universalising culture through its prior destruction would be terribly wasteful. It would be at best a desperate remedy in a Society where culture was mortally diseased. In any other case, we may reasonably look to the extension of culture and to its progressive transformation as it spreads over the whole people. We may hope to conserve and develop existing values, and to use them as a foundation on which new ones may be built. This is the Socialist meaning of the process of popular education; and it is natural and inevitable that, from Robert Owen's day, the demand for Socialism and the demand for education have always gone together.

The demand for universal education is, indeed, but another aspect of the demand for equality; and equality is but the political and social expression of the idea of fellowship. Those who value equality as a political concept do not mean that all men are really equal in any mathematical sense, or that all differences between them are due to differences of education or environment, or to remediable physical or inherited defects. They do not want to abolish the differences between men, but only those differences that stand in the way of fellowship. They want political and social equality in the sense that they want to stop any one man being treated merely or mainly as a means to some other man's ends.

The inmost life of Socialism, as I am conscious of it, consists largely in awareness of universal fellowship and social equality as the ideal, and demands, if a man who holds it is to live at peace with himself, that he should be reasonably active in furthering the practical advance of this ideal, and should in his own private affairs live reasonably in accordance with it. This inmost life is therefore essentially outward-looking and active or conative, rather than inward-looking or contemplative. Many of the faults of expression and much of the lack of clearness in this paper are due to the fact that it is only with an effort that I make myself look inward at all. For the Socialist, as for anyone else, an inner harmony is essential to happiness and well-being; but this harmony is like pleasure in that it comes most readily, not when we seek it, but when it lights upon us in the course of our seeking after something else. It comes to me with, or at least it cannot come to me without, the search for fellowship. If I sought happiness instead, I could not seek fellowship so well; and I should get both less fellowship and less happiness.

This, as I write it, sounds priggish. There are, of course, many ingredients in a man's happiness besides the consciousness of pursuing any ideal, even that which he counts the most important. A Socialist is not only a Socialist, but many things besides. He has in his mind many other ideals, values many other things besides fellowship, and sets out practically to do many other things besides furthering the cause of Socialism. His personal affections, his tastes, count for much in his life; and he need by no means attempt to co-ordinate them all with his Socialist ideal. If they conflict, then indeed comes at least some unhappiness, unless and until the conflict is resolved. But ideals and tastes need not conflict; they may live side by side in the mind without jostling.

This inmost life of Socialism that I have sought to describe is, then, not a complete way of living. I distrust the man for whom the Socialist ideal, or any other ideal, looms so large as to cover the whole of life. For that, I think, is a sign of inhumanity; and Socialism is above all a creed for ordinary men. Love of humanity need not submerge other loves—of wife, or children, or friends; indeed, these other loves are fires to keep it warm. Socialism is for me, I think, the most important single thing that exists. But I am not sure even of that. And I am quite sure that it is not the only thing that matters.

PRINTED IN GREAT BRITAIN BY
BILLING AND SONS LTD. GUILDFORD AND ESHER